African Refugees

African Modernization and Development Series

Paul Lovejoy, Series Editor

African Refugees: Development Aid and Repatriation,
edited by Howard Adelman and John Sorenson

Pawnship in Africa, edited by Toyin Falola and Paul E. Lovejoy

Slavery in South Africa: Captive Labor on the Dutch Frontier,
edited by Elizabeth A. Eldredge and Fred Morton

Politics and Economic Development in Nigeria,
Tom Forrest

Democracy and Socialism in Africa,
edited by Robin Cohen and Harry Goulbourne

South Africa's Labor Empire: A History of Black Migrancy to the Gold Mines,
Jonathan Crush, Alan Jeeves, and David Yudelman

Herders, Warriors, and Traders: Pastoralism in Africa,
edited by John G. Galaty and Pierre Bonte

*Children of Ham: Freed Slaves and Fugitive Slaves on
the Kenya Coast, 1873 to 1907,* Fred Morton

*The Black Man's Burden: African Colonial Labor on the
Congo and Ubangi Rivers, 1880–1900,*
William J. Samarin

Psychoses of Power: African Personal Dictatorships,
Samuel Decalo

African Cities in Crisis: Managing Rapid Urban Growth,
edited by Richard E. Stren and Rodney R. White

Patriarchy and Class: African Women in the Home and the Workforce,
edited by Sharon B. Stichter and Jane L. Parpart

The Precarious Balance: State and Society in Africa,
edited by Donald Rothchild and Naomi Chazan

African Refugees

Development Aid and Repatriation

EDITED BY

Howard Adelman
and John Sorenson

Westview Press

BOULDER • SAN FRANCISCO • OXFORD

York Lanes Press

NORTH YORK

African Modernization and Development Series

Copyright © 1994 by Westview Press, Inc.

Published in 1994 in the United States of America by Westview Press, Inc., 5500 Central Avenue, Boulder, Colorado 80301-2877, and in the United Kingdom by Westview Press, 36 Lonsdale Road, Summertown, Oxford OX2 7EW

Distributed in Canada by York Lanes Press, 4700 Keele Street, North York, Ontario, Canada M3J 1P3

Library of Congress Cataloging-in-Publication Data
African refugees : development aid and repatriation / edited by Howard
    Adelman and John Sorenson.
        p.   cm. — (African modernization and development series)
    Includes bibliographical references and index.
    ISBN 0-8133-8460-5
    1. Refugees—Africa.   I. Adelman, Howard, 1938–   .
II. Sorenson, John, 1952–   .   III. Series.
HV640.4.A35A36   1994
362.87'096—dc20
                                                                93-47501
                                                                CIP

Printed and bound in the United States of America

The paper used in this publication meets the requirements
of the American National Standard for Permanence of Paper
for Printed Library Materials Z39.48-1984.

10   9   8   7   6   5   4   3   2

Contents

Part Four
Refugees and Development

Acknowledgments

We wish to thank Kelli Morefield and Yohannes Gebresellasie of the Centre for Refugee Studies, York University, for their assistance in preparation of the manuscript for publication, Valerie Ahwee for editorial coordination and Barbara Schon for assistance with indexing. Special thanks to Professor Paul Lovejoy, History Department and the Centre for Refugee Studies, Barbara Ellington of Westview Press, and Stephanie Johnson and Arul Aruliah, York Lanes Press for their assistance in the publication of this book.

Howard Adelman
John Sorenson

Introduction

Refugees and Africa seem almost synonymous. Of the over fifteen million refugees in the world, Africa has more than five million. They are the product of ideological wars and nationalist conflicts, of environmental disasters and ethnic hatreds, of the brutal ambition for power of a few and the poverty of many. Ethiopia, Somalia and the Sudan have become known to most people in the West through the images of refugees on their TV screens, but Liberia, Ghana, Kenya, Chad, Angola, Rwanda, Burundi and, not least of all, South Africa, must all be included in the long list of African refugee-producing countries. There are one million Mozambican refugees alone, who make up 12.5 percent of the population of Malawi.

In no other continent is there such vast suffering. In no other continent do we find greater generosity in the local assistance given to refugees by surrounding states. They have a broader definition of a refugee and the obligations to assist, yet in some places the conflicts are so horrendous and the terrain so formidable that aid agencies cannot overcome the military and geographic obstacles to deliver needed relief supplies. In no other continent are the needs so vast and the capacity to assist so meagre.

This volume takes a thematic approach. The first brief section provides the legal framework for defining and assisting refugees. The second section considers the lack of resources that contribute to refugee production and inadequate relief aid. Since relatively few African refugees are able to avail themselves of one permanent solution to their plight—resettlement abroad—the third section discusses the two other permanent solutions utilized—settlement in countries of first asylum and repatriation.

However, the refugee problem is inseparable from the problem of economic development in Africa, both in preventing situations that create refugee flows and in dealing with either of the permanent solutions available—settlement and repatriation. Unless economic development occurs, neither solution is workable in the long run. The final section focuses on the issue of refugees and development.

Economic development is impossible without a proper legal framework. And a legal framework is necessary for preventing refugee flows and protecting the refugees produced by regimes not governed by the rule of law. The second sentence of the Organization of African Unity's (OAU) definition goes well beyond the narrow reference of the first sentence taken from the 1951 United Nations Convention relating to the Status of Refugees:

> The term "refugee" shall mean every person who, owing to well-founded fear of being persecuted for reasons of race, religion, nationality, membership of a particular social group or political opinion, is outside the country of his nationality and is unable, or owing to such fear, is unwilling to avail himself of the protection of that country, or, who, not having a nationality and being outside the country of his former habitual residence as a result of such events is unable or, owing to such fear, is unwilling to return to it. The term "refugee" shall also apply to every person who, owing to external aggression, occupation, foreign domination or events seriously disturbing public order in either part or whole of his country of origin or nationality, is compelled to leave his place of habitual residence in order to seek refuge in another place outside his country of origin or nationality.

Chris Bakwesegha's chapter focuses on the African legal regime. Before tackling the overall history of the Organization of African Unity and its approach to defining the legal context for an African refugee regime, Bakwesegha provides a comprehensive list of issues and figures by country on the number of refugees, low per capita incomes and the high ratio of refugees to the local population. He notes that the 1969 OAU Convention was created when African states were just achieving independence, when the African refugee population was one-fifth of its present size, and when the international convention was rooted in premises that were derived from the situation in Europe but expanded to apply to situations arising from the struggles for national liberation. His major concern is the appropriateness and inappropriateness of applying the OAU Convention to the current crisis.

Thus, though there are over five million refugees as defined by the OAU Convention, most of them are women, children, the disabled and the elderly, who are given no specific recognition by the Convention. There are an additional twelve million internally displaced persons in refugee-like situations. Further, the international aid available to the official refugees makes them privileged recipients of aid. Yet international efforts to provide aid to the internally displaced through the United Nations Disaster and Relief Organization (UNDRO) have to deal with the sensitive issue of the local state's political jurisdiction concerning its own citizens. Further, with regard to the externally displaced, the local population's hospitality towards refugees who fled colonial oppression has often been replaced by hostility now that refugees flee independent states. Hostility often exists between the local host population and the refugees, particularly when refugee aid arrives but does not take into account or make up for the depletion of the local food stores of the host population.

One aspect of the problem is whether the refugees are regarded as a burden or as an economic asset. Another aspect is the appropriate distance from the border for establishing the refugee settlements in an effort to balance safety, accessibility to aid agencies and the support of kith and kin. A third aspect is the paradox that requires refugees to conform to the laws and regulations of the host states and to refrain from political activity, thereby denying refugees any active economic role in their own settlement as well as any political role, which is often the very activity that forced them into exile in the first place. At the same time, this political inhibition provides the producing country with little incentive to change the situation and allow the refugees to return. Refugees thus often become warriors, resorting to armed struggle to go home, or else are the victims of wars in their host countries that may drive them back across the border in a form of repatriation that is anything but voluntary.

In the area of relief, which is explored in the second section of the book, specific cases are considered to indicate the problems faced, the agencies available to provide assistance and the attempt to deal with the problems by maximizing the refugees' capacities and willingness to help themselves. The three authors of the chapter on Tigray, Ethiopia, look at long-evolving historical, socio-economic and ecological forces to identify the key factors that led to resource depletion, famine and the creation of refugees. Understanding famine is the key to understanding the evolving politics of scarcity in the region. The authors make a key distinction between disaster—an event disabling humans in large numbers—and deprivation, the perceived cyclical gradual decrease in resources in an area dominated by sedentary subsistence agriculture with some areas of mixed cultivation and pastoralism. The local populations respond to deprivation with what the authors term "adaptive flux"—self-help, short-term tactics and long-term strategies that enable them to survive under fluctuating, harsh and erratic conditions that result in a system of local governing councils to facilitate concerted struggle against external threats and mobilizing local resources for increased food production through alternative farming strategies. Various forms of migration are coping strategies as socio-economic problems increase, though one form of migration—central government-enforced relocation and "villagization"—can scarcely be called a coping strategy in adaptive flux.

In this context, relief merely gets caught up in the political struggle. The donor community lacks the power or even the ability to coordinate efforts to ensure that supplies reach the vast rebel-controlled areas most affected by drought and famine, while the government-controlled food distribution centres are used as weapons of war and for militia recruitment, leading local populations to flee across borders as refugees. Thus, ironically, relief aid can be said to have contributed to refugee flows.

Gaim Kibreab also echoes the theme of self-help as applied to the refugees in their host states. In examining the situation in Sudan, he argues that in providing relief, refugees should be treated as an asset. Economic planning and development should include refugees as well as the local population and refugees should become an active element in the development process. He documents in detail the problem of obtaining accurate statistics, particularly with respect to self-settled refugees, but argues that international aid policy neglects the needs of the self-settled population and ignores the fact that years later, none of the settlements that received aid achieved self-sufficiency. Kibreab points out five reasons for the latter results in the settlements: marginality of the allocated land; a shortage of unoccupied cultivatable land; lack of clean water; lack of refugee participation in analysis, planning and decision making; and inadequate and inappropriate assistance. The wage-earning and semiurban settlements have also not achieved their objectives of either off-setting a labour shortage or making the refugees self-reliant, with the exception of Towawa, a settlement with a highly mobile labour force of young single men.

The self-settled refugees (the majority) present another problem altogether that requires new solutions for the refugees and the infrastructures of the areas where they have settled, but the Sudanese government and the aid agencies seem to be blind to the needs of urban refugees. Exacerbating both the rural and urban failures are the worldwide economic slump, the additional strain on already overloaded infrastructures, the Sudanese government's lack of vision and direction, and the failure to involve the refugees in policy making that affects their lives.

In contrast to Kibreab's pessimistic account of the policies and programs in the Sudan, but consistent with his recommendations, John Sorenson examines the work of the Eritrean Relief Association as an effective aid and development agency run by and for refugees in the midst of a most horrendous situation. Though there were problems with nepotism, distortions by established hierarchies and values that stressed kinship relations and undermined programs based on cooperatives, the main problems were inadequate international support and the war. In the process, Sorenson poses a major challenge to those who try to distinguish between political and economic refugees, at least in the case of Eritreans. His contention is that there was little difference, except the legal one, between the internally uprooted and the refugees who fled across an international border. In fact, echoing a theme throughout the book, Sorenson makes it clear that the political problems are central to the economic crises and must be recognized as part of the relief and rehabilitation effort. There can be no apolitical humanitarian aid.

The section on relief and rehabilitation forces us to look more closely at the reality of resettlement and the difficulties of repatriation as the two permanent solutions favoured in Africa. Peter Koehn's chapter examines the structural barriers to repatriation—perpetuation of the regime that induced the outflow, continuing or intermittent armed struggle and achieving acceptable repatriation conditions. Integration of refugees in the host society is not a factor because there is very little of it in contrast to the situation of the few refugees resettled abroad. The first barrier—regime perpetuation—can only be overcome after a protracted internal struggle. Thus, the first two barriers are joined, though continuing conflicts between states over unresolved territorial disputes may also inhibit repatriation. Governments that are legitimate and that rule by consent rather than force are a prerequisite to ending refugee flows and allowing repatriation.

To facilitate regime change and peace, a number of factors must be present: agreements to secure the interests of local populations, empowerment and self-determination and, most of all, the conviction by the warring parties that the benefits of peace outweigh the gains achievable through struggle. Even then, refugees will be required to undergo a process of readaptation to their home countries, a process helped by attending to the special needs of the children for whom the homeland is not home, refugee involvement in planning the return, and the creation of rehabilitation projects.

When repatriation is a remote possibility, emphasis is then placed on settlement and integration into the host society, yet key conditions for their successful implementation—such as giving development aid to the local population as well as to the refugees—have never been put in place. Numbers, host-country resistance and the failure to address long-term maintenance costs are all factors that Koehn stresses. But Koehn is hopeful even if only two of the recommendations proposed by other authors are followed—assistance to the host population and refugee participation in development projects. The same principles are applicable in repatriation, yet his hope seems belied by the admitted rarity of local integration and the failure of the developed countries to increase their intakes and more equitably share the burden of refugees. Further, if repatriation is to depend on international intervention by means of Western countries basing policies towards refugee-producing states on their human rights records, then utopia is at hand, for not only will conditions be in place for repatriation, but the situations that create refugee flows will have largely been eliminated. When Koehn recommends expanding international responsibilities, including those of the UNHCR, to the internally uprooted, it is clear that what is proposed is idealistic.

If Koehn proposes much greater activity and intervention by the West to facilitate repatriation, Tom Kuhlman reverts to the opposite theme raised earlier by Kibreab—the refugees' "spontaneous" activities in integrating themselves in countries of first asylum—the permanent solution considered most feasible when repatriation does not seem to be an imminent prospect. Self-settlement is again contrasted with organized settlement to assess which of the two is more conducive to economic integration.

Economic integration is not equivalent to self-sufficiency (either family self-sufficiency when refugees do not need to be given relief for basic necessities, or community self-sufficiency when refugees are able to finance community services, such as the water supply, health and educational needs) since self-settled refugees by definition survive without aid. Kuhlman offers complex criteria for defining integration in general, which is not merely economic, to include participation in the host society commensurate with skills and compatible with cultural values, attaining a standard of living that satisfies culturally determined minimum standards, retaining an identity of their own and adjusting psychologically. But these are just the criteria applicable to the refugees. The criteria for integration also apply to the hosts and the relationship between the hosts and the newly settled refugees. Thus, economic opportunities for the host population must not have deteriorated or friction between the two increased, and there cannot be any heightened discrimination by the host society beyond those suffered by previously settled groups. Clearly, this is a standard of integration that the developed world would have difficulty meeting. Even economic integration, one dimension of complete integration, refers to an ideal of social life in which material welfare is attained through the optimal allocation of resources, a situation never achieved anywhere.

Given this ideal, however, spontaneous and organized settlements of refugees can be compared in terms of economic participation, both proportionally and in relation to skills, incomes achieved, access to amenities and economic effects on the host population. However, a fair comparison in terms of employment, income and negative effects on the host population has to take into account the skills of both types of refugees in relationship to the hosts, the difference between short- and long-term effects and the conditions independent of the form of settlement utilized.

Now organized settlements are often preferred for reasons that have little to do with the economic and social benefit for the refugees, reasons that are particularly applicable in countries of first asylum, such as preventing the development of warrior refugees, obtaining and delivering aid and having the control to organize the repatriation of the refugees. Many reasons have to do with limiting alleged negative impacts on the host population, such as creating an ethnic imbalance, increasing the crime rates and overloading infrastructures of urban areas. Kuhlman dismisses these external convenience factors and unsubstantiated fears as insupportable. Further, organized settlements are more expensive, are used by only 20–25 percent of refugees and, in any case, have not been successful.

Since Kuhlman shows that these lessons were known as early as 1976, as indicated in the recommendations of the Arusha Seminar on Refugees in Africa held that year, why has the dominant policy for settling refugees in countries of first asylum not changed? One reason is that the conclusion, though known, was still academically controversial and conventional wisdom at the time favoured organized settlements. However, not only can some of the older evidence be reevaluated by bracketing a prior bias towards organized settlement, but evidence supporting the economic benefit of self-settlement has accumulated since that time, even if the data is limited and crude. Further, as indicated earlier, the reasons for the failure of organized settlements have also accumulated, such as inadequate allocations of land that is often marginal, inadequate provision for capital replacement and an inadequate base to support it. Even in wage-earning settlements, refugees' reliance on seasonal agricultural work without the supplemental provision of their own plots meant that they could never become self-sufficient. Nevertheless, whatever the other benefits of self-settlement, organized settlements seem to be better off in terms of the provision of infrastructure, such as water and housing, health, education and social welfare. The latter may be particularly important for both the refugees and the host society, but it is not clear that equivalent aid provided to the self-settled might not have allowed them to support the vulnerable members of their own communities more efficiently.

When impacts on the host population are considered, the impact of refugees has been either beneficial or benign except where refugees severely tax the natural resources available and contribute to ecological degradation or overburden the social infrastructure in place. But the impacts on the social infrastructure—water supplies, employment, housing, education and health services—are generally less than one might expect and, in any case, there are compensations that more than make up for the detrimental effects.

According to Edward Khiddu-Makubuya, it is the taxing of local resources by the refugees that provides a partial explanation for the decline in hospitality in contrast to the expectations of the OAU Convention as depicted by Bakwesegha in the opening chapter. Khiddu-Makubuya, however, provides a very different angle by focusing on the Rwandan refugees of the Tutsi tribe who self-settled in Uganda and then self-repatriated by force into Rwanda. The social, political and military aspects, rather than the economic issues, become the central focus, as the refugees repatriated in opposition to the dominant Hutu government but under increasing pressure (and possibly support) by their hosts in Uganda. The case also challenges the presumption that repatriation is always or should be a peaceful process and asks whether repatriation by militant means is a justified and legal act when the UN Charter generally prohibits a resort to force to resolve disputes and refugee warriors are denied UN assistance. Refugees' use of the territory of adjacent states to launch attacks on the home country is illegal according to the OAU Convention. On the other hand, how else were the refugees to acquire citizenship? Their prospect of obtaining Ugandan citizenship was diminishing. Further, their forceful repatriation can be considered an act of civil war or the exercise of self-determination.

Self-help is a major theme that runs through most of the chapters. The situation in Somalia at the end of 1992 and the beginning of 1993 was considered so desperate that outside intervention seemed to be welcome. In his concluding chapter to the section on refugee integration and repatriation, Roger Winter considers the issue of external intervention, not the contemporary ostensibly humanitarian intervention sanctioned by the UN, but the more traditional intervention of outside powers for their own political, military and economic interests. The supply of arms fuelled and prolonged the conflict and makes it much more difficult for aid workers today to work safely. In other words, external intervention in the past seems to necessitate external intervention in the present.

Roger Winter argues that repatriation must be pursued with vigour and enterprise if the opportunities for repatriation that have opened up in many places in the nineties are to be taken advantage of and if the refugee population is to be reduced by one half in this decade. Permanent settlement in countries of first asylum can no longer be considered realistic for the majority of refugees. Winter stresses international political will, organization and financial commitments made in advance rather than on the refugees' self-help potential since repatriation is the only real solution for most African refugees. And for that reintegration to be successful, the requisite form of external intervention is development assistance.

However, as my coeditor notes in the chapter that opens the section on development, although it has long been recognized that development aid and voluntary repatriation need to be linked, there has been little research on how to achieve this linkage. As mentioned in other chapters, there is a lack of adequate or accurate data on numbers of refugees or their situation. It is difficult to calculate the effects of refugees on the economics and politics of the host country, and any calculations we have seem biased by the disciplinary and theoretical perspectives of the researchers. There is a controversy between using organized versus spontaneous resettlement. There is the need to balance external assistance and intervention and refugee participation.

Sterkenburg, Kirkby and O'Keefe advocate a focus on sustainable development defined in terms of self-sustaining production, but their emphasis is on rural development. Like Kibreab, they criticize aid agencies for failing to take account of replacement factors and overemphasizing social services at the expense of production-oriented aid. They base their critiques on a detailed analysis of two of the projects considered by Kibreab—Sudan's Qala en Nahal and the Eastern Refugee Programme, as well as the Burundi refugee settlements in Tanzania—by assessing the discrepancies between the "real" conditions and the perceptions of the host countries, the donors, the delivering agencies and the refugees. This is another theme that runs through the book—an unwillingness of UN agencies, governments providing aid, aid agencies and host governments to face reality.

One advantage of Sterkenburg, Kirkby and O'Keefe's two-country study is that it demonstrates that the restrictions on refugees' movements, ability to work, pursue education or to form associations, which are discussed by Kibreab, also apply to Tanzania, which otherwise seems more open to the permanent settlement of the refugees. Tanzania built in plans for self-sufficiency and sustainability from the beginning. The authors make it clear that Tanzanian policy is more realistic in helping to create self-sufficient farms and in allowing long-stayers the opportunity to become citizens. Aid agencies, particularly the Dutch, are just as short-sighted as those in the Sudan in their emphasis on social services and their neglect of the productive sector. In both countries, soil-exhaustive agricultural practices without fertilizers or crop rotation practices in some settlements did not help. As in the case of Eritrea, the conflict between the cooperative-favoured policies of the authorities clashed with the family-based practices of the farmers.

Though the authors use different categories to examine the reasons for success or failure—such as project design features, adequate productive resources and the macroeconomic and policy environment of the country—the subcategories are virtually parallel to those used by Kibreab. Both chapters stress refugee participation, for example, for it was encouraged in Tanzania but prevented by the military style, hierarchical organization in Sudan. Also, aid agencies' biases towards social services rather than productive, self-generating enterprises were also cited in both articles as contributing factors to failure.

Véronique Lassailly-Jacob adds a more sceptical dimension. She provides additional evidence that government-sponsored land resettlement schemes favoured by government and international aid agencies for even a host population of involuntary migrants (as a result of national development policies, as in dam construction, war, political turmoil or natural disasters) take a long time to become self-sufficient, and then only through nonagricultural activities, clearly suggesting that the issue is not whether those being settled are refugees or not. The issue is the role, extent and mode of government and outside intervention. The obstacles to success are many of the same ones pointed out by Kibreab—the availability, quality and quantity of land, difficulties in providing water, improper use of the land provided and inadequate attention paid to the needs of future generations (resulting in subdivision of plots that were too small in the first place), inadequate provision for maintaining and replacing mechanized equipment, failure to involve the involuntarily uprooted in decision making, and a process that fosters dependence and paternalism as well as a resistant, conservative strategy by those being resettled and by the host community.

Robert Gorman's chapter stresses the need for research to identify the extent to which refugees impose a burden on host countries, their pattern of utilization of infrastructure, the effects on the local population and the responsiveness of the existing institutions. Thus, while identifying lack of assistance and inadequate local resources that other authors stressed, Gorman's emphasis is on the bureaucratic problems and imperatives. If two ideal models are considered, an international interventionist model at one pole and a refugee self-reliance model at another pole, Robert Gorman's chapter stresses coordination and the middle road. Though he points out the importance of the participation of refugees and the local population, his emphasis is on institutional cooperation of local government officials, national and international agencies, and representatives of donor countries. Such coordination can be institutionalized through mechanisms such as round-table talks.

When all the papers are read together, one is struck by the unanimity and the new intellectual consensus. First, a legal regime that provides protection for a wide spectrum of refugees is inadequate. We require a legal regime that protects everyone, the locally displaced as well as those who cross borders, women and children as well as men, those who move as well as those who remain in place. Most of all, a prerequisite to resolving a refugee crisis is the creation of a legal regime that ensures that a government rules by consent rather than force. This is particularly important if the resettlement option is marginal and settlement of refugees in countries of first asylum does not work. Secondly, the involvement of refugees is critical in all areas of relief, reintegration or development. Refugees and others cannot merely be passive recipients of aid; they must be empowered.

Thirdly, a targeted approach focused on refugees is inadequate. The results will be uneven, with refugees provided with inadequate land in areas with insufficient water, technological aid and capital to make the land productive. At the same time, the refugees may be given better infrastructural support in terms of housing, education and health services than the local population. Such an approach will create inequities and a social service sector that is too expensive for the meagre productive sector to support, thus ensuring perpetual dependence for the refugees.

Fourthly, spontaneous refugee settlement or repatriation is ignored. Further, settlement in countries of first asylum continues to be used extensively when, in fact, it is *not* one of the permanent solutions to the refugee problem. Only repatriation is a permanent solution if the political situation is altered to eliminate rule by coercion and replaced by a legitimate government that has the respect and trust of the population.

Most of the findings in the area of refugee development assistance are based on inadequate data and research. We do not build research budgets into development projects so that we can compare which ones work and which do not. In fact, the implications are that the research should shift from the economics of aid and development to the politics as the main criteria for success. The myth of emergency aid or long-term development aid divorced from politics can no longer be sustained. Perhaps the primary aid should go to reinforcing democracy in the countries that produce refugees and to which most refugees must eventually be repatriated. We could try comparative studies of which system of assistance produced the most return for the dollars invested—political aid for democratic development or economic emergency and development aid for refugees.

Since refugee involvement in any of the solutions or interim measures is critical, we will have to learn how to integrate the work of scholars, aid practitioners and refugees. The practitioners and researchers must be available to the refugees and the local populations as required. If the local populations do not take control of the investment priorities and become totally involved in effecting the solution, then refugee aid and development will perpetuate dependency and paternalism rather than self-help and self-governance. This collection does not answer all the questions, but it does help us focus on the critical issues.

H.A.

PART ONE

Background of the Legal Regime

1

Forced Migration in Africa and the OAU Convention

Chris J. Bakwesegha

In Africa, people have sought sanctuary long before the formal legal instruments on refugees were adopted by both the United Nations and the Organization of African Unity (OAU). Ethnic wars, famine, the search for better grazing land, slave raids and colonial occupation caused the flight of thousands of people across national frontiers in search of security or justice, food or shelter.

In traditional societies, where regional or national frontiers were changeable, some asylum seekers who crossed into neighbouring regions or countries were welcomed by kin. Assistance given to them was informal and unpublicized. Available resources were shared equitably between asylum seekers and host communities, and few distinctions were made between them. Early statistics on asylum seekers were neither institutionalized nor a subject of international concern. Most fundamentally, there were no refugee camps as we see them today.

However, asylum seeking in Africa today is viewed differently. It must be discussed in terms of the following: (1) people fleeing from wars of national liberation, internal strife or interstate conflicts that are often provoked from outside the continent but aggravated by strained relations between states, regional tensions arising from changes of governments or ideologies, exigencies of drought and famine, as well as territorial claims; (2) strains in political relations between refugee-generating and receiving countries;(3) security guarantees for those in flight and the host communities *vis-à-vis* pursuing security forces of the countries from which the asylum seekers have fled; (4) competition between asylum seekers and the local population over limited available resources; (5) confinement of refugees to designated zones, and the setting up of authoritarian administrative systems to deal with them; (6) suppression of refugees' political sentiments, even in host countries, and protection of rights and interests of concerned states; (7) international concern, evinced through resource mobilization and international organizations to care for refugees; (8) controversies over enumeration and statistics relating to those in flight.

Africa's refugee problem gained momentum towards the end of the 1950s when Africans started fleeing from the Algerian war of independence and from the South African regime and the Portuguese colonial administration. The problem, however, became an international concern in the early 1960s when masses of refugees also began to flee from other countries that were in the process of attaining independence from the colonial powers. As more countries attained independence, the continent's refugee population increased correspondingly.

For example, in 1964 when the refugee problem was first brought to the attention of the OAU, the estimated figure for African refugees was 700,000; in 1969 there were 900,000, an increase of 29 percent; one million in 1977, with an increase between 1969 and 1977 of 11 percent; 100 percent increases in both 1978 and 1979, followed by a further increase of 25 percent between 1979 and 1980. Thereafter, Africa's refugee population stabilized and subsequently appeared to assume a downward trend: 3.6 million in 1981 and three million in 1983 with a decrease of 17 percent over the two years. However, in 1988, once again there were five million refugees, a 67 percent increase. The refugee population again stabilized until early 1990 when events in Liberia and Somalia pushed the figure beyond the five million mark.

Africa's major refugee concentrations by order of magnitude are eastern Africa, southern Africa, central Africa and western Africa. The disheartening picture emerges in Table 1.1.

Furthermore, if statistics are important in appreciating the dimensions of the refugee problem borne by Africa's principal host countries, then, as an example, it should be noted that in 1989, Malawi, with a per capita income of U.S. $280, had a refugee/national population ratio of 1:10, while Ethiopia, with a per capita income of U.S. $120, had a refugee/national population ratio of 1:60, although in Itang (a shelter in southwestern Ethiopia for Sudanese refugees) this ratio was 1:5, indicating that Ethiopia, which has remained the largest refugee-generating country in the Horn of Africa, has now become a haven par excellence for refugees from the Sudan and Somalia.

What has the OAU been doing since its inception about this problem of refugees, which at the moment appears to have grown beyond the capacity of local states to deal with the issue?

TABLE 1.1: 1990 Refugee Populations in Africa by Region

	Region		Number of Refugees
Northern Region:	Algeria		170,000
	Egypt		1,600
		subtotal	171,600
Western Region:	Benin		1,200
	Côte d'Ivoire		210,000
	Guinea		310,000
	Nigeria		6,700
	Togo		3,500
	Senegal		50,000
	Sierra Leone		125,000
	Ghana		6,000
	Mauritania		22,000
		subtotal	734,400
Central Region:	Angola		56,500
	Burundi		267,500
	Cameroon		51,000
	Central African Republic		3,100
	Congo		2,100
	Rwanda		22,200
	Zaire		340,700
		subtotal	743,100
Eastern Region:	Kenya		12,500
	Uganda		112,000
	Tanzania		265,150
	Djibouti		1,300
	Ethiopia		679,500
	Somalia		834,000
	Sudan		745,000
		subtotal	2,649,450
Southern Region:	Botswana		2,100
	Lesotho		3,950
	Malawi		850,000
	Swaziland		28,800
	Zambia		143,600
	Zimbabwe		174,500
		subtotal	1,202,950
Africa's Total Refugee Population			5,501,500

Source: United Nations High Commissioner for Refugees, Information Division, Geneva, 1990. Countries with fewer than 1,000 refugees are not listed.

BACKGROUND TO THE OAU'S CONCERN WITH
THE ISSUE OF REFUGEES

The OAU's interest in refugee matters is reflected in the organization's Charter. The preamble affirms the will of African heads of state and government to work in concert by transcending ethnic and national differences to ensure the best conditions of existence for the peoples of Africa.

In February 1964, the Council of Ministers of the Organization of African Unity, in its Second Ordinary Session, established a special commission to study the refugee problem. The commission identified the guiding principles that govern the OAU's actions on behalf of refugees. Resolution AHG/Res. 26(II), adopted in October 1965 by the heads of state and government in Accra, Ghana, spelled out these principles as follows:

- Reaffirms its desire to give all possible assistance to refugees from any Member State on a humanitarian and fraternal basis;
- Recalls that Member States have pledged themselves to prevent refugees living on their territories from carrying out by any means whatsoever any act harmful to the interests of other states that are members of the Organization of African Unity; and
- Requests all Member States never to allow the refugee question to become a source of dispute amongst them.

These principles were further refined by the first major International Conference on the Legal, Social and Economic Aspects of the African Refugee Problem, held in Addis Ababa in 1967 under the joint sponsorship of the OAU, UNHCR, the UN Economic Commission for Africa and the Dag Hammarskjöld Foundation. The same principles were complemented and reproduced in the OAU Convention governing the Specific Aspects of Refugee Problems in Africa, adopted in September 1969 by the heads of state and government of the OAU in Addis Ababa and subsequently promulgated on June 20, 1974.

Note that this Convention was designed more than twenty years ago in 1969 when the number of refugees on the continent was merely 900,000 *vis-à-vis* the 5,501,500 refugee population of 1990. In 1969 the OAU member states' preoccupation was over the issue of refugees coming from the dependent territories of the continent, as buttressed by the principle of "non-interference in the internal affairs of other states," rather than refugees from the then emerging independent states. The political and economic situations were not as harsh and exacting as they are today. How does this Convention relate to the current situation of forced migration and mobility in Africa?

Previously, many thought that the refugee phenomenon was temporary and would eventually disappear. Most people believed that once Africa was rid of European colonial domination, the refugee phenomenon would automatically become irrelevant. The OAU founding fathers anticipated a united African state to replace the artificial state boundaries formed by the departing colonizers and sought *African solutions to African problems* in an African context.

The OAU Convention was thus adopted against the background of the formation of newly independent states with the primary objective of legitimizing their power and consolidating state control. Two fundamental premises governed the Convention's contents: the sanctity of borders that existed at the time of independence based on the principle of "territorial integrity," and "non-interference in the internal affairs of member states."

Earlier, the 1951 United Nations Convention relating to the Status of Refugees was adopted in Geneva on July 28, 1951. The provisions contained in this Convention were designed to address the refugee problems in Europe at the end of World War II. The 1951 UN Convention definition of "refugee" had two major shortcomings. Firstly, it was limited in terms of *time*, as it confined itself to events prior to January 1, 1951; secondly, it was limited in terms of *space*, as it confined itself to Europe. The new refugee situation that emerged after January 1951 outside Europe, especially in Africa and Asia, dictated the need to widen the temporal and geographical scope of the definition inherent in the 1951 UN Convention. This necessitated the adoption of the Protocol relating to the Status of Refugees on January 31, 1967. Both the 1951 UN Convention and its 1967 Protocol set forth minimum international standards for treatment of refugees.

To meet the unique situations of refugees in Africa, it was necessary to broaden the definition of "refugee" in the 1969 Convention governing the Specific Aspects of Refugee Problems in Africa. Recognizing that people become refugees not simply because of a "well-founded fear of being persecuted for reasons of race, religion, nationality," but also because of domestic political and social upheavals and struggles for national liberation, which force people to flee their homes and cross national frontiers in quest of protection, the heads of state and government made the following modification to the existing definition of the term "refugee," as spelled out in Article I, paragraph 2 of the OAU Convention: "The term 'refugee' shall also apply to every person who, owing to external aggression, occupation, foreign domination or events seriously disturbing public order in either part or the whole of his country of origin or nationality, is compelled to leave his place of habitual residence in order to seek refuge in another place outside his country of origin or nationality."

Although the OAU Convention is a regional complement to the 1951 UN Convention, it has contributed significantly to the development of refugee law and requires an in-depth analysis as a framework to deal with the patterns of forced migration that have characterized the African continent for the last twenty years or so. Thus, four questions may be posed:

- To what extent does the OAU Convention relate to the real problem of Africa's forced migratory patterns today?

- Given the fact that Africa's refugee problem has escalated ever since the adoption of the Convention in 1969, why have some member states of the OAU failed to ratify this important legal instrument of Annex A?

- For those states that have ratified the Convention, what difficulties do they face in implementing some of the provisions of this Convention?

- Is there a need to review and update the Convention to reflect the realities of time?

THE OAU CONVENTION'S IMPLICATIONS FOR AFRICA'S FORCED MIGRATORY PATTERNS

Article I: Definition of the Term "Refugee"

Paragraphs 1 and 2 of the 1969 OAU Convention on Refugees define a refugee as one who has been forced to flee from his or her country, either because of a well-founded fear of persecution or because of external aggression, occupation, foreign domination or events that seriously disturb public order. This definition implies that "refugeeism" has a geography; people are recognized as refugees *only after* they have crossed national borders. Yet civil war, domestic tension or natural disasters have caused hundreds of thousands of people to flee their homes to other areas within their national borders. Although still within their countries of origin, they are nonetheless in *refugee-like situations* and, therefore, deserve the minimum universal standards of treatment prescribed in the 1969 OAU Convention.

This classic definition, which ignores Africa's more than twelve million internally displaced and destitute persons, has encouraged some major donors to earmark aid exclusively for refugees and to place them in camps or settlements where, with their assured material assistance and physical protection, they are looked at as privileged classes amid the physical vulnerability, poverty and squalor of the surrounding local communities. This sometimes led to resentment and tension between the refugees and the host communities, resulting in the assault and eviction of the former by the latter, as demonstrated in the situation of Rwandan refugees in Uganda in 1982.

The OAU has recognized the role recently entrusted to the United Nations Disaster and Relief Organization (UNDRO) to meet the needs of internally displaced persons in Africa, a role recommended by the International Conference on the Plight of Refugees, Returnees and Displaced Persons in Southern Africa, which took place in August 1988 in Oslo, Norway. However, the *politics* that surround *internally displaced* persons might make the work of UNDRO rather difficult unless some arrangements are put in place to tackle particular political aspects of the problem with the seriousness they deserve.

Article II: Asylum

Paragraph 2 of this article clearly states that "The grant of asylum is a peaceful and humanitarian act and shall not be regarded as an unfriendly act by any member state." The drafters of this clause had in mind the refugees who were fleeing colonial territories in the early 1960s and who, therefore, constituted a source of unity and cooperation among and between states. But today's refugees, the majority of whom come from independent states, can be a source of friction. Some member states regard those who flee into exile with suspicion. Sometimes the government of the refugee-generating country feels that "whoever gives asylum to my enemy is also my enemy," a feeling that has often led to protracted disputes and interstate conflicts over refugee issues.

In situations where political relations between states are strained, the flow of refugees may aggravate the situation. The host government, fearing hostilities within the country of origin, may decide to settle refugees in remote camps and set up authoritarian administrative structures to ensure safety and security, but this in turn restricts the freedom of movement espoused in Article VI of the OAU Convention. Refugees are thus forced to remain on the dole and to suffer accusations of "dependency syndrome"— a way of blaming the victim. Freedom of movement is an essential element in the effort to maximize refugee skills and energies in productive ways that will make them self-reliant and enable them to contribute to the economic base of the host country.

Paragraph 4 of Article II sees refugees as a burden that ought to be shared by the member states of the OAU. Admittedly, the responsibility of hosting refugees is not evenly distributed among the OAU member states. Some of the poorest countries, such as Ethiopia, Sudan, Somalia and Djibouti, bear the brunt of hosting refugees. The tendency to see refugees as a "burden" evokes the misinterpretation that refugees, regardless of their qualifications, are a problem. Indeed, refugees are increasingly portrayed not as people who genuinely need help, not as people whose lives need to be stabilized to enable them to become productive and self-reliant, but rather as people who themselves are the problem. They are considered "lazy" and "parasitic," and as such constitute a liability. But, time and again, we are reminded that the development of the agricultural economies of countries like the United States, Canada, Australia, Brazil and France owes much to the skills and energies of immigrants, many of whom were refugees.

While appreciating that Africa's economic hardships have been aggravated by large numbers of refugees, our failure to utilize the resources that often exist among the refugees might also contribute to Africa's socio-economic malaise. Refugees are indeed part of Africa's socio-economic problem, yet under special conditions, they can also be part of the solution. In a speech at the Pan-African Conference on the Situation of Refugees in Africa, Tanzania's former president Julius Nyerere remarked, "All refugees are certainly victims, but they do not consequently lose their individual ideas about life and their own purpose. They will include the ambitious, the optimist, the honest hard-working man and the sly delinquent; the person who will make the best of things, and the man who will grumble about everything. And so on. Generalizations about refugees are very dangerous" (1979).

Paragraph 6 of the same article calls upon countries of asylum (for reasons of security) to settle refugees at a reasonable distance away from the frontiers of their countries of origin. In large countries like the Sudan and Zaire, "reasonable distance" may mean 50 kilometres or more from the border. In tiny Lesotho, "reasonable distance" may mean just a kilometre away from South Africa. It is no wonder then that there have been so many cases of abduction of South African refugees in Lesotho and Swaziland by South African security forces.

In pursuit of this principle, some member states settle refugees in inhospitable and remote parts of the country, far away from the host communities and mainstream of development. This practice not only hinders integration of refugees into host communities, but creates suspicion and hostilities between refugees and local people. All this undermines the process of naturalization of refugees espoused in the 1951 UN Convention.

However, some refugees prefer to settle close to the border, a practice that violates the 1969 OAU Convention and hinders integration. Reluctance to settle far from the border is based on a desire to maximize existing cultural affinities between them and the host communities at the border and their hope that conditions at home will change and make it possible for them to return to familiar environments.

Article III: Prohibition of Subversive Activities

Paragraph 1 stipulates that refugees have duties to their countries of asylum and that they should conform to the laws and regulations necessary for public order. Evidently the issue of the rights of refugees is not raised because these were adequately covered in the 1951 UN Convention. However, what is missing is a delineation of ways and means of disseminating information related to the rights of refugees, not only among the refugees and the host population, but also among such institutions as the local police, the state security apparatus and immigration authorities.

The second part of this paragraph requires refugees to abstain from subversive activities against any member state of the OAU and from attacking any member state by any activity likely to cause tension. Paragraph 2 urges member states not to allow their territories to be used by refugees as launching pads for attacks against any other member state. By implication, while refugees are allowed to stay in exile until circumstances that drove them out of their country change, they are not allowed by word or deed to help bring about the desired political change. Put most simply, the refugees' stay in a member state that offered them asylum is contingent upon their passivity and silence, even though the motive behind their flight might have been the search for freedom of expression, as well as the right to development.

Article V: Voluntary Repatriation

Unlike the 1951 UN Convention, Article V of the OAU Convention assumes that at one time or another, refugees will want to return home. Voluntary repatriation means that the refugees will decide when they want to return. This decision is to be based on the refugee's conviction that the circumstances that initially led to their flight have improved. But since it is the prerogative of the refugee-generating country, and not the refugees, to change these circumstances, the government of the refugees' country of origin, which sees the refugees as the "enemy across the border" is bound to take its time in changing these circumstances; therefore, refugees remain in limbo, sometimes for decades, without being allowed to make a decision to return home. Some governments, in fact, declare a general amnesty for their nationals living in exile without even attempting to change the circumstances that led to their flight.

Two situations have emerged from this. Firstly, as a result of being denied the right to return to one's country of origin sometimes for decades, and out of cumulative frustrations that usually accompany life in exile, refugees have decided to resort to armed struggle, contrary to Article III of the OAU Convention. The Rwandan refugees' invasion of Rwanda from Uganda in October 1990 is a recent example. Secondly, the refugee situation has remained permanent, especially due to the OAU's cardinal principle of "non-interference in the internal affairs of other member states." This helped to undermine the political and humanitarian will of the host governments, voluntary agencies, international and intergovernmental organizations in facilitating the refugees' safe return, as called upon by paragraphs 2 and 5 of Article V of the OAU Convention.

Political changes that led to the flight of an individual might indeed have changed in the refugee's favour, but the economic situation might have deteriorated greatly. Examples of refugees who have refused to take such a risk or who have had to go back into exile abound. Related to this are situations in which refugees are forced to return home by exigencies such as war in the host country. The recent case of Ethiopian refugees who sought asylum in Somalia and who, due to the civil war there, had to return to Ethiopia, reveals how complicated Africa's refugee scene has become.

Article VI: Travel Documents

Paragraph 1 of Article VI requires OAU member states to issue refugees travel documents for travel outside their country of asylum, unless compelling reasons of national security or public order require otherwise. Under the 1951 UN Convention, member states are also expected to issue refugees identification cards to facilitate internal movements in the country of asylum, at least for education and employment purposes, but if some member states perceive that granting asylum to refugees contains a political risk, freedom of movement may be restricted.

The necessity of incorporating a "return clause" in a refugee's travel document to travel abroad with a view to returning to the first country of asylum has not always been respected by all member states, especially those in southern Africa. Getting one refugee out of a country is a way of reducing the "burden." Paradoxically, accepting one more refugee for resettlement is to accept one refugee too many. Due to such restrictions of movement, many refugees find it difficult to avail themselves of opportunities for education and employment, either in countries of asylum or abroad.

Article VII: Cooperation of National Authorities with the OAU

This article calls upon member states of the OAU to furnish the OAU secretary-general with all relevant information and statistical data regarding refugee situations. However, there is debate about refugee statistics. Some host governments are accused of inflating numbers of refugees to maximize international assistance, while others are accused of underestimating numbers to minimize costs. For example, in 1987 the OAU General Secretariat was informed that 38 percent of the refugees in the Sudan were receiving direct assistance from the UNHCR. The remaining 62 percent were spontaneously settled refugees who, technically speaking, were beyond the UNHCR mandate, were not being assisted and were causing considerable strains on the economic base of the country to the extent that the local population began to resent the refugees.

Reasons for not offering international assistance to spontaneously settled refugees include such ethnocentric views as "traditional African hospitality" and "ethnic cultural compatibility" across borders. However, host communities sometimes do not offer hospitality because of antagonism between the peoples concerned, or fear of socio-economic competition, or poverty, all of which render refugees vulnerable to starvation. Unfortunately, these ethnocentric arguments are being advanced at a time when Africa's economies are deteriorating, when public opinion in many parts of the world is hardening against refugees, and when some European countries are not only tightening their immigration laws but also flagrantly violating the 1951 UN Convention.

TABLE 1.2: **List of Countries That Have Signed, Ratified or Adhered to the African Charter on Human and Peoples' Rights**

No.	Country	Date of Signature	Date of Ratification	Date Deposited
1.	Algeria	10/04/86	01/03/87	20/03/87
2.	Angola	02/03/90	09/10/90	—
3.	Benin	20/01/86	25/02/86	—
4.	Botswana	17/07/86	22/07/86	—
5.	Burundi	28/07/89	30/08/89	—
6.	Burkina Faso	05/03/84	06/07/84	21/09/84
7.	Cameroon	23/07/87	20/06/89	18/09/89
8.	Cape Verde	31/03/86	02/06/87	06/08/87
9.	Central African Republic	26/04/86	27/06/86	—
10.	Chad	29/05/86	09/10/86	11/11/86
11.	Comoros	01/06/86	18/07/86	—
12.	Congo	27/11/81	09/12/82	17/01/83
13.	Côte d'Ivoire	—	—	—
14.	Djibouti	—	—	—
15.	Egypt	16/11/81	20/03/84	03/04/84
16.	Equatorial Guinea	18/08/86	07/04/86	18/08/86

(Continued)

No.	Country	Date of Signature	Date of Ratification	Date Deposited
17.	Ethiopia	—	—	—
18.	Gabon	26/02/82	20/02/86	26/06/86
19.	Gambia	11/02/83	08/06/83	13/06/83
20.	Ghana	24/01/89	01/03/89	
21.	Guinea	09/12/81	16/02/82	13/05/82
22.	Guinea-Bissau	—	—	—
23.	Kenya	—	—	—
24.	Lesotho	07/03/84	—	—
25.	Liberia	31/01/83	04/08/82	29/12/82
26.	Libya	30/05/85	19/07/86	26/03/87
27.	Madagascar	—	—	—
28.	Malawi	23/02/90	17/11/89	23/02/90
29.	Mali	13/11/81	21/12/81	22/01/82
30.	Mauritania	25/02/82	14/06/86	26/06/86
31.	Mauritius	—	—	—
32.	Mozambique	22/02/89	07/03/90	—
33.	Namibia	—	—	—
34.	Niger	09/07/86	15/07/86	21/07/86
35.	Nigeria	31/08/82	22/06/83	22/07/83
36.	Republic of Rwanda	11/11/81	15/07/83	22/07/83
37.	Saharawi Arab Dem. Republic	10/04/86	02/05/86	23/05/86
38.	Sao Tome and Principe	23/05/86	28/07/86	—
39.	Senegal	23/09/81	13/08/82	25/10/82
40.	Seychelles	—	—	—
41.	Sierra Leone	27/08/81	21/09/83	27/01/84
42.	Somalia	26/02/82	31/07/85	20/03/86
43.	Sudan	03/09/82	18/02/86	11/03/86
44.	Swaziland	—	—	—
45.	Tanzania	31/05/82	18/02/84	09/03/84
46.	Togo	26/02/82	05/11/82	22/11/82
47.	Tunisia	16/03/83	22/04/83	—
48.	Uganda	18/08/86	10/05/86	27/05/86
49.	Zaire	23/07/87	20/07/87	28/07/87
50.	Zambia	17/01/83	19/01/84	02/02/84
51.	Zimbabwe	20/02/86	30/05/86	12/06/86

Source: Office of the Secretary-General, Organization of African Unity, Legal Division, Addis Ababa.

Article X: Signature and Ratification

In paragraph 1 of this article, member states are urged to accede to the 1969 OAU Convention. While the African Charter on Human and Peoples' Rights, which became effective in 1981, has been ratified by forty member states of the OAU (see Table 1.2), the 1969 OAU Convention has so far been acceded to by only forty-one member states (See Table 1.3). Interestingly, some member states have ratified the 1951 UN Convention, but not the OAU Convention. Some believe that ratification of this Convention will undermine voluntary repatriation as a durable solution. They support encouraging voluntary repatriation by not allowing integration between refugees and host communities. It should not, however, be perceived that those member states that have not yet ratified the Convention do not assist or admit refugees. In fact, despite their very limited socio-economic opportunities, countries like Djibouti have not closed their borders to asylum seekers, even though Djibouti has only 142 hectares of cultivable land. But the value of ratifying the OAU Convention lies in the fact that organizations like the UNHCR find it relatively easy to legally apply or invoke provisions of the Convention in countries that are parties to the Convention.

TABLE 1.3: OAU Convention Governing the Specific Aspects of Refugee Problems in Africa

No.	Country	Date of Signature	Date of Ratification	Date Deposited
1.	Algeria	10/09/69	24/05/74	20/06/74
2.	Angola	30/04/81	03/12/82	—
3.	Benin	10/09/69	26/02/73	12/03/73
4.	Botswana	"	—	—
5.	Burundi	"	31/10/75	10/12/75
6.	Burkina Faso	"	19/03/74	16/08/78
7.	Cameroon	"	07/09/75	10/01/86
8.	Cape Verde	16/02/89	09/03/89	—
9.	Central African Republic	10/09/69	23/07/70	09/08/70
10.	Chad	"	12/08/81	10/09/81
11.	Comoros	"	—	—
12.	Congo	10/09/69	16/01/71	01/02/71
13.	Côte d'Ivoire	"	—	—
14.	Djibouti	—	—	—
15.	Egypt	12/06/80	17/11/80	—
16.	Equatorial Guinea	10/09/69	08/09/80	28/01/81
17.	Ethiopia	"	15/10/73	25/10/73

(Continued)

No.	Country	Date of Signature	Date of Ratification	Date Deposited
18.	Gabon	21/03/86	26/06/86	—
19.	Gambia	10/09/69	12/11/80	16/03/81
20.	Ghana	"	19/06/75	19/06/75
21.	Guinea	"	18/10/72	16/04/73
22.	Guinea-Bissau	27/06/89	12/07/90	—
23.	Kenya	10/09/69	—	—
24.	Lesotho	18/11/88	30/12/88	—
25.	Liberia	10/09/69	01/10/71	07/02/72
26.	Libya	25/04/81	17/07/81	—
27.	Madagascar	10/09/69	—	—
28.	Malawi	04/11/87	02/12/87	—
29.	Mali	10/09/69	10/10/81	16/11/81
30.	Mauritania	"	22/07/82	07/09/72
31.	Mauritius	"	—	—
32.	Morocco	"	13/05/74	16/07/74
33.	Mozambique	22/02/89	07/03/90	—
34.	Namibia	—	—	—
35.	Niger	10/09/69	16/09/71	29/09/71
36.	Nigeria	"	23/05/86	24/06/86
37.	Republic of Rwanda	"	19/11/79	04/02/80
38.	Saharawi Arab Democratic Republic	—	—	—
39.	Sao Tome and Principe	—	—	—
40.	Senegal	10/09/69	01/04/71	21/05/71
41.	Seychelles	11/09/80	24/09/80	—
42.	Sierra Leone	28/12/87	14/03/88	—
43.	Somalia	10/09/69	—	—
44.	Sudan	"	24/12/72	12/01/75
45.	Swaziland	"	16/01/89	09/02/89
46.	Togo	"	10/04/70	28/05/70
47.	Tunisia	"	17/11/89	18/12/89
48.	Uganda	"	24/07/87	07/08/87
49.	Tanzania	"	10/01/75	24/01/75
50.	Zaire	"	14/02/73	04/05/73
51.	Zambia	"	30/07/73	15/08/73
52.	Zimbabwe	"	28/09/85	17/10/85

Source: Organization of African Unity, Addis Ababa.

CONCLUSIONS

Since the adoption of the 1969 OAU Convention, major changes have taken place. The number of refugees jumped from less than one million in 1969 to over five million today, exceeding the total population of more than the ten least populated African states. Most of these refugees are women, children, the disabled and the elderly, all of whom deserve mention in the 1969 OAU Convention.

Armed conflicts in Africa that give rise to mass exodus of refugees and displaced persons have almost become endemic. Refugees have become increasingly vigilant, inspired by the events of eastern and central Europe that took place towards the end of the 1980s. They have, out of desperation, resorted to armed struggle to force their way back home. This practice has not only wreaked havoc on the civilian populations and on the environment as a whole, but has also led to flagrant violation of the OAU Convention.

Displaced persons are not given any place in the Convention, yet this problem poses a greater challenge than refugees. Political difficulties that displaced persons usually generate cannot be ignored. Humanitarian efforts aimed at alleviating the plight of uprooted communities are undermined by armed struggle. Convoys carrying relief supplies to or through zones of conflicts are either attacked or not allowed to reach their destinations, aggravating the lot of many refugees and displaced persons.

Finally, host communities may exhaust their food stocks to assist refugees or displaced persons during the early stages of a crisis, yet when the international or donor community finally arrives to assist the uprooted, host communities are usually ignored. This kind of situation has led to an emergence of a somewhat privileged class of people who receive international assistance while needs of local inhabitants are ignored.

Involuntary migration in Africa is, to a large extent, a manifestation of our failure to recognize the link between the politics and the economics of the refugee-producing or receiving countries: the failure of a government to provide citizens with basic human rights relating to physical security, subsistence, political participation and freedom of movement. If these basic needs were provided, forced migration would be reduced. Once asylum is found, political and economic factors determine to a large measure not only prospects for refugees to live a normal life in the host country but also prospects for voluntary repatriation. Whatever solutions are taken to address the political and economic problems confronting refugees and member states of the OAU, they can only be successful *if they are built on an assured respect for the minimum but universal standards of treatment of refugees.*

REFERENCES

Bakwesegha, Chris J. 1991. "Armed Conflicts in Africa: Their Effects on Civilian Populations." A paper prepared in honour of the World Red Cross Day 1991 under the theme "Protecting War Victims," March.

Harrell-Bond, Barbara E. 1990. "Breaking the Vicious Circle: Refugees and Other Displaced Persons in Africa." In *The African Social Situation: Crucial Factors of Development and Transformation*, African Center for Applied Research and Training in Social Development, 92-143. London: Hanszell Publishers.

Nyerere, Mwalimu Julius. 1979. Statement at the 1979 Pan-African Conference on the Situation of Refugees in Africa, May 7.

Organization of African Unity. 1969. Convention governing the Specific Aspects of Refugee Problems in Africa, September 10.

Press and Information Division of OAU General Secretariat. 1964 OAU Charter and Rules of Procedure.

United Nations. 1951. Convention relating to the Status of Refugees, July 28.

———. 1967. Protocol relating to the Status of Refugees, January 31.

PART TWO

Basic Needs and Refugees

2

Resource Depletion, Famine and Refugees in Tigray

Tsegaye Hailu
Tsegay Wolde-Georgis
Peter W. Van Arsdale

Recent political developments in Ethiopia have been nothing short of phenomenal. In February 1991 the Ethiopian People's Revolutionary Democratic Front (EPRDF)[1] made rapid advances from its base area in Tigray to the north-central regions of Gonder, Gojam, Welega and many parts of rural Shewa and Welo. By mid-spring the city of Addis Ababa was surrounded. On May 21, 1991, Lieutenant Colonel Mengistu Haile Mariam, the long-standing president, fled to Zimbabwe. He was succeeded by his newly appointed vice-president, Lieutenant General Tesfaye Gebre-Kidan.

A London conference between the Ethiopian government and the armed opposition forces was previously scheduled to begin on May 28. The United States was serving as conference broker. Opposition participants were to include the EPRDF, the Eritrean People's Liberation Front (EPLF) and the Oromo Liberation Front (OLF). On May 27, just hours before the conference was to begin, Acting President Tesfaye reported to the United States Embassy in Addis Ababa that his government was now unable to control its army. He feared that administrative chaos, prison killings and localized looting would erupt.

The EPRDF, which remained outside the city limits of Addis Ababa so as not to interfere with the talks the next day, was forced to enter the city to maintain law and order. Herman J. Cohen, the American mediator, consented to this move.[2] There was fear that if swift action were not taken, a Somali-type civil war would erupt in the capital.

The talks went ahead as scheduled. However, with the establishment of the interim EPRDF regime in Addis Ababa, the representatives of the Mengistu-Tesfaye government dropped out. The three rebel groups became the principal players. Several decisions were reached, the most important of which was to hold a national conference beginning July 1, 1991. When the conference took place, a broad-based transitional government representing two dozen opposition groups was formed.[3] Another important development was that for the first time, the United States accepted the right of the Eritrean people to self-determination.

Subsequently, some of the other key concerns raised at the July conference and immediately thereafter have been clarified or addressed. One dealt with the resumption of relief to drought-affected areas of the country. Another dealt with free press and assembly, as well as related human rights issues. Another (with which two of the authors were directly involved) dealt with planning and seeking funds for village-level, diversified water development. Yet another dealt with reestablishing relations with refugees and citizens of Ethiopia living elsewhere; such people are now welcome and perceived as valuable resources for the country.

The broad-based and democratically established transitional government under President Meles Zenawi, the former rebel leader, appears to have consolidated its position. The main antagonist of the EPRDF is now an inherited bureaucracy that is, at the least, unsympathetic to the causes for which the EPRDF fought. Although many are optimistic, time will tell if the EPRDF—through the new national government—will be able to institutionalize the changes it seeks.

This chapter is not so much about contemporary politics or opportunities in the "new Ethiopia," although these are covered, as it is about the ramifications of long-evolving historical, socio-economic and ecological forces. Using an implicit systems analysis framework, we attempt to clarify salient factors that have contributed to the interrelated situations of resource depletion, famine and refugee creation, with particular attention to Tigray. We introduce the concept of "adaptive flux" to help explain the remarkable resilience demonstrated by refugees and settled villagers alike.

Historically, the boundaries and constituent regions of Tigray have varied, depending on the centre of political power in Ethiopia. The contemporary Tigray region is a land-locked area immediately south of Eritrea. Tigray can be geographically classified into three distinct regions: (1) the eastern escarpment and the Rift Valley, which is very sparsely populated; (2) the central plateau, which is heavily populated, overgrazed, prone to erosion and extremely susceptible to minor climatic changes; and (3) the western lowlands, which are relatively fertile and yet less densely populated than the central highlands (English et al. 1984).

The people of Tigray historically occupied the northern highlands of Ethiopia. They are identified by their use of the Tigriyna language, which evolved from the ancient language of Geez. (Amharinya also evolved from Geez, a point that will be important in a later section.) The Tigriyna language is spoken in the contemporary province of Tigray, in the highland provinces of Eritrea and in the northern parts of the provinces of Welo and Gonder. The region is home to the Tigray people, the Raya and Azebo Oromos, the Afar and the Saho. The Tigray are predominantly Christian and comprise about 70 percent of the population (Markakis 1987, 251).

Virtually all economic activities are at subsistence level and hence easily disrupted by prolonged droughts and/or socio-political instability. Indeed, droughts and destructive wars have characterized the history of Tigray. To understand recent disruptions and the adaptive flux that will be discussed is to understand the history of the region. To understand famine in the region, as Finn and his colleagues (1990) emphasized, is to understand politics.

Causally interrelated are successive famines, civil war and certain policies of the Ethiopian government, which all contribute to the displacement of thousands of Tigrayans within and outside of Ethiopia. Unfortunately, the distinction between disaster—including famine—and deprivation is seldom recognized, yet it is critical to understanding the ways in which displaced people cope and to understanding our interpretations of the factors that have created Tigrayan refugees.

Disaster and deprivation are not mutually exclusive. Whereas a disaster can be defined as an event that disables humans in significant numbers, deprivation can be defined as "a decremental shift in resource availability which is perceived by most or all of the actors as being cyclical or repetitive and therefore at least partially predictable in occurrence" (Laughlin and Brady 1978, 18). The concept of adaptive flux is based upon the work of Van Arsdale elsewhere in the Horn of Africa. It is defined as short-term tactics and long-term strategies that enable survival under fluctuating, harsh and erratic conditions in a socio-economically peripheral area (Van Arsdale 1989, 72).[4]

Adaptive flux reflects people's own self-help capabilities and motivations, as opposed to externally-derived interdependencies. When new organizations are formed, as with the *baito* system discussed in the chapter's concluding section, it reflects empowerment strategies. The concept encompasses those tactics and strategies that enable people, such as many of the Tigrayan refugees, to cope successfully with deprivation—in its interactive ecological, economic and political manifestations. In northern Ethiopia, adaptive flux has been manifested primarily through various types of migration, in alternative farming strategies, and in the formation of the *baito* system.

HISTORICAL BACKGROUND

Environmental Degradation, Political Instability and Resource Depletion

Contemporary Tigrayans are predominantly subsistence cultivators. Notable exceptions are the Afar nomads of the Danakil area, and the Raya Oromo who are mixed cultivators and pastoralists. The Saho, who inhabit the escarpment region, are also involved in mixed cultivation.

Prior to the twentieth century, the main socio-economic system in northern Ethiopia was a form of feudalism. However, unlike European feudalism, northern Ethiopian feudalism was based more fully on the extraction of surplus in labour and in kind. Even though there were many variations of landholding, the predominant system was based on communal ownership of land among kinship groups. The *rist* system of landholding has been described in detail by Markakis (1974, 75–80) and Hobben (1973, 137). Church and state lands were also widespread. Peasants paid tribute to the state, individual nobles and the church. Broadly speaking, northern Ethiopian feudalism was based on the class relationships between the priests, the nobility and the peasantry—the "classic trinity" (Markakis 1974, 73).

A mixture of "plough culture" and cattle raising were predominant. Important stocks and varieties of cereals and other crops were developed, including durum, wheat barley, sorghum, linseed, finger millet and chick-peas.[5] In the sixteenth century, a Portuguese missionary named Alvarez visited northern Ethiopia and reported on an area of Tigray called Maitsaeda. He wrote of dense populations and abundant crops. In southern Tigray he reported seeing thick maize fields and a surplus of crops (Pankhurst 1966, 47). Yet the years following the visit of the Portuguese missionaries were not favourable for the northern Ethiopian economy and productivity in many areas declined. While a number of factors were at work (Markakis 1974, 15ff.; McCann 1990, 393–95), we believe that environmental degradation, resource depletion and increases in rural population caused a rural crisis that has lasted into the twentieth century. Ecological and socio-economic analyses provide the underpinning, while political analysis provides the overlay. Politics, in large part, became "the evolving politics of scarcity," to borrow a phrase from Ophuls (1977).

Population pressure increasingly led to the cultivation of traditional pasture areas and steep slopes. Such pressure also led to more demand for housing materials and firewood, with subsequent deforestation. Over time, the use of crop residues and animal manure for fuel deprived the land of these traditional fertilizers (Kebbede and Jacob 1988, 68). Lack of pasture led to fewer cattle owned by farmers. Moreover, the system of fallowing used to regain land fertility, while still practised, was attenuated; the cultivation of steep slopes and the deforestation that followed led to excessive soil erosion. The consequence was evident in decreased agricultural productivity. We believe these pressures created pressures to internally migrate and expand into new lands, rather than intensify production and improve technologies in local areas. As will become apparent, this can be seen as an antecedent of the twentieth century's refugee movements.

Civil wars and associated political instability also contributed to agricultural and resource decline. The years between 1769 and 1855 are known as the "Age of Princes" in Ethiopian history. There was virtually continuous warfare among the nobility, with severe consequences for manpower and agriculture in Tigray and elsewhere. The absence of a permanent army led to deterioration in the economic well-being of peasant farmers. It was the norm for passing militia to take farmers' savings or supplies without compensating them. Many communities were pillaged and ransacked. While the Christian Emperor Tewodros II did much to reduce the internecine conflicts and unify the country, members of his administration severely depleted peasant resources.[6]

In the late nineteenth century there were additional external and internal conflicts that battered northern Ethiopia. External conflicts included the 1867–1868 British invasion against Tewodros II, the Egyptian invasion in the mid-1880s, the 1889 invasion by the Sudanese Mahdists that led to the death of Emperor Yohannes IV, and the 1895–1896 Italian invasion that led to the Battle of Adwa. Internally, the socio-economic life of northern Ethiopia was disrupted significantly (McCann 1990). In 1898 Menelik II (who ruled from 1889 to 1913) took an army of some 50,000 to 100,000 men to northern Welo and Tigray in order to vanquish Ras Mengesha Yohannes, the traditional ruler and contender for the throne as the son of Emperor Yohannes IV. Resources were depleted again. In 1909 Dejazmach Abate led a Shewan army of 10,000 to establish his command in Tigray. They were all supported by local resources. In 1914 an imperial army of 30,000 was sent to Tigray in response to the intense rivalries among local factions. Only the exhaustion of Tigrayan resources and associated epidemics (including dysentery) led to the army's withdrawal.

Disruption continued. The 1916 coup d'état in the Ethiopian capital that led to the accession of Tafari Makonnen (later known as Haile Selassie) resulted in the mobilization of Tigrayan troops. Between 1916 and 1921 the deposed king Lij Iyasu organized an antigovernment resistance movement from eastern Tigray and Welo. In response, the central government sent punitive expeditions. Iyasu was caught five years later. From 1928 to 1930 eastern Tigray and Welo were involved in a resistance movement against imperial efforts at centralization. Troops from both the north and south were mobilized. Furthermore, the Italian occupation of Ethiopia (which lasted from 1935 to 1941) required local peasants to provide resources not only for the anti-Italian partisans but also for the Italian soldiers. In 1943 the Woyane rebellion in Tigray led to intensive fighting that was also accompanied by the intervention of British bombers. McCann (1990) argued that the need for the provision of food for unsalaried troops in several instances damaged smallholder agriculture in Ethiopia.

By the mid-twentieth century, the pressures and constraints briefly outlined in this section took a tremendous toll on Tigray. Lack of technical support for peasant farming systems, resource mismanagement and inadequate soil conservation measures led to further environmental degradation. As of the mid-1970s, topsoil in the central plateau was drastically eroded and aquifers severely depleted (Hailu 1991). Successive Ethiopian governments clearly had not invested in the management of natural resources (Dejene 1990). Socio-economically, this was compounded by the fact that there were few nonagricultural employment opportunities to ease the burden on the land. The seeds were sown for the civil war during the Mengistu regime and for the devastating famines of the past decade.

Government Constraints and the Oppression of Tigray

From the Tigrayans' point of view, they have experienced environmental as well as human degradation in the latter part of the twentieth century. During the 1980s open political conflicts developed in the region against the oppression of the central government in Addis Ababa. Two of the Tigrayans' major problems were the continued economic and political weakness of the region (Henze 1985). Viewed in this light, the oppression of Tigray can be historically associated with the shift of political power from the north to the south, and the central government's generalized policy of national oppression.

Historically, there was a struggle between Tigrayan leaders and those of the Amhara for the domination of the kingdom of Ethiopia. Since the fall of the ancient Axumite kingdom in the ninth century A.D. Tigrayans have not been able to gain political ascendancy except for a brief period during the second half of the nineteenth century. The only Tigrayan emperor to ascend to power was Yohannes IV (1872–1889). His death, while fighting against the Sudanese Mahdists, shifted the power to the most influential chief of Shewa, who crowned himself as Menelik II in 1889. This was the beginning of the Tigrayans' downfall. The cornerstone of Menelik II's policy was the suppression of Tigray. As a polity, Tigray was not able to again consolidate its power until 1990–1991.

The Tigriyna-speaking frontier provinces to the north were occupied by the Italians to form the colony of Eritrea in 1890. The various leaders of Tigray were divided, leading to instability in the region. Any sign of revolt was crushed by the government. In the late 1890s, an Amhara from outside the region was appointed governor of Tigray. Thus, Tigrayans were losing their control by the dual intervention of colonialism from the north and an internal Amharic presence from the south. As the Tigray and Amhara represent the broadest historical divisions within traditional Ethiopian society, the ominous nature of this presence from the Tigrayan perspective can be better understood.

The quality of life in Tigray was one of the lowest in Ethiopia. Illiteracy, malnutrition and disease were widespread in the early decades of this century.[7] Even though the Ethiopian government was responsible for constructing schools and hospitals throughout the country, key informants interviewed by two of the authors in Tigray indicated that resources spent on this province were minimal. The few schools, hospitals and other services that were established were located in the provincial capital of Mekele. Even then Tigrayans had difficulty in getting government staff to teach in the schools and work in the health facilities. Most outlying facilities and side roads had to be developed by local initiative. The main roads were constructed by Italian occupiers in the 1930s.

Furthermore, development inputs from the central government were reduced after the 1943 Woyane revolt. Thus, even though the literacy rate of Tigrayans was very low, over half of the town schools were closed in 1949 on the grounds that Tigray did not bring in enough revenue (Hammond 1990, 18).

This may have been a ruse, as we believe there was no direct relationship between regional revenues and central government investments in other parts of the country. Remarkably, there were only two high schools for the whole of Tigray until the people took the initiative in the late 1960s and early 1970s to build more themselves.

The conflict between Tigray and the state, as reflected in resource constraints, continued after the 1974 revolution. For example, in order to alleviate the shortage of health facilities, the people of the Tigrayan town of Adigrat decided to build a hospital in the late 1970s. Within a few years the people were able to raise more than half a million dollars. The completed structure contained 120 beds, yet a request to the Ministry of Health for medical personnel and medicine was refused. Our field interviews indicated that only the intervention of the Ministry of Defence, when it perceived the facility's value as a regional army hospital, led to support from the Ministry of Health.

The Woyane I and II

An important event in recent Tigrayan history was the 1943 revolt against Amhara domination, popularly known as the Woyane. Unlike previous revolts, this involved the collaboration of different social classes. It had popular grassroots involvement and many peasants participated. The leader of the revolt, Blata Hailemariam Reda, was a man of peasant origins. The revolt was organized around democratic principles not previously practised definitively in Tigray (Tareke 1984).

The main cause of the rebellion was a new taxation policy set by corrupt government officials appointed from Shewa, in concert with the oppression and abuse by the unsalaried government militia. The revolt challenged the legitimacy of Emperor Haile Selassie's government, a structure restored after the defeat of the Italians. The revolt was so widespread that it was crushed only after British ground and air intervention. Bombs were dropped in market-places and other civilian areas during October 1943 (Haggai 1986, 189-94; Tareke 1984, 80). The leaders of the revolt were exiled to a remote part of the country. As the rebellion was being suppressed, many peasants (especially in southern Tigray) lost their cattle and land as a collective punishment for their participation. Such land alienation was the first ever in Tigray (Tareke 1984, 81) and exacerbated pressures related to land use that were discussed earlier.

The central government clearly recognized that land was the single most important resource and the basis of power. Depriving the people of land meant disarming them. Therefore, to prevent Tigray from mounting any future revolt, the central government confiscated the province's most productive agricultural areas. The boundaries of Tigray were redrawn so that two districts in the west (Wolkait and Tselempt) were annexed to the province of Gonder, and one in the south (Raya) was annexed to the province of Welo. The area of Tigray was reduced to about 66,000 square kilometres. It was only in the 1980s that the TPLF reclaimed the lost districts as part of Tigray, expanding the area to approximately 102,000 square kilometres, encompassing an estimated population of five million.

The political and military struggle that began in 1975 under the leadership of the Tigrayan People's Liberation Front (TPLF) eventually called itself the Woyane II, in memory of the peasant struggle in the early 1940s. A primary difference between earlier revolts and the Woyane II was the level of organization and political consciousness engendered, and adaptive flux must be understood in light of this organization. It meant learning lessons from past failures, as well as learning how to be more resourceful in the face of significant odds.

In its formative years, the TPLF emerged as an organization with a seemingly strident political vision combining aspects of orthodox socialism and Marxism. Many members of the policy-making TPLF Standing Committee apparently belonged to the Marxist-Leninist League of Tigray, a situation in the 1980s that engendered either praise or condemnation (depending upon one's orientation). Accusations that dissident members of the TPLF were purged from membership may have been true, but as the organization evolved and gained increasing grassroots support, its rhetoric mellowed and its ability to effectively handle diversity of opinion increased. While the TPLF's military strategy was based on traditional guerrilla warfare, the main program became the establishment of cultural, economic and political autonomy in Tigray *(People's Voice* 1990). We believe that more than any espoused political orientation, this program—coupled with a remarkable resilience in the face of long-term stress—enabled this organization to succeed. The expressed desire for equal democratic participation in Ethiopia and its corollary, the eradication of national oppression, were well-intended but less directly linked to grassroots successes. Ironically, it was in March 1989, exactly one hundred years after the imposition of Shewan Amhara rule, that the TPLF completed the expulsion of the Mengistu government's provincial administration from Tigray.

PATTERNS OF MIGRATION

Having concentrated on sedentary agriculture and raising livestock for centuries, Tigrayans were not known as migrant people. Movements traditionally were restricted to short-term internal shifts, usually in response to seasonal food shortages. These were followed by a return to the place of origin. There are indications that a few significant migrations in the distant past had occurred in what is now northern Ethiopia, and that refugees were later sent to Axum by the prophet Muhammad, as mentioned earlier. While not directly involving Tigrayans, major movements took place elsewhere during the period of the great Ethiopian ethnic migrations (ca. 1520–1660).

The Increase of Out-Migration

Some authors have argued that Tigray's economic decline led to increased migration as early as the middle of the nineteenth century (McCann 1990, 396). McCann believed that there was a gradual movement of some of Tigray's rural agricultural population towards the south. Ecological constraints and economic pressures on small farmers, exacerbated by periodic droughts and political instability, caused internal migration to increase. He argued that Tigray's political unrest in the late nineteenth century was not a cause of the decline in agricultural productivity but a result. We agree.

In the early 1880s, according to McCann (1990, 396), Tigriyna-speaking migrants from Eritrea settled further south. They also settled in northern Welo as farmers and penetrated the north-south caravan route in attempts to become more commercially engaged. In the eastern part of Tigray, income from trade was becoming an increasingly important supplement to agriculture. By the late 1960s, petty trade was an entrenched strategy of income generation for this part of the province (Bauer, cited in McCann 1990, 396). Thus, nonagricultural employment and trade—together with migration—were becoming important coping mechanisms for Tigrayans decades before the most recent droughts and political disruption occurred.

Migration as a Long-Term Strategy

Migration became more established as a coping strategy as socio-economic problems increased. Famines exacerbated the problems, but did not create them. Those that occurred after World War II were not necessarily worse than those of previous decades, but were better documented and contributed to a greater degree of out-migration (and eventual refugee creation) in Tigray than famines in the past. One of the worst occurred in 1958–1960 when an estimated 397,000 people died as a result of locust infestations and epidemics (Wolde-Mariam 1984, 13). This disaster is remembered as the Zeben Anbeta ("Epoch of the Locusts"), and also is remembered for its devastating effects on both urban and rural people. It should be added that the government was very slow to respond, thus contributing to the deaths of many Tigrayans. This encouraged migration even further.

Migration as a long-term strategy has taken on additional dimensions. Since World War II young men and women have moved into the larger cities and the more promising agricultural development areas in other regions as seasonal labourers. Agricultural development centres in Humera and the Awash Rift Valley have attracted many Tigrayan labourers. School drop-outs also move out of Tigray because of minimal employment opportunities. The most important urban centres outside of Tigray that have major concentrations of Tigrayans are Asmara and Addis Ababa. The extent of the out-migration has been noted by Henze (1985), who stressed that one can find Tigrayans even in the most remote parts of Ethiopia, where they work as labourers or small business people. A study by Kloos and Adugna (1989) showed that the highest rate of population growth in Ethiopia was in the central and southern regions, partly at the expense of the north (which includes Tigray). The study also showed that Tigray had the lowest rate of population growth, a fact partly attributable to out-migration.

In the 1980s the fact that the government was being challenged by the TPLF meant that people were not free to move about; the government of Ethiopia suspected many of them of being rebel sympathizers. Bombing and strafing by government aircraft caused people to flee to TPLF-held areas for safety. Those we interviewed indicated that when government troops came to a village that was visited by TPLF cadres, the whole village would flee from fear of government reprisal. People were also forced to flee when government troops destroyed their homes as part of a process of intimidation. The migratory coping strategy was being curtailed.

Government-Sponsored Forced Relocation

One type of migration is forced relocation. In the 1980s the Ethiopian government began the policies of resettlement and so-called "villagization." These began after the 1984–1985 drought, the most severe of the past century in Tigray. These policies also followed on the heels of the strengthening of the TPLF. The government rationalized this policy as a partial solution for the drought-prone regions of the north. It argued that the land degraded in Tigray could be rehabilitated only by removing people to other areas. The program was to take people to the supposedly fertile and sparsely populated regions of the south and southwestern parts of Ethiopia.

In fact, the program was neither properly studied nor voluntary. The central government did not couch the relocations in appropriate socio-economic contexts, nor did it properly assess the effects they would have on the host populations in the south. One case illustrates the severity and mismanagement of the problem. In October 1985 the Ethiopian army entered the town of Korem where there were many Tigrayan relief recipients and rounded up about 600 residents for resettlement. The ultimate result was the dispersal of 10,000 others (including hospital patients) into the surrounding hills (U.S. Committee for Refugees 1986, 44).

The relocation of Tigrayans coincided with the revolt of the people in the area. Those we interviewed, who opposed the forced relocation program, argued that the drought itself was not the primary cause of the 1984–1985 famine in Tigray. We agree. Instead, proximate causes were a combination of government mismanagement and war. The involuntary movement of people during the time of deprivation was neither humanitarian nor developmental in nature, as Clay and Holcomb noted (1986, 84–88). Those we interviewed stated that the program was aimed at depriving the liberation movement of the support it was receiving from the peasantry. It is estimated that thousands of people from Tigray died during the process of resettlement. Many others ended up as refugees in the Sudan.

FAMINE, GOVERNMENT POLICY AND
THE CREATION OF REFUGEES

During the last century there were more than fifteen famines in northern Ethiopia (Degefu 1987). Since 1970 there have been four, two of which were very severe and the other two less so. Wolde-Mariam (1984, 37) estimated that about two million people were displaced from their homes in Harerge and the two northern provinces of Welo and Tigray during the 1972–1973 famine. The numbers displaced in 1984–1985 were likely even greater (Hendrie 1991).

As mentioned earlier, in the 1980s population movements in Tigray were caused by famine and the government's policy of resettlement and villagization. These problems, in concert with the inadequacy of relief distribution, also led many Tigrayans to migrate within Tigray, especially to the TPLF-held areas with the help of the Relief Society of Tigray (REST) and other aid agencies. At the height of the 1984–1985 disaster, tens of thousands of Tigrayans spontaneously migrated to the Sudan as refugees in search of relief. This movement was exacerbated by the Ethiopian government's refusal to allow the safe passage of relief supplies into contested areas of Tigray (Hendrie 1991, 201–2; Clay 1988).

The suffering of Ethiopians under the Mengistu government was summarized by one former official as follows: "In the last 10 years, 2.6 million people have died as a result of the war and famine; over 3 million have been made refugees in the neighbouring countries and around the world; 6 million have been displaced internally; 500,000 children have either been abandoned or orphaned; and more than 400,000 people disabled, while the entire population lives in permanent poverty, fear, and terror" (Wolde Giorgis 1989, 370).

Even though Tigrayans were oppressed intermittently for several centuries, we believe that the experiences of the 1970s and 1980s can be considered the worst. Political oppression, killing, famine, forced resettlement and exile were all evident. The migrations of the 1980s were exacerbated by the problems of the 1970s, one of the most ominous of which was the so-called "Red Terror." This infamous campaign of the Ethiopian government has been described by several authors (Bulcha 1988, 101–4). The government turned against its civilian and student opposition in the late 1970s, with ominous results. The greatest toll of casualties (next to Addis Ababa) occurred in Tigray, especially in its capital, Mek'ele (Wolde Giorgis 1989, 370).

Yet famine and food allocation programs became even worse. While the 1984–1985 famine enabled the central government to receive massive influxes of international aid, it did not allow the free flow of food to Tigray.

Food distribution was limited only to the urban areas controlled by the government. The donor community did not have the coordination or power to force the central government to freely distribute food to the most needy (U.S. Committee for Refugees 1986, 44).

The limited food supplies that reached the rebel-held areas came through REST via its cross-border operation in the Sudan. However, in early 1985 aid to the rebel-held areas equalled only about 5 percent of the total amount provided to the government (U.S. Committee for Refugees 1986, 44). This was a very limited amount, considering that rebels controlled more than 85 percent of the rural areas that were most affected by drought and famine at that time. We believe that relief agencies were afraid to support the cross-border operation through the Sudan, lest the Ethiopian government expel them from the country.

People in the rural areas under TPLF control or influence were initially allowed to go to the feeding stations that were set up, but they soon realized that the government was using the relief stations as centres of militia recruitment, as well as for resettlement purposes. People who came for food rations were told that they should resettle in the fertile lands of southern Ethiopia. Some did not even have the chance to consult their families and friends before being shipped south. Some Tigrayan farmers interviewed in 1986 by one of the authors stated that people were involuntarily taken to new settlements by bus. Many were taken away at gunpoint. Some were targeted in market-places, a few even at wedding ceremonies. Others were removed while harvesting their crops. Disruption of everyday life was part of the government's plan. Others reported that they were able to save their family members from forced resettlement by bribing officials (Wolde Giorgis 1989, 299).

Although emergency feeding stations were the main centres of forced recruitment, whole villages were also rounded up in some instances (Wolde Giorgis 1989, 299). Some people died while trying to escape from trucks carrying them to the resettlement collection centres. Others were forced to fly to the resettlement areas in military cargo planes. Indeed, a short-term tactic exemplifying adaptive flux came to be used by some villagers who heard of this—they started refusing to go to the government-run relief stations. This was followed by the long-term strategy (again exemplifying adaptive flux) of migrating to the Sudan as refugees.

The Ethiopian government wanted to capture peasants in Tigray and the surrounding rebellious areas when they were vulnerable and weak because of the famine. Rather than the stated aim of enhancing Tigrayans' socio-economic opportunities through resettlement, the actual aim was to move people to areas where they would have less opportunities to rebel against the government. It was no coincidence that during the height of the famine in 1985 the government was planning to resettle about 1.5 million people. By November 1985 it had already moved 600,000 peasants from the north, many of them Tigrayans.[8]

Although not a primary theme of this chapter, it should be stressed briefly that some believe widespread interethnic bigotry and prejudice served as the underpinnings to a number of key decisions made regarding the forced resettlement program. Sergeant Legesse Asfaw is accused by one author (Wolde Giorgis 1989, 300) of having targeted frail Tigrayans, both old and young, for modes of transport to resettlement areas that purposely contributed to large numbers of deaths. Buses were used when aircraft were available. Legesse had a "primitive theory that mixing the Tigrayan settlers with the Amharas . . . would make the Tigrayans somehow loyal" (Wolde Giorgis 1989, 300).

Special concentration camps were established for those who refused to be resettled. Those who were caught trying to escape were executed by firing squad. Many others died because of illnesses exacerbated by the climatically different lowland areas. According to the French relief agency, Médecins Sans Frontières, some 100,000 people perished during this phase of resettlement (U.S. Committee for Refugees 1986, 45).

Thus, many of the Tigrayans who fled to the Sudan as refugees were pushed in part by their inability to access internationally-donated food supplies, as well as the government's policy of forced resettlement. Details of this exodus—for Tigrayans and other ethnic groups—and its impact on the Sudan have been detailed by Bulcha (1988), whose conceptual model of the five types of refugees created in Ethiopia over the past two decades is most useful.

All five nonmutually exclusive types are representative of those leaving Tigray: (1) revolutionary activists, (2) contenders for power, (3) opponents of change (many espousing conservative social ideologies), (4) persecuted minorities and (5) displaced masses (Bulcha 1988, 81). Interestingly, refugees representing all of these categories also have been repatriated to Ethiopia.

In summary, Western-donated food was used as a trap to resettle starving Tigrayans. As Wolde Giorgis (1989, 285) said, "from the very beginning resettlement for Mengistu was not a development program but a solution to his social and national security problems." As seen during the 1980s in other countries of the Horn of Africa as well (e.g., southern Sudan), food became the most insidious of all the methods of oppression used. While government-initiated advance warnings for the drought and famine conditions in 1988 indicated some improvement (Ruiz 1990, 1), the manipulation of food aid and distribution systems continued, unfortunately.

ECOLOGICAL ADAPTATION AND SOCIAL
CHANGE BY FARMERS

Adaptive flux is exemplified among Tigray's sedentary farmers as well as refugees. According to Clay and Holcomb (1986, 60–61), as well as the senior author of this chapter (based on work in the province in 1991 and again in 1992), there is an ecological adaptation that reduces risk of crop failure and a set of modified social relationships that help villagers respond to drought.

Farmers are increasingly planting different types of crops on different parcels of land (i.e., diversifying), thus increasing chances that at least some of them may be successfully harvested. While mixed farming and eco-niche crop diversification were common in certain areas of Tigray before the most recent droughts and famines, this recent adaptation in large part was triggered by the political situation.

In terms of modified social relationships, the recent droughts and accompanying socio-economic pressures eliminated many draft animals. This in turn led to the sharing of draft animals by different farming households. While the sharing of paired oxen was previously common among relatives so that they would not miss the optimum part of the planting season, more extended patterns of sharing with unusual social components have emerged. Fewer oxen also has led to sharing land equally with farmers who can afford to plough it. The most common "equal share strategy" is based on the contractually-enforced concept that the tenant and the landowner will provide equal labour and equal quantities of seeds in all stages of farming and harvest. The elderly and infirm, men and women, those without labour capabilities nor oxen also do the same. People without oxen also borrow them in exchange for straw for animal feed after the harvest. A landowner can also give over his land for planting, without contributing labour and seeds, in return for a previously agreed-upon portion of the future harvest.

These changes must be viewed in concert with land reforms that have been implemented under the auspices of the TPLF. As described by Asfaw (1990, 24), a more equitable distribution of land was sought. It now neither can be sold nor inherited. All men older than twenty-four and all women older than seventeen have the right to own and use the land, as long as their direct livelihood is dependent upon it. (The age distinction was made owing to the fact that, on average, women marry and assume greater responsibilities some seven years earlier than men.) When land is distributed, factors of parcel size, quality and location relative to water and grazing resources are taken into account.

Thus, while before land reform the ownership of land was deemed as being more important, the ownership of the means of production has now become more important. The absence of the means of production in a society where there is egalitarian distribution of land has, in a sense, reversed the traditional notion of landlord/tenant relationships. Wealthier individuals who own oxen are acting like tenants in order to get more income.

Other long-term strategies have evolved recently as well. Barriers against female ploughers have been broken, in part because most of the young males joined the TPLF. Pressures on women continue as water resources are depleted, necessitating ever longer journeys to meet daily demand (Hailu 1991).

INTERPRETATIONS AND CONCLUSIONS

Recent refugee flows from Ethiopia—mainly by Tigrayans and Eritreans—were triggered by the former government's policy of oppression. It took many forms. Urban dwellers, students and teachers were imprisoned, killed and tortured for real or imagined sympathies for antigovernment liberation forces. As a result, many refugees were created. Many peasants also escaped for fear of recruitment into the government militia. The most insidious element was the government's use of food as a political weapon. The following statement is attributed to Lieutenant Colonel Mengistu Haile Mariam, the deposed president, when he spoke at a meeting of party secretaries and administrators: "The people are like the sea and the guerrillas are like fish swimming in that sea. Without the sea there will be no fish. We have to drain the sea, or if we cannot completely drain it we must bring it to a level where they will lack room to move at will, and their movement will be easily restricted" (Wolde Giorgis 1989, 298).

Yet the creation of Tigrayan migrants—most recently refugees—is by no means a recent phenomenon, nor one tied exclusively to political unrest. Since the 1960s, Tigrayans have consistently used temporary or long-term migration to other parts of Ethiopia as a coping strategy. Less regularly but nonetheless still definitively, various forms of migration were used for decades prior to that. As demonstrated in this chapter, the antecedents to migration and refugee generation are long-standing and deeply rooted in a number of factors.

An understanding of contemporary refugees requires an understanding of historical, socio-economic and ecological factors spanning more than a century. Contemporary politics, as related to the deposed Mengistu regime, provide the overlay but, we believe, are not the root of the problem. Resource depletion, famines, ethnic strife, power shifts and corollary changes in Tigrayans' economic patterns are the causes.

It is important to note that Ethiopia is "the only African state below the Sahara whose boundaries have been determined by an internally induced natural process of expansion carried out in the classic manner of military conquest" (Markakis 1974, 25). Northern Ethiopian history shows that pressures of population expansion and conquest promoted internal migration and expansion to new lands, rather than agricultural and technical innovation on existing lands. Unity, divisiveness, resource depletion, famine and refugee issues must be understood within this context.

As well, adaptive flux must be understood within this context, as it has contributed to refugees' abilities to cope and rebound against seemingly insurmountable odds. One example of a short-term tactic used by Tigrayans (as previously noted) occurred during the period of forced resettlement and villagization, when many began refusing to go to government food stations. One example of a long-term strategy was refugee migration to the Sudan. As defined herein, both tactics and strategies of this sort constitute elements of adaptive flux.

Understanding adaptive flux is partially tied to understanding resilience. This was shown during the Woyane I and II, and in the organizational resilience that Tigrayans demonstrated in coping with numerous decades of externally-imposed limitations, resource constraints and calamities. Most recently, the TPLF also exemplified this resilience, which proved far more important to their success than any Marxist, socialist or even democratically-oriented philosophy they may have professed.

The concept of adaptive flux is lent its strongest support in the 1980s development of the *baito* (local council) system in Tigray. It was conceived and employed "from the grassroots up." As described by Abreha (1990), this was part of a two-pronged strategy aimed at self-empowered survival. One prong was aimed at bracing for a more concerted struggle against opposing forces, the other for mobilizing resources for increased food production. Local-level *baito* decisions led, for example, to the mobilization of some 6,000 peasants from western Tigray (which was less severely affected by the 1984–1985 drought and famine) to construct a dry-weather road to eastern Sudan. Relying on their own food resources, the peasants completed the project in only four months. This "life-line," as Abreha describes it, enabled much-needed relief assistance to reach Tigray from the Sudan. The new government hopes that the *baito* system can be extended effectively across the country.

Cultural-ethnic factors are important in understanding refugee creation, but have not been covered in-depth herein. For example, in interviews with educated Ethiopian and Eritrean refugees living in Colorado, we were told that there are twenty to fifty identifiable ethnic groups in their homelands. The work of Sorenson (1990, 1991) in Canada makes it clear that ethnicity among Ethiopians and Eritreans is by no means monolithic.

Indeed, it has been defined historically—and is being redefined today—by a combination of internal and external political, economic and cultural forces.[9] To the extent that earlier concepts of "Ethiopian unity" were shaped by the "shared experience of domination," to borrow a phrase from Sorenson (1990, 301), current concepts of ethnicity in the Meles Zenawi era are being debated and possibly shaped more by external players and factions. To the extent that one ethnic faction has pressured another, the refugee situation has been exacerbated.

NOTES

1. The EPRDF is a coalition of four liberation movements, including the Tigrayan People's Liberation Front (TPLF), the Ethiopian People's Democratic Movement (EPDM), the Oromo People's Democratic Organization (OPDO) and the Ethiopian Democratic Officer's Revolutionary Movement (EDORM).

2. Details concerning evolution of the U.S. position and some of the diplomatic negotiations that took place are in "Statement of Assistant Secretary of State Herman J. Cohen, Before the House Foreign Affairs Committee, Subcommittee of African Affairs on the Political Crisis in Ethiopia, June 18, 1991."

3. The authors have found that, as the transitional government has become increasingly clear on its positions on issues, such as resource development, famine relief and political representation of various ethnic groups, a backlash of sorts has occurred among certain Ethiopians living in the U.S. Some, such as the Amhara interviewed in Colorado, insist that there is increasing danger that Ethiopia will become less—rather than more—democratic. They also fear that the Amhara in particular will be oppressed or, at least, forced out of virtually all positions of importance. Others insist that plans for more equitable ethnic representation in government and the opportunity for pursuing self-determination on the part of some ethnic groups *qua* nationalities is nothing more than a charade. One recent article on the recognition of ethnic identities and new rights is "In New Ethiopia, Main Tribe Takes Peaceful Route to Reclaim Rights," *Christian Science Monitor*, July 15, 1991.

4. The concept of famines as unpredictable "resource scarcity events" has been given credence in the literature (Ember and Ember, cited in Cohen 1990, 481). However, we believe that the number that have occurred in northern Ethiopia over the past century alone, in concert with the other ecological, economic and political factors discussed in this chapter, warrant the reconsideration of famines (at least for this area) as a somewhat predictable type of disaster that results in deprivation. This is lent support by other researchers in Ethiopia (Hendrie 1991, 201–2), as well as those studying what are known as "famine tracts" (Learmonth 1978, 136–41). A detailed discussion of the conceptual differences among the terms disaster, drought, famine and deprivation is found in Van Arsdale (1989).

5. It has been estimated that U.S. farmers benefit to the extent of $150 million annually from a variety of barley developed in Ethiopia, as noted in the *Christian Science Monitor*, April 25, 1990.

6. Henry Blanc, who was a prisoner of Emperor Tewodros, estimated that his camp had between 500,000 and 600,000 people who were continuously fed by the peasant population (Mengisteab 1990, 41).

7. It is possible that such diseases as tick- and louse-borne relapsing fever, among other maladies, were prevalent. One authority has indirectly linked relapsing fever to the Italian invasion of 1935 (Hartwig 1978, 226).

8. The large movement of people within and from Tigray began with the drought of 1982. In March and April of 1983 about 400,000 displaced people from the central highlands spontaneously moved westward. The Relief Society of Tigray (REST) had seventeen reception centres in the area to facilitate the displacement. By July 1983, about 56,000 family heads returned to the central highlands for the cultivation period. REST provided them with two to three months of provisions (especially targeting the most needy) until the harvest was gathered. To everyone's disappointment, the harvest failed again and the people migrated westward once more. In their areas of new residence, the migrants formed their own councils for the purpose of administration. Relief committees in the host villages were able to provide them with some commodities (English et al. 1984, 12–14).

9. The latest developments in Eritrea are covered in a series of articles in a special issue of the journal *Africa Today* 38, no. 2 (1991).

REFERENCES

Abreha, Aseffa. 1990. "People's Participation and Sustainable Development in Ethiopia, Tigray's Case: An Overview." In *Proceedings:1st Annual Symposium, Tigray Development Association (TDA)*, edited by Yasmina Sam Atsbeha and Abraham Teklu. Washington: Howard University.

Asfaw, Netsanet. 1990. "Revolutionary Democracy in Tigray, As a Force of Restructuring the Ethiopian Society." In *Proceedings: 1st Annual Symposium, Tigray Development Association (TDA)*, edited by Yasmina Sam Atsbeha and Abraham Teklu. Washington: Howard University.

Bulcha, Mekuria. 1988. *Flight and Integration: Causes of Mass Exodus from Ethiopia and Problems of Integration in the Sudan.* Uppsala: Scandinavian Institute of African Studies.

Clay, Jason W. 1988. "Famine Returns to Ethiopia." *Cultural Survival Quarterly* 12, no. 2:48–50.

Clay, Jason W., and Bonnie K. Holcomb. 1986. *Politics and the Ethiopian Famine, 1984–85.* Cambridge: Cultural Survival.

Cohen, Alex. 1990. "A Cross-Cultural Study of the Effects of Environmental Unpredictability on Aggression in Folktales." *American Anthropologist* 92, no. 2:474–81.

Degefu, Workineh. 1987. "Some Aspects of Meteorological Drought in Ethiopia." In *Drought and Hunger in Africa: Denying Famine a Future*, edited by Michael H. Glantz, 23–26. Cambridge: Cambridge University Press.

Dejene, Alemneh. 1990. *Environment, Famine, and Politics in Ethiopia: A View from the Village*. Boulder: Lynne Rienner.

English, John, Jon Bennett and Bruce Dick. 1984. *Tigray 1984: An Investigation*. London: OXFAM/UK. Unpublished report.

Finn, James, ed. 1990. *Ethiopia: The Politics of Famine*. Lanham: University Press of America.

Haggai, Erlich. 1986. *Ethiopia and the Challenge of Independence*. Boulder: Lynne Rienner.

Hailu, Tsegaye. 1991. "Brief Report on the Reconnaissance Survey of Water Resources of Tigray (February 27 to March 29, 1991)." Denver: Water and Sanitation Consultancy Group. Unpublished report.

Hammond, Jenny. 1990. *Sweeter Than Honey: Ethiopian Women and Revolution*. Trenton: Red Sea Press.

Hartwig, Gerald W. 1978. "Louse-Borne Relapsing Fever in Sudan, 1908–51." In *Disease in African History: An Introductory Survey and Case Studies*, edited by Gerald W. Hartwig and K. David Patterson, 207–23. Durham: Duke University Press.

Hendrie, Barbara. 1991. "The Politics of Repatriation: The Tigrayan Refugee Repatriation 1985–1987." *Journal of Refugee Studies* 4, no. 2:200–18.

Henze, Paul. 1985. *Rebels and Separatists in Ethiopia: Regional Resistance to a Marxist Regime*. Santa Monica: Rand Corporation.

Hobben, Allen. 1973. *Land Tenure among the Amharas of Ethiopia: The Dynamics of Cognatic Descent*. Chicago: University of Chicago Press.

Kebbede, Girma, and Mary Jacob. 1988. "Drought, Famine and the Political Economy of Environmental Degradation in Ethiopia." *Geography* 73, no. 318:65–70.

Kloos, Helmut, and Aynalem Adugna. 1989. "The Ethiopian Population: Growth and Distribution." *Geographic Journal* 155, no. 1:33–51.

Laughlin, C.D., and Ivan Al Brady. 1978. "Introduction: Diapasis and Change in Human Populations." In *Extinction and Survival in Human Populations*, edited by C.D. Laughlin and Ivan A. Brady. New York: Columbia University Press.

Learmonth, Andrew. 1978. *Patterns of Disease and Hunger: A Study in Medical Geography*. North Pomfret: David & Charles.

Markakis, John. 1974. *Ethiopia: Anatomy of a Traditional Polity*. Addis Ababa: Oxford University Press.

————. 1987. *National and Class Conflict in the Horn of Africa.* Cambridge: Cambridge University Press.

McCann, James C. 1990. "A Great Agrarian Cycle: Productivity in Highland Ethiopia 1900–1987." *Journal of Interdisciplinary History* 20, no. 3:389–416.

Mengisteab, Kidane. 1990. *Ethiopia: Failure of Land Reform and Agricultural Crisis.* New York: Greenwood Press.

Ophuls, William. 1977. *Ecology and the Politics of Scarcity: Prologue to a Political Theory of the Steady State.* San Francisco: W.H. Freeman.

Pankhurst, Richard. 1966. "Some Factors Depressing the Standard of Living of Peasants in Traditional Ethiopia." *Journal of Ethiopian Studies* 4, no. 2:47–98.

People's Voice. 1990. "Interview with Meles Zenawi, Secretary General of the TPLF." *People's Voice* 12, nos. 2 and 2 (January–June): 4–16.

Ruiz, Hiram A. 1990. "Insufficient Aid, Increased Fighting Further Threaten Famine-Stricken Northern Ethiopians." *Refugee Reports* 11, no. 2:1–5.

Sorenson, John. 1990. "Opposition, Exile, and Identity: The Eritrean Case." *Journal of Refugee Studies* 3, no. 4:298–319. 1991. "Politics of Social Identity: 'Ethiopians' in Canada." *Journal of Ethnic Studies* 19, no. 1:67–86.

Tareke, Gebru. 1984. "Peasant Resistance in Ethiopia: The Case of the Woyane." *Journal of African History* 25, no. 1:77–92.

U.S. Committee for Refugees. 1986. "Country Reports: Africa." *World Refugee Survey: 1985 in Review.* New York: American Council for Nationalities Service.

Van Arsdale, Peter W. 1989. "The Ecology of Survival in Sudan's Periphery: Short-Term Tactics and Long-Term Strategies." *Africa Today* 36, nos. 3 and 4:65–78.

Wolde Giorgis, Dawit. 1989. *Red Tears: War, Famine and Revolution in Ethiopia.* Trenton: Red Sea Press.

Wolde-Mariam, Mesfin. 1984. *Rural Vulnerability to Famine in Ethiopia, 1958–1977.* New Delhi: Vikas Publishing House.

————. 1985. "The Socioeconomic Consequences of Famine." In *Challenging Rural Poverty*, edited by Fassil G. Kiros. Trenton: Africa World Press.

3

Refugees in the Sudan: Unresolved Issues

Gaim Kibreab

The Sudan had one of the most generous refugee policies in the world until 1987. Despite an economic crisis, it still kept its doors wide open to the victims of war, persecution and famine. As a result of the alleged pressure from the large number of refugees on the national economy, infrastructure and natural environment of the country, the government "adopted a stricter policy towards refugees in 1987" (United Nations High Commissioner for Refugees 1988). After 1987 only those who were fleeing persecution and war were allowed to enter the country. The new policy excluded environmental refugees. However, under the conditions prevailing in northern Ethiopia and Eritrea, it was difficult to isolate environmental factors from the political problems and the war, and the government was not able to enforce this policy.

No country can choose its neighbours. The Sudan is surrounded by countries that have distinguished themselves in generating refugees and famine victims. (The Sudan itself was also one of the earliest refugee-producing countries in Africa, and it is still both a producer and receiver of refugees.) The problem of refugees is unique in the Sudan because in most other African countries (except Malawi), the numbers of refugees have either remained relatively unchanged or have decreased following their repatriation after cessation of the causes that first prompted their flight. Recently there has been some progress in voluntary repatriation. From 1985 to 1986, for instance, about 160,000 Ethiopian refugees from Tigray returned home (United Nations High Commissioner for Refugees 1987a). These were mainly famine victims. Between January 1986 and September 1987, over 170,000 Ugandan refugees voluntarily repatriated (United Nations High Commissioner for Refugees 1987c), partly because the present government has brought peace to the country and partly because of the armed attack on the camps. A larger number of Chadian refugees also returned home from western Sudan following the government's declaration of a general amnesty and a policy of national reconciliation (United Nations High Commissioner for Refugees 1987b). There was a slight decrease in the numbers of refugees in the country as a result of these repatriations. (In December 1986 the estimated total number of refugees was 1,164,000, while in July 1987 the estimate was in the range of 974,200.) By the end of 1991, there were 700,000 Ethiopian refugees in the Sudan, with an additional 29,200 refugees from other countries (United Nations High Commissioner for Refugees 1992).

During the 1980s the influx in the eastern region continued unabated and the situation is likely to be exacerbated by the recurrent drought that devastated northern Ethiopia and Eritrea. The situation was further aggravated by the Ethiopian government's resettlement and villagization programs. The total number of people who would have been affected if the government's plans for the resettlement and villagization programs had materialized were two million (Colchester and Luling 1985) and thirty million respectively (Waldron 1985). It is reported that tens of thousands fled as a result of the government's resettlement program and over 100,000 fled to the Sudan because of villagization (Waldron 1985).

To the casual observer, the refugee problem in the Sudan seems to be under full control. A closer look, however, reveals an underlying explosive situation. Most of the attempts that were made and the measures taken hitherto have not succeeded in resolving the basic issues. The plight of the refugees, as well as that of the poor hosts and the strain on the social and physical infrastructures in the affected areas, continue unabated.

In the following section I shall discuss the government of Sudan's attempts, in collaboration with the UNHCR and some NGOs, to enable the refugees to attain self-reliance. I shall concentrate on the long-term solutions and the efforts made for emergency relief. In order to shed light on some of the unresolved issues, I shall briefly discuss the main problems facing the organized rural refugee settlements and the spontaneous settlements (self-settlements). (For the major constraints on achieving economic and social viability of the land and wage-earning settlements in the eastern and central regions of the Sudan, see Kibreab 1987a and 1990a, respectively.)

ORGANIZED SETTLEMENTS

There are three types of organized refugee settlements in eastern and central Sudan. These are rural land settlements, wage-earning settlements and semiurban settlements. The total number of the refugees in the organized settlements was about 110,000 (United Nations High Commissioner for Refugees 1983a), but by 1992, 370,000 Ethiopian refugees were receiving

UNHCR assistance in twenty rural settlements and three reception centres in Sudan. Since most of the Ugandans in southern Sudan and Chadians in western Sudan have returned home, the overwhelming majority of refugees were from Eritrea and Ethiopia.

Following the repatriation of 160,000 famine victims to Tigray, most of the remaining refugees in northern Sudan were of Eritrean origin. There is no exact breakdown of the refugee statistics with regard to their origin in eastern and central Sudan. According to the estimate of the International Labour Organisation survey, of the total 67 percent were Eritreans, 14 percent were Tigrayans and 18 percent were Oromo and Amhara (International Labour Organisation and United Nations High Commissioner for Refugees 1984). This estimate cannot, however, be anything more than very crude because, in the absence of reliable population figures from which a sample is drawn, it is always difficult to estimate the population from the sample proportion.

Compared to the total number of refugees in the eastern region, the number of refugees relocated to organized settlements was very small—about 25 percent of the total number of refugees outside the camps. As of August 1988, there were 18,483 Tigrayan refugees in reception centres at Hilat Hakuma I and II and 55,816 Eritreans in Shagarab I, II and III and Wad Sherife living on UNHCR emergency assistance. There were also another 31,344 new arrivals—30,010 in Wad Sherife, 174 in Wad Kowli and 1,160 in Safawa or Hilat Hakuma I (see Table 3.1). This shows that of the estimated total of 630,000 Eritrean and Ethiopian refugees in eastern and central regions of the country, only 261,059 or about 40 percent were assisted. About 60 percent of the total refugee population received no assistance. These were the self-settled refugees in both rural and urban areas who were outside the international refugee support systems. These figures are, however, nothing more than indicative. Even though the government has been taking the liberty of estimating the total number of self-settled refugees in the Sudan, the truth is that nobody knows how many self-settled refugees there are in the rural and urban areas.

At the end of 1986 the total number of self-settled refugees, according to the government's estimate, was about 623,000 (United Nations High Commissioner for Refugees 1987a). According to the available statistics at the end of 1991, however, the total number of self-settled refugees was 327,000 (U.S. Committee for Refugees 1992).

In the absence of adequate statistical sources, different organizations and individuals came up with any figure that seemed to support their arguments. Those officials who had failed to deliver the essential goods and services to the capital's population increasingly resorted to statistical fabrications in order to attribute the acute shortages in the city to the refugees.

TABLE 3.1: Number of Refugees in Organized Settlements in Kassala and Blue Nile Provinces 1969–1983

Name of Settlement	Population	Province	Year of Establishment	Type of Settlement
Qala en Nahal (six villages)	28,626	Kassala	1969–1972	Land
Aburakham	3,460	"	1979	"
Wad Awad	1,325	"	1980	"
Mufaza	3,211	"	1983	"
Hawata	3,418	"	1982	"
Abuda	4,779	"	1981	"
Umgurgur	8,244	"	1976	"
Um Ali	3,000	"	1981	"
Karakora	11,928	"	1978–1985	"
Khashm el-Girba	11,645	"	1978–1985	Wage
Kilo 26	11,648	"	1979–1985	"
Fatah el Rahman	2,338	Blue Nile	1978	"
Awad es Sid	2,549	"	1978	"
Kilo 7	1,560	"	1980	"
Umrakoba	20,620	Kassala	1976–1985	Land
Tenedba	2,413	"	1981	"
Umgulja	5,282	"	1978	Urban
Tawa	13,063	"	1980	"
Wad el-Hilew	12,007	"	1984–1985	Land
Fau V	4,300	"	1987	Wage
subtotal	155,416			

Number of Refugees in Reception Centres in Eastern Sudan		
Hilat Hakuma I (Safawa)	2,352	1984
Hilat Hakuma II	16,131	1985
Shagarab I	20,023	1985
Shagarab II	12,333	1986
Shagarab III	13,354	1986
Wad Sherife	10,354	1982
subtotal	74,547	

New Arrivals as of August 1988	
Wad Sherife	30,010
Wad Kowli1	74
Safawa	1,160
subtotal	31,344

Total UNHCR-assisted refugees in eastern and central regions=261,307

Source: Data drawn from United Nations High Commissioner for Refugees records, Branch Office, Khartoum.

In the mid-1980s it was fashionable for politicians to blame all economic and social problems on refugees. For example, despite the fact that the Commissioner's Office for Refugees' (COR) estimate of the total number of refugees in Khartoum was about 55,000, the commissioner of the capital put the figures at more than 160,000 (*El Siyasa* 1987). The commissioner further stated that the solution to many of the capital's problems lay in evacuating the refugees (*El Siyasa* 1987). It is important to observe, however, that the results of the recently completed census of the refugee population in Khartoum came as a surprise to those who have been exaggerating the level of the burden imposed by the presence of a "large" number of refugees. The results, which were based on total enumeration, showed that only 31,500 were residing in the capital.

The problem of statistics is not only limited to self-settled refugees but to the refugees in organized settlements. Statistics on refugees are not only unavailable and incomplete, but even when they are available, they are fraught with contradictory data derived from different sources. (For the factors underlying refugee statistical inaccuracy, see Kibreab 1990b.)

THE RURAL LAND SETTLEMENTS

Whenever the prospects for voluntary repatriation did not seem foreseeable, the establishment of rural land settlement was historically considered as the most feasible solution to the problem of African refugees (Kibreab 1987b, 1990a, 1990b). Accordingly, between 1962 and 1982 106 organized settlements were established in Africa, ninety-nine of which were land settlements. Of the remaining seven, five were wage-earning settlements located in the Kassala and Blue Nile regions of the Sudan, and two were semiurban settlements located in Kassala province. By 1988 the total number of organized settlements had increased to about 170, but this included those that were closed due to voluntary repatriation.

Rural land settlement in the Sudan refers to the agriculturally-based settlements established with UNHCR assistance. The initial investment costs, such as housing, elementary school premises and furniture, health services, water supply, roads, etc., were met by the UNHCR. The World Food Programme supplied the refugees with free rations of food for the first two years, after which the refugees were expected to be self-sufficient. In the land settlements in Kassala province, the refugee families were allocated cultivable land donated by the government of Sudan varying from 5 to 10 *feddans* (see Kibreab 1985, 1987a). The fundamental aim of the land settlements was to enable the refugees to become self-reliant in food and other essential commodities. Initial production inputs, such as agricultural machinery, hand tools and seeds, were supplied by the UNHCR. Since agricultural production was based upon partial mechanization, the refugees were entitled to free cultivation in the first two years following the establishment of the settlements. After two harvesting seasons, the refugee farmers were expected to pay the full operational costs of the tractors. However, owing to the low level of agricultural income (due to the small size of holdings, low productivity or low producer price) and high recurrent costs, the tractor-hire service is still heavily subsidized by the UNHCR or other voluntary agencies. Refugee farmers can hire tractors from this service.

Between 1969 and 1988 nineteen land settlements, six wage-earning and two semiurban settlements were established in the eastern and central regions. The populations in the land, wage-earning and semiurban settlements were 103,031, 34,040 and 18,345, respectively. Although the number of refugees in the organized settlements is small, most international aid is directed to them, to the neglect of the self-settled refugees.

The international donor community is indifferent and insensitive to the plight of the refugees outside the settlements, despite the fact that none of these settlements are self-sufficient, although they have existed for a decade or more. Even though the settlements were established with high capital investment costs and maintained with a substantial amount of funds, they are still dependent on international assistance for their survival. For example, of the total amount of money given by the UNHCR to Sudan between 1968–1985, a lion's share was spent on the settlements.

Between 1968 and 1985 the total UNHCR expenditure in the Sudanese settlements was U.S. $114,572,539 (United Nations High Commissioner for Refugees 1987a). Since the UNHCR records I consulted did not contain a breakdown of the annual budgets for the settlements in the eastern and southern regions for some of the years, it was not possible to determine exactly how much was spent on the settlements in the eastern region. Since the settlements of the Ugandan refugees in the southern region were established from 1979 onwards (except for Rajaf), the largest amount of the budget provided was spent on the refugee settlements in the east.

Considerable amounts were spent by nongovernmental organizations on medical, agricultural, nonagricultural, income-generating, educational and other projects. For example, the expenditure of the Euro-Action Agency for Cooperation and Research in Development (ACORD), one of the NGOs operating in the settlements in the Qala en Nahal agricultural project between 1981 and 1988, was £6,781,468.31. What is disquieting is that despite such a huge investment, none of the settlements in the eastern region had become self-sufficient.

What are the main problems faced by the land settlements? The main constraints on the achievement of economic self-sufficiency are, among others, marginality of the land allocated to the refugees, lack of unoccupied cultivable land in the areas where the refugee settlements are located, lack of clean water supplies for human and livestock consumption, lack of refugee participation in the development process and inappropriate international assistance.

Marginality of the Land Allocated

Most of the land settlements in eastern Sudan, with the exception of the six villages in Qala en Nahal, are located in the low rainfall areas and, consequently, agricultural output varies from year to year, depending on the amount and distribution of rainfall.

Except for the settlements located in the relatively high rainfall area, namely, Qala en Nahal, Hawata and Mufaza, where the average annual amount of rainfall from 1960–1979 has been about 486 mm in Qala en Nahal and 488 mm in Mufaza (Kibreab 1985, Appendix 2). Rainfall is not only inadequate but unevenly distributed. This makes life in the settlements highly precarious. In the 1981–1982 season, for instance, there was sufficient rainfall and the refugee farmers with enough land and adequate family labour or capital to hire labour earned an acceptable agricultural income, but there were complete crop failures in 1982–1983, 1983–1984 and 1984–1985. The fact that most land settlements are located in marginal areas means that the risk of crop failure is very high, and settlers are consequently reluctant to commit themselves to an economic activity that cannot guarantee them a minimum and stable income to ensure their survival.

Land Shortage

The Sudan, as the largest country in Africa with an area of 2.5 million square kilometres and a population of about twenty-one million, is often believed to have abundant land. On the contrary, availability of unoccupied cultivable land is one of the most serious problems facing the existing land settlements. No new land settlement has been established after 1983 in the east due to shortage of suitable land. The inadequacy of the allocated land forced refugee farmers to cultivate their holdings continuously without allowing the land to lie fallow (Kibreab 1987a, Chapter 5). This has, in many cases, led to crop nutrient depletion in the soil and a decline in yields. According to refugee farmers, after five seasons of continuous cultivation, the return per unit of land declines substantially, often to subeconomic levels. This is exacerbated by using tractors for cultivation. If the refugee farmers were to use hand tools or other traditional forms of cultivation, some of them would not be able to cultivate all their plots intensively. Those families whose plots are 10 *feddans* or more would have been indirectly forced to leave part of their plots uncultivated. Even though there are no time series data on settlement yields, there are clear indications that this represents one of the major problems facing the agriculturally-based refugee settlements in the east. Kiflemariam Sebhatu, who has many years of experience in agricultural extension service in the Qala en Nahal settlement, observes that "there is an indication of yield decline and the case is serious, particularly in some villages and farms of the scheme. The consequences may be more serious in the future unless something is done, with the escalation of human and animal population" (Sebhatu 1988, 25). The old refugee settlements in eastern Sudan are faced with declining soil fertility caused by monocropping and failure to allow the land to rest over a long period.

In the central rainlands of Sudan, where the refugee land settlements are located, there is a strong correlation between scheme age (continuous cultivation) and decline of yield (Simson and Khalifa 1976). The older the scheme, the lower the yield. This is mainly because neither fertilizers nor organic manure are used to maintain soil fertility.

Often Sudanese farmers abandon their old holdings and shift to virgin land when the yield decline is below an acceptable level (Agabawi 1969). Because of existing institutional and legal restrictions, refugee farmers cannot cultivate land outside the designated area. In the old settlements the problem of land inadequacy also leads to overfragmentation of holdings, in which parents share their holdings with their landless married sons. Forty-five percent of the refugee households that possess less land than what they were originally allocated gave part of their holdings to their children (Kibreab 1987a).

Some settlements also faced very serious problems of land allocation. In Abuda, Um Ali and Umrakoba, the area that was supposed to be allocated to the refugees was claimed by local Sudanese farmers who threatened the refugees when the latter tried to clear the land allocated to them (Agrisystems 1983). In 1983 only 49 percent of the settler families in Abuda had received 5 *feddans* of land. The rest had no land allocated to them. In a report prepared by the Agrisystems Consultants for the UNHCR, it was observed that "The project agreement states that each family should be allocated 10 fd. and therefore serious land allocation problems are likely to continue into the 1983/84 season" (Agrisystems 1983).

Of the 688 families in Um Ali, only 210 had cultivated in the 1982–1983 season. In Umrakoba, though it was claimed that 400 families out of 1,060 received land, only sixty to ninety families reported having cultivated their holdings in the 1982–1983 season. The problems were associated with land allocation and clearing (Agrisystems 1983). The nearest land allocated was about a ninety-minute walk from the settlement (Agrisystems 1983). The effect of farm distance on productivity and use of labour time is detrimental to farm families' efforts to attain self-reliance.

My own findings in the six settlements of Qala en Nahal, as well as Aburakham, also show that there was a serious shortage of land, whereby a considerable number of the refugee households were either landless or possessed inadequate amounts of land to generate sufficient income to meet the households' requirements for food and other essential commodities. In Aburakham, despite the fact that the settlement was in a low rainfall area, the refugee families were allocated 5 *feddans* of cultivable land, regardless of their family size. There were many vulnerable groups, such as the elderly, disabled, unaccompanied orphans and families headed by women. Some of these groups were unable to cultivate their plots because they do not have able-bodied family members or enough capital to hire labourers.

All these findings suggest that in the settlements with no land allocation problems, no adequate planning was exercised because the question of natural population growth and the need to leave part of the land fallow were not crucial considerations. Since the settlements are agri-culturally-based, wherever there are problems with land allocation, refugees should be provided with adequate cultivable land if they are to become self-reliant. The question of land shortage, which is facing the already established settlements, throws light on the feasibility and relevance of the traditional approach to the durable solution of the refugee problem in the eastern region. The problem would have been overcome if there was adequate rainfall or water for irrigation. Thus, the shortage of land will remain a reality as long as the Sudan is unwilling to share the waters of the Nile with the refugees.

Lack of Water Supply

One of the major problems in eastern Sudan is that of water supply (United Nations High Commissioner for Refugees 1982). The development of water resources is a major expenditure in the east. Despite the substantial financial commitments from the UNHCR and some donor countries, some of the settlements still do not have reliable access to water. The establishment of three refugee villages near the old refugee settlement of Qala en Nahal has, for instance, been delayed due to a lack of water resources (National Committee for Aid to Refugees 1980). These villages were to be established in Balos, Bia and Huweig (Gifford and Partners Consulting Civil Engineers 1981). In Qala en Nahal cattle owners used to be denied access to water in the settlement during the dry season. In the last few years, however, in Qala en Nahal the problem of water supply for the livestock has been partially solved after the construction of large livestock watering *hafirs* by ACORD. According to the refugee farmers, lack of water is one of the problems faced by livestock owners. Thus, availability of clean water for human and livestock consumption is a major problem facing some of the existing land settlements and in the establishment of new ones.

Lack of Refugee Participation

"Refugees themselves have been ignored throughout the decision-making process in the three phases of relief, rehabilitation and development" (Karadawi 1983, 532). The refugees in the eastern settlements are not participating in the identification of their own needs, planning, implementation, management and evaluation of projects. The manner in which assistance is delivered and the way settlements are managed has, in effect, relegated the refugees to a role as passive receivers. The refugees lack all the necessary institutional structures through which to influence the outcome of decisions that affect their lives directly or indirectly.

An institution known as *legina* (residents' committee) has emerged in the settlements since 1976 as a go-between for the settlements administration (the *modir*'s office) and the refugees, but it still has no part in any substantial decision making. In many cases, the institution of the *legina* is undemocratic and is dominated by the traditional religious or clan elite. The question of participation is central to any refugee development work.

The refugees are settled in a country with which they do not identify. Hence, they must be committed to their settlements in order for development to occur. Owing to bitter experience, refugees are suspicious even of those who genuinely try to help them. Until one has gained the refugees' trust, they often assume that everyone wants to take advantage of their vulnerability. Even the most genuine effort to help is often regarded with reservations because the refugees have lost confidence in authorities.

Therefore, securing their participation has two advantages. Firstly, it helps the refugees to regain their dignity. Secondly, it enables them to participate in creating economically and socially viable communities. Since people are the central purpose of development, the human factor is indispensable in the process. Because they have been uprooted from their homeland and forced to flee, refugees are always marginalized in the political, social and economic life of the host country. They need to feel empowered to take the initiative without being dependent on outside authorities in order to feel included in the mainstream of society. This can only be possible by reawakening their confidence and self-respect through cooperative work, in which all take part in identifying needs, setting priorities, and formulating and implementing projects. A development strategy that does not involve their participation from the outset contains the ingredients for failure. The settlements in eastern Sudan are typical cases of refugee nonparticipation.

The Nature of International Assistance

One of the major obstacles to self-reliance for the agriculturally-based rural refugee settlements is the substantial cost of agricultural machinery and other settlement infrastructures. Under the existing resource endowments and household income levels, it seems highly improbable that the refugees will ever be self-sustaining.

The Sudan, as one of the twenty-one least developed countries in the world, cannot meet these financial costs after international assistance is phased out. For the settlements to maintain the agricultural machinery, they must be able to generate the necessary foreign exchange to replace worn-out machinery, purchase spare parts, fuel, lubricants and hire skilled labour to maintain and operate the tractors. The management implication is also very serious. The refugees, especially the former pastoralists and agro-pastoralists, cannot manage the tractor-hire services without being trained.

When the UNHCR withdrew its financial assistance from Qala en Nahal in 1974, the responsibility was handed over to the Commissioner's Office for Refugees, which in turn handed it over to the local government of the town of Qala en Nahal. Since the refugees were never involved in planning or managing the program, the withdrawal of UNHCR's assistance caught them unaware. The recurrent costs and the technical and the management skills required proved beyond the reach of the local government. By 1975 the settlement was on the verge of total collapse (Kibreab 1987a, Chapter 8). In 1978 the UNHCR was forced to intervene financially. The settlement infrastructure reached rock-bottom by 1980. In 1981 ACORD took over the management of the tractor-hire service and other related activities, and is still running it very effectively. The question is what will happen after its withdrawal?

For the other settlements outside Qala en Nahal, Valmet Corporation, on behalf of the Finnish government, has been implementing a project since 1983 to support mechanization of agriculture in the refugee settlement areas of the eastern Sudan. The objective of the project was to establish a workshop at Showak, to supply fifty tractors (including spare parts), trailers and agricultural implements (especially disc harrows) and to provide technical assistance for supporting the workshop and training the drivers and mechanics (Joint Finnish-Sudanese Project Review Mission 1984).

The fact that the project contains a training component is appropriate, but a problem of retaining the trained manpower, as in many of the other projects, will arise when the project is handed over to the government of Sudan. The history of Qala en Nahal is likely to repeat itself in the other settlements following the phasing out of outside assistance. Outside assistance cannot, however, be expected to continue indefinitely. But if international assistance is one of the forces responsible for creating structures that cannot be sustained by existing knowledge and financial resources, it is unacceptable to phase it out when it is clear that withdrawal will most probably lead to collapse.

The available evidence suggests that the settlements depend on outside assistance. The problem is equally worrying to the international organizations because they have unintentionally become prisoners of their own making. The continuity of the settlements has become a function of their presence. This is a classic example of a dependent situation. Dependence means a structure's inability to maintain and perpetuate itself without relying on outside forces over which it lacks control.

The mistake was made at the planning stage. If the planning had taken into account the eventual hand-over of the settlements to the government of Sudan (the government's financial restraints were no secret), the donors' heavy and well-intentioned investments would have been avoided as obstacles to achieving self-reliance. If oxen and/or *seluka* (plough-sticks) were used instead of tractors, the acquisition price and recurrent costs, as well as the required technical and management skills, would have been within the reach of the refugee farmers.

Another important problem closely related to international assistance is a significant bias towards supplying social services and equipment, as opposed to agricultural and other production-oriented program funding. Investments in production were very limited compared to the amounts invested in administration and the provision of social services. This can easily be seen from the total expenditure during 1982-1983 in the settlements (see Table 3.2). Even though the data is only for one year, the settlements have similar expenditures for other years.

Although agricultural production was supposed to represent the settlements' economic basis for self-reliance, less than 12 percent of the annual budget was allocated for this purpose. About 65 percent of the total expenditure was allocated to health and administration within and beyond the settlements.

This was also the case with the projects submitted to the second International Conference on Assistance to Refugees in Africa (ICARA II). The projects submitted by the technical team, consisting of representatives from the UN, United Nations Development Programme, UNHCR and the Organization of African Unity (OAU), in consultation with the fourteen countries involved in ICARA II, placed undue emphasis on expanding infrastructural services as opposed to creating income-generating activities.

Of the total U.S. $362.3 million requested, 76 percent was for strengthening the infrastructures of the countries concerned. Only 24 percent was to

TABLE 3.2: Total Expenditure in the Settlements in Eastern Sudan by Sector

	1982–1983 Amount in Sudan£	*Percentage of Total Expenditure*
Medical	4,432,000	36.8
Agriculture	1,392,000	11.6
Nonagricultural income-generating projects	601,000	5.0
Aid to vulnerable groups	571,000	4.7
Education	1,456,000	12.1
Miscellaneous expenses	247,000	2.1
Administration in Settlements	1,843,000	15.3
Administration in Gedaref, Showak, Kassala excluding Khartoum	1,494,000	12.4
Total	12,036,000	100.0

Source: Data drawn from "Sectoral Analysis of Resources Flows in the Refugee Settlements of Eastern Sudan," United States Embassy, Office of Refugee Affairs, Khartoum, December 1983.

be used for agriculture, forestry and fisheries (United Nations High Commissioner for Refugees 1984).

It should also be pointed out that the expenditure on administration beyond the settlements is understated by about 40 percent (United States Embassy, Office of Refugee Affairs 1983). Only about 21 percent of the total expenditure was allocated for activities designed to enable refugees to achieve self-reliance. This strong bias towards delivery of social services and relief activities, to the neglect of funding long-term, production-oriented programs, reflects the obsession of donor organizations with obtaining quick and visible results that they can show to their constituencies.

It is often easier to obtain immediate results in activities related to food aid, medical care and delivery of goods and services than in activities related to helping people to grow their own food.

Wage-Earning Settlements

These settlements are located partly within the irrigated agricultural schemes of New Halfa in the eastern region and Es Suki in the Blue Nile region, and partly on the outskirts of the towns of Gedaref and Khashm el-Girba in the east. The settlements of Kilo 7, Fatah el Rahman and Awad es Sid are near the Es Suki pump scheme, while Kilo 26 is near the New Halfa scheme. The Khashm el-Girba refugee settlement is about 2–3 km from the town of Girba and not very far from the New Halfa scheme. (For an extended discussion on the history and economic viability of the refugee wage-earning settlements, see Kibreab 1990a.) Umgulja is located about 12 km from Gedaref. The refugees in these settlements (except those in Umgulja, who were expected to become self-supporting by working in the rain-fed agricultural schemes) were expected to support themselves by working in the irrigated agricultural schemes. In the past, it was believed that one of the major problems facing Sudan's irrigated schemes in the eastern and central regions was the shortage of seasonal labour for cotton picking. Thus, the major aims of establishing the wage-earning settlements were to enable the Sudanese tenants to fill the labour shortage, to improve the performance of the irrigation schemes on which the country depends for foreign exchange, and to enable the refugees to become self-reliant. There is indisputable evidence that shows that the irrigated scheme's major problem is not only a shortage of labour. The problem is more complex and cannot by any means be reduced to a single factor (Ministry of National Planning 1979; World Bank 1980; Ministry of Finance and Economic Planning [Planning] 1982; Sorbo 1985). The government's intention notwithstanding, the establishment of the refugee settlements has not led to the achievement of any of the planned objectives (Kibreab 1990a; National Committee for Aid to Refugees 1980).

Semiurban Settlement

Towawa, a semiurban settlement, is about 7 km outside the town of Gedaref. The refugees are expected to become self-reliant by working partly in Gedaref and partly in the surrounding agricultural area. According to the staff of the UNHCR subbranch office in Gedaref, Towawa was one of the most successful projects in the east. This was mainly due to the demographic characteristics of the settlers who, owing to their age and unmarried status, could move easily from place to place in search of employment opportunities. A high proportion of the residents were single men. Unlike the refugees in the other settlements, most of the refugees are in their most productive age. In 1983 when there was no organized reception of newly arriving refugees, Towawa became a reception centre for new arrivals from northern Ethiopia who were not receiving assistance from the UNHCR subbranch office in Gedaref. The new arrivals relied mainly on the old settlers for subsistence and shelter.

Self-Settlement

Self-settled refugees are those who are outside the organized settlements and transit camps. It is not known how many refugees are self-settled in the Sudan in general and in northern Sudan in particular. According to government estimates, there were about 623,000 self-settled refugees in rural and urban areas (United Nations High Commissioner for Refugees 1987a). According to data from the end of 1991, however, the total number of Ethiopian and Eritrean refugees was estimated at 700,000, almost half of whom were self-settled. It is not clear either what percentage of the self-settled refugees were in the urban areas, but educated guesses varied from 65–75 percent. This does not mean that all the refugees in the urban areas were of urban origin. Those refugees who were originally from rural areas but who fled without any livestock, often settled in the towns near the border areas, mainly in Kassala and Port Sudan. However, the social composition of the Eritrean refugees was unique because, unlike the overwhelming majority of African refugees, a high proportion of them were of urban origin and had subsequently settled in the various cities and towns in the Sudan.

This is significant for several reasons. Firstly, this situation has given rise to a need for new solutions, as the conventional approaches of land and wage-earning settlements are not applicable to them. Secondly, the impact of these large influxes on the social and economic infrastructures of the affected areas was such that in some places, the services had almost reached breaking point. However, the decline of the economic and social infrastructures is not only due to the presence of refugees. Even in the areas where there were no refugees, the supply of basic amenities was extremely limited. It is often claimed that the effect was more pronounced on housing, health services, schools, transport and on the availability of strategic commodities. However, no serious attempts were made to measure the real impact of refugees on the social and economic infrastructures of the affected areas. This was mainly due to lack of readily available data and partly due to problems of measurement. My own attempts to quantify the refugees' impact on health services in the neighbourhoods with high refugee concentrations in Khartoum and in the main hospitals were frustrated because no separate records were kept for refugee patients. This gap in our knowledge has led to untenable speculations and unreasonable claims about the refugees' negative impact on the social and physical infrastructures of the affected areas (Sudanow 1979; *El Siyasa* 1987). Thirdly, owing to lack of assistance and absorptive capacity of the modern sector, the refugee labour force in the urban areas, no matter how skilled, could not be completely absorbed into the labour market. Hence, the overwhelming majority of urban refugees were leading precarious lives.

All former city and town dwellers head for the urban areas in search of employment, resettlement in third countries, education and/or to get in touch with relatives abroad. Even those without any hope of employment or resettlement opportunities preferred the towns to the unfamiliar and hostile rural environment. The government was then opposed to the presence of refugees in the urban areas, especially Khartoum. The refugees in Khartoum were from time to time rounded up and evicted to the countryside. However, since there were no settlements suitable for urban refugees, and since rural settlements had limited available services and resources, refugees who were unable to emigrate abroad tended to stay in urban areas despite police harassment and economic hardships. According to official policy, no refugees except those in following categories were allowed to reside in Khartoum: (1) those who already had employment; (2) medical cases referred to Khartoum by qualified medical doctors through the UNHCR suboffices; (3) students admitted to universities and higher technical institutes, as well as those funded by the Refugee Counselling Services; (4) children and wives who lived with a legally resident father in Khartoum or a husband who joined his wife if she was working in Khartoum with a work permit (Commissioner's Office for Refugees 1987, 1989).

This policy notwithstanding, it is claimed that tens of thousands were residing in Khartoum "illegally." As long as the refugees remain "illegal" residents, they will always be vulnerable to police harassment, extortion and exploitation by greedy employers. "Illegal" residents, when aggrieved, could not seek redress because this might result in their exposure and subsequent deportation to the countryside, often without any means of survival, so they were forced to maintain a low profile even when their fundamental human rights were violated flagrantly. The overwhelming majority of urban refugees had no official papers. As long as there was peace in Khartoum and elsewhere, their security was not threatened substantially, but in a political and economic crisis, their situation became extraordinarily precarious.

Forcible relocation of urban refugees to the countryside is not, however, a solution to the problem because this attempt has only led to a vicious circle. The relocations took place without any prior planning. Often they reflected a policy that suffered from lack of direction and vision. The population density in the settlements was already very high and a further influx of people without simultaneous expansion of housing facilities, water supply, land resource, medical and educational facilities was likely to strain the settlement's economic and social infrastructure to the breaking point. Besides, the so-called "illegal" residents were mostly young people with relatively good educational backgrounds who disliked and were unfamiliar with rural life, so they were unlikely to fit into the rural settlements.

It was often believed that urban refugees receive the lion's share of international assistance to the neglect of rural refugees. Chambers (1979), for instance, noted that "moreover, urban refugees, often educated, articulate and politically active, demand attention and usually receive it. They queue for interviews daily, they protest, and they do not go away. Understaffed as they are, UNHCR branch offices in Africa have to handle rural as well as urban problems; but the urban are immediate and take priority."

The reverse is true in the Sudan. The urban refugees in Khartoum were living like fugitives and were not even in a position to protest against the crimes that were being committed against them, let alone make their economic demands openly. As pointed out earlier, all assistance (except the insignificant amount spent on individual solutions) was directed to the rural organized settlements that were only accommodating a small proportion of the total number of refugees. The anomaly of the situation was that the government and aid agencies had until then remained insensitive to the abysmal misery of the poor urban refugees, primarily because (despite its conspicuous prevalence) urban self-settlement was not recognized at a policy level. Hence, no assistance was directed towards it. The relief organizations were closing their eyes to the plight of the poor urban refugees. What was overlooked was the fact that the lives of people were at stake.

THE UNRESOLVED ISSUES

The issues involved in the politics of refugees and refugee assistance in the Sudan are complex and can only make sense if approached within the wider developmental measures encompassing all the populations in refugee-affected areas. It is impossible to create employment opportunities in the urban areas without increasing the absorptive capacity of the economy of the areas concerned. Providing infrastructural services to self-settled refugees is impossible without upgrading the supporting capacity of the public services so as to benefit both the refugees and the local population. But in reality, the problem is not so easy to solve. The financial and management implications of such an approach, no matter how theoretically sound, are difficult to achieve when the world is in the grip of an economic crisis and international aid is increasingly politicized. It has now become fashionable to state that refugees should be treated as a regional development problem and host governments should be provided with additional assistance to enable them to cope with the problem. But unless host governments are willing to eliminate the constraints that prevent refugees from participating in the economic, social and cultural life of the host society on an equal footing with nationals, such assistance will not have an impact.

The problem facing the Sudan is how to turn this liability into an asset, whereby measures undertaken to alleviate the plight of the refugees would simultaneously contribute to economic development and growth that will benefit the local population in the refugee-impacted areas and the refugees themselves. One way is to stop looking at the refugee population as a problem. Given the industriousness of the Eritrean refugees in the country, eliminating the barriers that restrain their movement and participation in the economic life of the country would automatically constitute an asset. The key to solving the problem is not providing additional assistance but allowing the refugees freedom to engage in any legal activity.

For example, the tremendous task of integrating the German refugees and expellees in an already devastated and overstrained economy after World War II would not have been possible without the financial and technical assistance extended to West Germany under the Marshall Plan. The arrival of refugees was followed by an ever-growing demand for industrial labour, so even the refugees from rural areas were absorbed by industry. Instead of overstraining the economy, the refugees contributed to expanding its capacity to absorb the increased labour supply. According to Paikert, the refugees "brought invaluable assets with them from their old homelands. Among these their almost fanatical determination to work, their enterprising spirit, their individual imaginations, their special skills and their vocational background" (1962, 35). Without the necessary capital and proper policy and practice, however, even the most skilled and industrious labour force can be wasted. The three major factors that facilitated West Germany's attempt to turn the liability into an asset were the refugees' commitment, the availability of capital to reconstruct the devastated West German economy, and the government's correct and far-sighted refugee policy. As noted by Paikert, "The exceptional recovery made by the Federal Republic of Germany since 1951 has demonstrated that the refugees were a major national asset rather than a burden" (Paikert 1962, 35). But he further observed that the credit for the successful integration of the German refugees and expellees "must be given not only to the refugees themselves but also to the West German leadership, *which from the very outset has treated the expellee problem not as a distinct and specific issue but as an integral part of the Bund's general plan of reconstruction*" (emphasis added) (Paikert 1962, 35).

This suggests that in order for refugees to become an important factor in national development in the countries of asylum, three conditions must exist simultaneously. Firstly, the refugee influx must coincide with economic growth, so that the country is able to cope with the challenge and the refugees are able to use their creativity and industriousness. Unfortunately, the uprooting of African refugees is occurring at a time when the African national economies are on the verge of collapse and when the world economy is experiencing one of the most serious crises since the Great Depression of the 1930s. This has exacerbated the refugees' plight due to insufficient international assistance and strained the already inadequate infrastructures available to the nationals of the host countries, who are in a state of need. Hence, host countries cannot help regarding the refugees as an additional burden and an aggravating factor in their already miserable situation. The local population's attitude towards newcomers is, among other things, determined by the national economic situation.

The second condition is the host government's policy. Does government policy treat the problem of refugees as a separate and distinct question or as an integral part of the country's development problem? This is crucial because it is the foundation on which all refugee relief and development assistance rest. Although there has been much talk in the Sudan about the need to perceive the refugee problem in the country's development perspective, little is *done* at a policy level to allow the refugees to participate in the country's social and economic life on an equal footing with the nationals. As long as their freedom of movement and their right to obtain business licences, work permits and land, etc., remain limited, the refugees will continue to be on the margin rather than in the mainstream of the host society.

One of the major constraints on the performance of the Sudanese national economy is the shortage of transport facilities (Ministry of National Planning 1979). This is especially true of the agricultural sector, where the transport of machinery, fertilizers, fuel, lubricants, labour and products require an efficient transport network. This is the only branch in the economy where the restrictions on business licences are not applied to refugees. Within a relatively short time, a considerable number of Eritrean refugees have already entrenched themselves in the transport industry as owners of fleets of trucks. Most of the capital was earned outside the Sudan mainly by refugees residing in the Middle East and the Organisation for Economic Co-operation and Development countries. The refugees' contribution to the task of overcoming the transport shortage is evident and even government officials admit this. If the refugees were allowed to participate freely in other economic activities, their contribution to national development would be more significant.

Though there are no accurate data, it is known that a substantial number of urban refugees possess skills that are indispensable to the development needs of the Sudan. If the restrictions on business licences, work permits and freedom of movement were lifted, the refugees might be encouraged to release their potential productive energy. Government officials and even academics argue that the Sudan cannot be expected to do this unless there is financial and technical commitment from the international donor community to enable it to cope with the huge task of national development in hosting a large number of refugees. The lifting of restrictions without simultaneously increasing the national economy's absorptive capacity may lead to acute competition between refugees and nationals for scarce resources. However, instead of leading to conflict, the competition may give an impetus to economic growth and social progress, as well as to better economic and social interaction between the refugees and the nationals.

The third condition is the role government policy and practice assign to the refugees. No matter how skilled and industrious refugees may be, their enthusiasm and ability to release their productive energy can be stifled by a policy that does not encourage them to become involved in the development process. There is a tendency to assume that increased assistance to African refugees is a panacea that can improve the refugees' social and economic conditions and ease the strains on the host countries' underdeveloped economies and social services. While the latter may be achieved as a result of increased assistance, the former is by no means a guaranteed result of increased material assistance. Even though material assistance is crucial, it is not the only solution to alleviating the refugees' economic and social plight.

A durable solution to the problem of African refugees should not be sought in just one or two variables. Inasmuch as the problem is caused by an interplay between political, economic and social factors, the solution requires more than a focus on supplying material goods. Although 50 percent of the world's refugees are in Africa, the per capita share of the overall refugee budget for the African refugee was still far below that for other refugees. Allocation of large amounts of assistance without host country policies and short- and long-term planning that recognize refugees' rights of participation will create dependency instead of promoting development.

A greater awareness has been generated lately for the need to tackle the African refugee problem within an overall economic and social development plan for refugee-affected regions. So far, the idea has not really taken off.

The major objectives of the first International Conference on Assistance to Refugees in Africa (ICARA I) were to focus public attention on the plight of African refugees, to mobilize additional resources for refugee programs and to increase international assistance to countries adversely affected by refugees so that they would be able to cope with the problem and the burden on their services. However, ICARA "fell short of its third objective" (United

Nations High Commissioner for Refugees 1983a). Even though U.S. $573,943,000 was pledged at the conference, "a number of difficulties were encountered," such as "lack of clarity concerning pledges made" (United Nations High Commissioner for Refugees 1983a). It is also admitted in the same report that "the overall results of ICARA have fallen short of expectations" (United Nations High Commissioner for Refugees 1983a).

There are even some who argue that the assistance allocated to African refugees has declined since ICARA. According to Birido (1982), "the assistance provided by the UNHCR general programme to refugees in Africa was U.S. $173 million in 1980, U.S. $168 million in 1981 and U.S. $158 million in 1982." A meeting of experts on refugee aid and development held in Mont Pèlerin also reaffirmed the need to solve the African refugee problem within the regional and national development context of the countries of asylum (Meeting of Experts on Refugee Aid and Development 1983). A meeting of the OAU Secretariat and voluntary agencies held in Arusha also called on the UNHCR to link its "humanitarian assistance programmes to development endeavours in the countries of asylum, as this is the path that is likely to lead to durable if not permanent solutions to the refugee problems" (Scandinavian Institute of African Studies 1983). International awareness of this need culminated in the ICARA II conference, held in July 1984 in Geneva. The response at the conference was positive, but the promises made were overshadowed by the 1984–1985 famine, which devastated most of sub-Saharan Africa.

Recognizing the African refugee problem as an integral part of the overall development problem is a significant step forward, but it is important to guard against a potential tendency to use refugees as a pawn to seek development assistance. If refugees do not have any right to influence the outcome of decisions, and if future development projects are implemented by a host government and not by a neutral agency accountable to the host government, donor agencies and the refugees, how can one ensure that refugees will benefit from development projects funded by international assistance on an equal footing with nationals?

The question of operationalism is a tricky issue in refugee work. In Tanzania, Zaire and Zambia, the operational partners of the UNHCR are neutral third-party voluntary agencies that provide technical assistance and manage UNHCR and other funds in accordance with the governments' policies in a tripartite agreement with host governments and the UNHCR. In eastern Sudan, except in the field of health and the tractor-hire service of Qala en Nahal (where voluntary agencies are allowed to operate), COR is the UNHCR's sole operational partner, i.e., all settlements are implemented and funds are administered by COR. There are advantages to having a voluntary agency as an operational partner. Firstly, whenever the host government, the refugees or the donor agencies feel that the operational partner is not performing its duties as agreed upon, it is possible to take corrective measures and even dismiss it. Secondly, whenever the refugees feel aggrieved by something the implementing voluntary agency did or did not do, they can seek redress from the host government. If the implementing partner is the government itself, and if it fails to play its implementing role properly, no measures can be taken against it. Assigning the role of an implementing partner to a host government may also divert the host country's scarce skilled manpower resources that could be used else-where in the country.

In situations where refugees are self-settled among local populations, supply of services must be based upon the provision of international assistance to upgrade existing health services, housing facilities, schools, etc., so that both refugees and the local populations will benefit equally. The creation of employment opportunities also requires, as noted earlier, an increase in the absorptive capacity of the national or regional economy by establishing different income-generating activities designed to benefit refugees and nationals equally. It is easy to talk about this in the abstract, but in reality, all discussions have so far overlooked the crucial questions of how to finance such efforts and how to ensure the mix. Assuming that international assistance is used for investments to upgrade or create social services and income-generating activities in refugee-affected areas that will be accessible to both refugees and the local population, and assuming that the refugees do not participate through their elected representatives in implementation, and that the operational partner is the host government, how can one guarantee that refugees will benefit equally from such services and employment opportunities?

Inasmuch as there is a need to perceive and tackle the African refugee problem within the host country's development context, it is also important to realize that only when the refugees are allowed to participate in all decisions through their democratically-elected representatives that the mix can be ensured. Before this can happen, host governments should be convinced that refugees, if given an opportunity, can manage their own affairs effectively. According to the National Committee for Aid to Refugees in the Sudan, "the two symptoms which constitute the most important constraints usually express themselves as an emotional and practical inability to plan for the future, and a much reduced openness towards innovations. The combination of these symptoms ... produces a situation which makes resettlement of refugees a task that differs considerably from conventional development activities" (National Committee for Aid to Refugees 1980).

This perception of refugees cannot be conducive to promoting policies and practices that encourage refugee participation. It is sometimes argued that the nature of the decisions or the refugees' lack of knowledge required in planning may constrain their participation. It is true that sometimes a project may require skills beyond the technical knowledge of the beneficiaries. What happens in such a situation? Participation must include freedom of choice and if the refugees are involved in the planning from the outset, the question of technical expertise will not arise because the structures that will be created will develop within their own institutional and cultural milieu.

CONCLUSION

Some of the unresolved issues that have been raised indicate that the refugee problem in the Sudan requires a serious and imaginative new look based on careful reassessment of the situation, as well as of the government's policies and practices. As noted, the politics of refugees and refugee assistance is complex. One has to consider the short- and long-term interests of the refugees themselves, the interests of the host country, the populations in the affected areas and the financial limitations of the donor governments and the voluntary agencies. Often some of these interests can be difficult to reconcile, but somehow a balance has to be struck and this is not easy to achieve without the refugees' full participation and commitment.

The history of the land settlements in eastern Sudan shows that it is important to take into account in the planning stage the eventual hand-over of the settlements to the refugees themselves and to the host government. Failure to recognize this has led to the development of structures that cannot be sustained without outside assistance under the present resource endowments and technical and management skills.

Despite the fact that only a small fraction of the refugees are in organized settlements, the government's plan is to put all the refugees in those settlements. Already in 1980 during the June conference in Khartoum, the government declared its decision to phase out spontaneous settlement (National Committee for Aid to Refugees 1980). Its policy notwithstanding, however, the overwhelming majority of the refugees are still self-settled. The country's short-term interests may require putting refugees in spatially-segregated sites where all their needs can be met by the international donor community. But the crucial question is where will the money and cultivable land come from? If such is the case, does the host government perceive these organized settlements as a way of keeping refugees separate until their eventual repatriation or as a means of facilitating integration? A report prepared by two staff members of COR and a researcher from the Economic and Social Research Council of Sudan states that "the unorganized settlement (whatever its *examples* of success, may be cited) is bound to be unwelcome. *Its advantages as seen by the outsiders are irrelevant to the affected host community. Once external aid comes in, it should cover all needs of refugees"* (emphasis added) (Osman et al. 1984, 17–18). This clearly indicates that the government perceives organized settlements not as a means of facilitating refugee integration but as a means of keeping refugees separate so that the responsibility of meeting all their needs would rest indefinitely on the international donor community. The criterion for preferring one settlement form to the other is not determined by whether such a settlement will succeed or fail but by the criterion of cost minimization for the host community. The host community's willingness to integrate refugees into itself and consequently to incur some costs in the form of shared access to public utilities can be influenced positively through provision of assistance to offset the strain caused by refugees. Self-settled refugees in urban areas have been almost totally excluded from international assistance mainly because their presence in the cities is not recognized by the government of Sudan. However, the fact remains that these refugees have nowhere else to go. Their problem requires a solution within the urban setting. Since the government does not recognize their presence, no assistance (this is mainly true of Khartoum) can be given to offset or to upgrade the urban infrastructure and consequently the host community cannot help but disapprove of their presence in the urban areas. Given the shortage of cultivable land and the financial constraints of international assistance, the government's determination to phase out self-settlement is unrealistic.

REFERENCES

Agabawi, K.A. 1969. "Some Developments in Rainfed Agriculture in Central Sudan." *Sudan Notes and Records* I.

Agrisystems. 1983. "Agricultural Survey of Land Settlements in the Eastern Sudan." Mimeo.

Birido, Omer. 1982. "International Conference on Assistance to Refugees in Africa (ICARA) and Its Aftermath." A paper presented at the Khartoum Seminar on Refugees, Khartoum, September 11–14.

Chambers, R. 1979. "Rural Refugees in Africa: What the Eye Does Not See." A paper presented at the African Studies Association Symposium on Refugees, London, England, September 13–14.

Colchester, M., and V. Luling, eds. 1985. *Ethiopia's Better Medicine: Settling for Disaster*. London: Survival International.

Commissioner's Office for Refugees. 1987 and 1989. Interview with the head of the Individual Case Unit, Khartoum, Sudan, March and April.

El Siyasa. 1987. Arabic newspaper, no. 269, April 28.

Gifford and Partners, Consulting Civil Engineers. 1981. "Water Supplies for Qala en Nahal and Gedaref Initial Appraisal Report." Prepared for UNHCR, August. Mimeo.

International Labour Organisation and United Nations High Commissioner for Refugees. 1984. *Towards Self-Reliance: A Programme of Action for Refugees in Eastern and Central Sudan.* Geneva: ILO and UNHCR.

Joint Finnish-Sudanese Project Review Mission. 1984. "Mechanization of Agriculture in the Refugee Settlement Areas of the Eastern Sudan." Summary report of the Joint Finnish-Sudanese Project Review Mission, December. Mimeo.

Karadawi, A. 1983. "Constraints on Assistance to Refugees: Some Observations from the Sudan." *World Development* 11, no. 6:537–47.

Kibreab, G. 1985. "A Study of Organized Land Settlements for Eritrean Refugees in Eastern Sudan." Ph.D. dissertation, Department of Economic History, Uppsala University, Uppsala, Sweden.

———. 1987a. "How Viable Are the 'Durable Solutions' for the Refugee Problem in Africa?" Overview paper for the IDRC Refugee Research Network Workshop, Nairobi, Kenya, December 14–17.

———. 1987b. *Refugees and Development in Africa: The Case of Eritrea.* Trenton: The Red Sea Press.

———. 1990a. *From Subsistence to Wage Labour: Refugee Settlements in the Central and Eastern Regions of the Sudan.* Trenton: Red Sea Press.

———. 1990b. "The State of the Art Review of Refugee Studies in Africa." A paper presented at the International Seminar on Refugees in Africa, sponsored by the International Development Research Centre, Arusha, Tanzania, July 30–August 3.

Meeting of Experts on Refugee Aid and Development. 1983. Mont Pèlerin, Switzerland, August 29–31.

Ministry of Finance and Economic Planning (Planning). 1982. "Prospects, Programmes and Policies for Economic Development 1982/83–1984/85." Khartoum: Ministry of Finance and Economic Planning. Mimeo.

Ministry of National Planning. 1979. "An Analysis of Agricultural Production Trends and Policies in the Sudan." Khartoum: Ministry of National Planning, Agricultural Section. Mimeo.

National Committee for Aid to Refugees. 1980. *Documentation for the June 20–23 Conference.* 4 vols. Khartoum, Sudan. Unpublished.

Osman, A.M., et al. 1984. "The Outcome of the International Conference on Assistance to Refugees in Africa (ICARA I)." Khartoum: Economic and Social Research Council. National Council for Research. Mimeo.

Paikert, G.C. 1962. *The German Exodus: A Selective Study on the Post-World War.* The Hague: Martinus Nijhoff.

Scandinavian Institute of African Studies. 1983. *Meeting of the OAU Secretariat and Voluntary Agencies on African Refugees.* Uppsala: Scandinavian Institute of African Studies.

Sebhatu, K.K. 1988. "Refugees and Agricultural Development Challenges: The Case of Qala en Nahal, Eastern Sudan." Diploma dissertation, Agricultural Extension and Rural Development, University of Reading, England, May.

Sorbo, G.M. 1985. *Tenants and Nomads in Eastern Sudan: A Study of Economic Adaptations in the New Halfa Scheme.* Uppsala: Scandinavian Institute of African Studies.

Sudanow, G. 1979. Interview with General Omar Mohammed el Tayeb, State Security Chief, Khartoum, Sudan.

United Nations High Commissioner for Refugees. 1982. *UNHCR Information,* no. 4. Khartoum: UNHCR, August.

———. 1983a. "ICARA: Report of the Secretary-General." E/1982, 65. Geneva: UNHCR, June 10.

———. 1983b. "International Conference on Assistance to Refugees in Africa, ICARA II." Information prepared for the Executive Committee.

———. 1984. "Summary of Needs." A/Conf. 125/1. Geneva: UNHCR, January.

———. 1987a. *UNHRC Fact Sheet,* no. 15. Khartoum: UNHCR, March.

———. 1987b. *Refugees,* July.

———. 1987c. *Refugees,* September.

———. 1988. "Briefing Note on Refugees in the Sudan." Khartoum: UNHCR. United Nations High Commissioner for Refugees and Commissioner's Office for Refugees. 1980. "Planned Rural Refugee Settlements in Kassala Province: Report on a Technical Appraisal Mission." Geneva: UNHCR and COR, December. Mimeo.

———. 1992. "UNHCR Activities Financed by Voluntary Funds: Report for 1991–1992 and Proposed Programmes and Budget for 1993." A/AC. 96793 (Part I). Geneva: UNHCR.

United States Embassy, Office of Refugee Affairs. 1983. "Sectoral Analysis of Resource Flows in the Refugee Settlements of Eastern Sudan." Khartoum: United States Embassy, Office of Refugee Affairs. Mimeo.

U.S. Committee for Refugees. 1992. *World Refugee Survey.* Washington: U.S. Committee for Refugees.

Waldron, S . 1985. "Resettlement in Ethiopia: Where Angels Fear to Tread." *Refugee Issues* 3, no. 2.

World Bank. 1980. "New Halfa Irrigation Rehabilitation Project, Staff Appraisal Report no. 2608a-su." Washington: World Bank.

4

Refugees, Relief and Rehabilitation in the Horn of Africa: The Eritrean Relief Association

John Sorenson

Research on refugee issues typically overlooks steps taken by refugees themselves to improve their situation. The focus is frequently on external interventions and concentrates on assistance during a crisis. Furthermore, the formal definition of what constitutes a refugee may exclude a majority of the uprooted and dispossessed (Bulcha 1988, 80). However, research and effective policies must examine how refugees cope with their situation, attend to internally displaced populations not formally recognized as refugees, and consider prevention, preparedness and development (Kozlowski 1982). A particularly striking example of effective work done by and for African refugees and displaced people is that of one indigenous organization, the Eritrean Relief Association (ERA). Much of Eritrea's internally displaced population was completely dependent on ERA for survival during the long war and famine that afflicted the region, and ERA's work in providing emergency aid was impressive regardless of one's views on Eritrean nationalism.

CONFLICT IN ERITREA

Eritrea's strategic location on the Red Sea coast made it a target of occupations by the Ottoman Turks, Egyptians and Italians. Italian colonialism transformed economic and social relations and established the basis of a distinct national identity (Araia 1986, 1987; Jordan 1989). Following Italy's defeat in World War II, Eritrea came under British administration for a decade. Unlike other colonies, Eritrea did not gain independence but was federated with Ethiopia in 1952 by a UN decision, largely due to pressure from the United States. Ethiopia disregarded the terms of the federation and annexed Eritrea in 1962. For three decades, Eritreans fought for independence and, in 1991, seemed to achieve their goals with the collapse of the Mengistu regime (known as the *Derg* in Amharic). The cost was high. The conflict created one of the largest refugee populations in the world, exacerbated famine and drained the economy of the entire region.

THE ERITREAN RELIEF ASSOCIATION

ERA was formed in 1975 to help Eritrea's rural population who were affected by war and drought. Eritreans who fled war and political repression in Eritrea were asked to return to assist with these efforts. A number of skilled professionals responded and gave up relative comfort and security abroad for spartan conditions in the war zone. ERA went to work in remote and rugged areas that were inaccessible to Ethiopian troops, although the danger of aerial attack persisted. ERA's aims were to solicit and distribute emergency aid, to undertake relief and development projects that could contribute to self-reliance, to stop the flow of refugees by improving socio-economic conditions in Eritrea, and to advocate human rights, including those of refugees. While clearly supportive of Eritrean nationalism, ERA advocated a peaceful solution to the conflict. Its goals included transforming traditional life through education and health care and rebuilding the agricultural base.

ERA established semiautonomous committees in fourteen countries; most members were Eritrean refugees. The committees met every two years and were expected to contribute to the development of policies, as well as raise the financial and material support necessary to implement them. Most committees had subbranches; in Canada, for example, there were fifteen. The organization covered the coordinator's living expenses, but most work was done by volunteers, unless individual subcommittees could obtain local support for staff salaries. At the local and international levels, ERA worked with churches, trade unions, community organizations and other nongovernmental organizations (NGOs).

Until February 1991, ERA was based in Khartoum, with an international coordinating office in Köln, Germany, and a central field office in Sahel province of northern Eritrea. With the original assistance of several church-based NGOs in Khartoum, ERA transported relief supplies from Port Sudan across the border into Eritrea, usually at night to avoid aerial attacks. This operation lasted until the end of the war.

Almost to the end, the *Derg* characterized Eritrean nationalists as bandits and refused to acknowledge that it was fighting a full-scale war. It also rejected proposals for the internationally-supervised safe passage of relief aid. Western governments were "cautious in raising concerns that might appear to violate diplomatic protocol in relation to Ethiopian sovereignty" (Hendrie 1989, 353). As a result, ERA's operations were not acknowledged as an effective means of reaching famine victims and, consequently, remained severely underfunded. Lack of support contributed to the continuing movement of refugees across the border into the Sudan (Hendrie 1989, 354). Gradually, ERA's demonstrated efficiency won some support from donors. The U.S. government recognized the cross-border relief operation as a means of avoiding the destabilizing impact of huge refugee inflows on Sudan, a Western ally, and support for the operation prevented a large influx following crop failures in 1987 (Hendrie 1989, 355).

Following decisive military victories in 1989 by the Eritrean People's Liberation Front (EPLF), ERA moved its central office to Eritrea in response to the huge expansion of its area of operations. When the EPLF took control of Massawa in 1990, ERA began to coordinate much of its work from the port. However, the continuing threat of attack limited its activities. The *Derg* retaliated with a massive attack on Massawa, which was clearly intended to destroy the port facilities, and used Israeli-supplied cluster bombs against the civilian population. Some limitations on ERA's activities were lifted with the end of the war in 1991, but enormous tasks remained in relief, rehabilitation and repatriation.

THE REFUGEE SITUATION

Estimates of the number of Eritrean refugees varied, but some were as high as 800,000, over a quarter of the population. Most went to the Sudan, but the war scattered Eritreans around the world; thousands were internally displaced and lived in ERA camps.

When war erupted in 1961, fighting was concentrated in Eritrea's western lowlands. The first major wave of refugees left in 1967. They were mainly Muslim pastoralists fleeing attacks on villages suspected of assisting the early nationalist organization, the Eritrean Liberation Front (ELF) (Kibreab 1987). The Ethiopian air force used U.S.-supplied napalm and other weapons to slaughter villagers in a deliberate policy of terrorizing the civilian population to eliminate support for nationalist forces. This included poisoning wells and killing livestock, tactics that were particularly effective against nomadic herders who were dependent on scattered water-holes. By 1967 25,627 refugees had fled to the Sudan (Smock 1982). In response, the Sudanese government set up six camps near Kassala. As conflict spread, larger numbers of refugees began to pour across the border to escape massacres. When the Ethiopian military deposed Emperor Haile Selassie in 1974, Eritrean refugees in the Sudan numbered 54,000 (Smock 1982). The military junta continued the emperor's policies and intensified violence against civilians. This was directed previously mainly at rural areas, but in 1975 a reign of terror was imposed on Asmara, Eritrea's capital, and unprecedented violence swept the highlands. The ethnic composition of the refugee movements changed as more urban people from Christian back-grounds fled these attacks.

By 1977 nationalist forces controlled most of Eritrea, but continuing attacks on civilians ensured a steady exodus of refugees. In 1978 the *Derg's* switch of allegiance to the Soviet Union gave it the weapons to launch a huge offensive. The ELF and its offshoot, the EPLF, clashed in a civil war that made them doubly vulnerable to Ethiopian attacks. Both groups were forced to retreat and their withdrawal was accompanied by a massive displacement of civilians who feared Ethiopian reprisals. Unlike the refu-gees who left earlier, most did not go to the Sudan but, as the EPLF emerged victorious in the civil war, settled in the organization's liberated zones. Defeated, the ELF splintered into several smaller groups, with many fighters and supporters fleeing to the Sudan. Throughout the 1980s the *Derg's* hold on Eritrea remained unstable and it continued a strategy of depopulating rural Eritrea, poisoning wells, burning crops, slaughtering livestock and forcing people to go the EPLF areas, relocate in "strategic hamlets" or flee the country.

REFUGEES IN THE SUDAN

Whereas there were 28,000 Eritrean refugees in the Sudan in 1967, by 1984 there were 500,000 Eritreans and Ethiopians. Most were spontaneously settled and received no services from international organizations. Oppos-ing self-settlement, the Sudanese government tried to place the refugees in camps. This was understandable from the Sudanese point of view, but many refugees did not want to settle in permanent camps. They felt that this conflicted with their self-perception as refugees, their desire to return home and their identification as Eritreans (Bascom 1983, 71; Kibreab 1990b; Smock 1982). Strong identification with place of origin is noted in uprooted populations in general (Ingram 1988). In particular, those who were young, educated and from an urban background saw the camps as dead ends, ridden with disease and despair. Many hoped to go Europe or North America or to jobs in the Middle East; however, such opportunities were limited.

While the Sudanese government attempted to assist the refugees in becoming self-sufficient, land and resources provided for settlements were inadequate and inappropriate (Kibreab 1987). Most refugees hoped to return to Eritrea and aside from physical safety, little else motivated them to stay in the Sudan. Much of the Sudanese population lived in squalor and as the economy degenerated, most refugees suffered grim conditions. They faced a general lack of facilities, few employment opportunities, and received no support from UNHCR, not even food. Despite any goodwill of national policies, the refugees were at the mercy of local officials. For example, in July 1987, *New African* magazine reported the deaths of two unaccompanied children in a camp in eastern Sudan. They died from lack of water, which they tried to get from six camps in the area; UNHCR had installed water pumps, but local officials sold the spare parts and oil so that water shortages forced thousands to line up at one sporadically-working pump.

As the situation deteriorated, refugees became scapegoats for political and economic crises, suffering harassment and pressure as officials sought to portray them as the cause of insecurity. Some antirefugee demonstrations occurred, but, fortunately, these were limited.

Smock (1982) described the Eritrean approach to refugees in the Sudan as ambivalent. While ERA worked to establish schools and provide medical care, the EPLF encouraged refugees to return to Eritrea. However, ambivalence was not limited to the Eritrean side. Noting that the EPLF's cooperation was essential to the success of potential settlement schemes in the Port Sudan area and that ERA was an effective channel for mobilizing refugees, Smock pointed out that neither the Sudanese government nor UNHCR worked formally with either organization. Eventually, ERA was legally recognized in Sudan; however, UN agencies and other governments continued to avoid working directly with ERA and most relief aid to Eritrea went through Ethiopian government channels.

WAR, REFUGEES AND THE INTERNALLY DISPLACED

The war and consequent outflow of refugees weakened the whole region. Eritrea suffered devastating attacks for thirty years and many areas literally became underground societies; Ethiopia ruined its own economy by insisting on a military solution. There were enormous casualties and much productive labour was lost. Famine ravaged the weakened countryside.

Rogge (1977) suggested that one can differentiate nonpolitical refugees (who migrated due to ecological factors) from political refugees because in the case of the former, repatriation usually followed immediately after amelioration of the conditions that caused flight. This distinction is not applicable in the Eritrean case. Apart from the probability that many political refugees would also return after an amelioration of the circumstances that caused them to flee, it would be simplistic to view famine as a "natural" disaster. Despite increasingly sparse rainfall in the Horn over the last decade, famine is directly linked with political and military events.

War and drought combined to weaken the entire region. As noted, Ethiopia directed a campaign against Eritrea's civilian population in an attempt to destroy the economic base of the nationalist movement. This exacerbated the effects of drought and created conditions for the spread of famine. Years of conflict eroded Eritrea's food-producing capacity. Ethiopian forces specifically targeted crop fields and livestock, and large areas went uncultivated due to fear of attack.

The psychological effect of the war was devastating. Continuous attacks terrorized the population, traumatized many (which made it impossible for them to continue with productive activities), and created massive displacement. Industrial growth was choked off in urban areas as movement was increasingly restricted, and much of the educated population fled as refugees. Coastal trade and fishing were limited as well. Because conflict reduced agricultural productivity, there was little chance of harvesting a surplus to be stored as a safeguard during severe drought. Conservation efforts were curtailed, and as drought persisted, the situation worsened. Weakened farmers cultivated smaller areas, depleted their cash and food resources, and were forced to consume their seeds and sell their tools and animals. This meant ever-decreasing production, growing dependency on food aid and greater numbers of refugees.

Some argued that these should not be considered refugees because they did not flee from political persecution, but clearly the famine cannot be separated from military conflict; there is no basis for regarding these people as economic migrants. Conditions in the Sudan were grim for many. In the past, Eritreans crossed into the Sudan for economic reasons, but Smock stated that "economic motives have not, however, stimulated the periodic waves of Eritreans entering since 1967. Most were far better off economically in their home country than in the Sudan; they fled for survival" (1982, 451).

War and famine created massive internal displacement in Eritrea. Because these people did not cross an international boundary, they were not classified as refugees, yet their conditions were similar to those of many refugees.

> There is little difference between the displaced and the refugee, save the fact that one remains in his or her country of origin, while the latter crosses a recognized international boundary. Both have been stripped of their livelihood and are in imminent danger of loss of life. They are poor, malnourished, vulnerable to disease and unable to survive without outside help. What difference there is tends to lie in the fact that the refugee is more visible and more likely to attract the attention of the international community (Eritrean Relief Association 1983, 10).

In the Eritrean case, refugees and the internally displaced were the results of politics. ERA sought international assistance for both. It hoped to stop the refugee flow by providing aid to drought-affected villages and to camps for the displaced. During the last decade, ERA focused on providing emergency aid. For much of the population, ERA was the main source of food rations. Until Massawa was opened to ERA, supplies were received at Port Sudan and then trucked across the desert and into Eritrea. Ethiopian attacks constantly threatened distribution, so ERA worked at night to avoid detection. ERA also attempted to design and implement effective strategies to rebuild the shattered rural economy. It not only attempted to halt the refugee flow but to establish conditions for repatriation of those in exile and for return of the internally displaced.

DROUGHT AND DISPLACEMENT

There was insufficient rainfall throughout the 1970s, but by 1980 the drought worsened, affecting 1.25 million people. Of these, 350,000 needed food aid, while 100,000 entered camps for the displaced and were totally reliant on ERA for food, clothing and shelter. New camps opened as the situation deteriorated. In 1981 infestations of army worms damaged the crops. In 1982 the *Derg's* Red Star Offensive, launched during the planting season, further disrupted food supplies. In 1983 the rains failed during the planting season and ERA assisted 650,000 displaced people in ten camps. Long before the BBC finally broadcast the terrifying scenes of starvation in Ethiopia, ERA warned of impending disaster and appealed for assistance to the displaced population. It was ignored, although independent researchers substantiated the spread of malnutrition and anaemia in rural Eritrea. Overcrowding in the camps, poor hygiene, lack of proper clothing and harmful traditional healing practices increased the incidence of disease. The threat was particularly great to women and children. The health situation deteriorated further with the failure of rains again in 1984. Many wells dried up completely and ERA estimated that only 10 percent of food requirements were being met. Bondestam, Cliffe and White (1988) suggested this was an underestimation, but they disputed UN reports that 70 percent of needs were being met through official Ethiopian channels.

In October 1984 ERA claimed it was able to deliver food aid to 85 percent of Eritrea and estimated that approximately half a million people were on the verge of starvation, while another million were hungry. It reported hundreds of people dying of starvation, most of them children. Diseases such as tuberculosis, malaria, measles and typhoid tore at a population weakened by food shortages and deprived of proper medical treatment. Lack of water meant severe livestock losses and erosion of the subsistence base for the seminomadic population. By providing relief aid, ERA attempted to help people remain in their villages, but the shortfall in food supplies meant ration cuts and resulted in a large migration to the Sudan. One study estimates that 150,000 Eritrean refugees fled to the Sudan at the height of the famine (Bondestam, Cliffe and White 1988).

ERA stated that drought and war displaced 10 to 15 percent of the population at this time. Many of those who did not go to the Sudan became totally dependent on ERA for survival. ERA was forced to create more camps for the displaced and supply them with water, which had to be transported through rugged terrain.

ERA's transportation capacity was extremely limited. Until 1984, ERA had only ten trucks. The EPLF gave ERA forty of its trucks for transporting food to the displaced population. However, as most of the available trucks were old, rough terrain meant that almost a quarter of them might be off the road for repair at any one time. Relief convoys faced attacks by the Ethiopian military. This made it impossible for ERA to rent trucks in Sudan because commercial truckers would not risk destruction of their vehicles. Therefore, ERA had to seek resources to purchase trucks, as well as soliciting food aid. Further difficulty was posed by the fact that most of the rural population were in remote areas inaccessible by road. Therefore, food aid had to be distributed by pack animals. Beneficiaries were encouraged to provide these pack animals, but drought had made animals scarce, so ERA was forced to purchase pack animals as well.

Pack animals were also used to transport relief supplies into areas held by the *Derg*. Such operations were dangerous and required much caution. ERA appealed for an agreement to allow free access for emergency aid, but its proposals were rejected, making the supply of aid uncertain in large areas.

The situation had worsened by December 1984. Thousands more were displaced and two million people were now affected by drought and famine. Although there was still a lack of rainfall, conditions were worse in 1984 because the drought had extended over several years and there were no surpluses from previous years to fall back on. Insects attacked the crops, and because drought had affected a greater area, the Sudan was also suffering and was forced to ban exports of grain.

ERA's emergency relief request to aid 750,000 people included provision of food aid, transportation costs and medical supplies. Fortunately, publicity concerning famine in the region encouraged increased aid. In 1985 resumption of rainfall allowed planting and the harvest of a small surplus. In thirty-one camps for the displaced, ERA supported food production by distributing seeds. It also encouraged refugees to return from the Sudan by providing them with rations and seeds.

While there was some improvement in 1985, there was still a danger of aerial attack. Ethiopian forces attacked villages, targeted crop fields and mined some areas to prevent planting. By 1986 ERA's estimate of those affected by drought was 1.5 million, with 650,000 still dependent on food aid. Rainfall in 1986 brought a small increase in crop production, but ERA continued its appeal for food aid. Response was encouraging and led to an improvement in health conditions. A survey by the International Committee of the Red Cross (ICRC) in Senhit province reported a 10 percent decrease in malnutrition among children (Pateman 1990a, 186). ERA was also able to proceed with its effort to rebuild Eritrea's agricultural base by distributing seeds and tools to farmers around Nakfa. ERA also gave money to 150 families in the Barka region to purchase oxen (Eritrean Relief Committee 1986). By 1986 it seemed that the crisis had passed and ERA was turning to recovery and development plans.

However, long-term effects of famine presented real problems. The population was weakened and much of the livestock was dead. The subsistence base of the seminomadic people was wiped out. The farmers' ability to work their fields was severely diminished due to lack of draft animals and their own malnourished state. The war left large areas uncultivated. With farming restricted to smaller areas, no surplus could be harvested, so the population remained dependent and at risk.

In 1987 rainfall was irregular and did not coincide with the growing season. Locusts and army worms destroyed much of the crops. The *Derg* prohibited international organizations from aerial spraying in Eritrea. ERA and the EPLF undertook ground-spraying by hand; despite limitations, efforts to stop the locusts were successful, although 3,500 hectares of crops were destroyed (Bondestam, Cliffe and White 1988, 50).

Drought continued into 1988, leading to crop failure of 85 percent in Eritrea. ERA's emergency relief request estimated that 2.5 million people were in danger and one million were totally dependent on relief, which was a substantial increase. Food shortages were predicted for the entire year and the outlook was bleak as growing numbers of displaced people moved into the ERA camps. ERA stated it could distribute food to 75 percent of the needy, approximately 825,000 people. Half of this was to be distributed in Sahel, Senhit and Barka provinces, the EPLF-held areas. Another 25 percent was to be distributed in areas under conflict and the remaining quarter was to be distributed by ERA behind Ethiopian lines.

ERA's food distribution was based on the standard World Health Organization daily ration, and included food grains, edible oil, milk powder, pulses and corn-soya milk, although the unreliability of aid meant that minimum requirements were often unmet. The usual ration was for a two-month period, although those travelling from dangerous areas sometimes received a larger ration. The most vulnerable were those in hospitals and clinics, as well as children in schools and orphanages. In addition to the standard ration, these groups received supplementary rations of sugar, biscuits, canned beef, egg powder, whole and skim milk and soap whenever they were available. Those in ERA camps were severely affected by drought and war; often they had no resources whatsoever. These people received the usual ration, plus a supplementary ration of sugar, soap and household utensils (cooking pots, etc.). Those who remained in their villages were assumed to be less affected. Depending on the extent of the supply, supplementary food could be distributed to the general population, but if amounts were limited, distribution was restricted to vulnerable groups. In 1989 the situation deteriorated further. Lack of rain meant total crop failure and extensive livestock losses. ERA's October 1989 appeal estimated that 1.9 million people would face starvation in the following year. ERA requested 270,000 metric tons of cereals and 63,000 metric tons of various supplementary foods, as well as medical supplies and trucks.

As always, transportation remained a major problem. ERA's 1988 appeal included plans to upgrade distribution through the purchase of new trucks. Since 1985, ERA had acquired 318 trucks with a transport capacity of 3,755 metric tons per trip. These were serviced by an ingenious network of hidden repair shops and gas stations, but with the rough roads and the war, twenty-five trucks were taken off the road and another twenty-six were awaiting repair. This reduced the number of trucks to 267, with a capacity of 3,301 metric tons per trip. ERA estimated that due to flooding and slow travel during summer, the total actual transport capacity would be 103,981 metric tons per year. In 1991 a lack of transportation continued to present problems for effective food distribution, creating a monthly shortfall of 13,000 metric tons and requiring 226 twenty-ton trucks to make up the difference.

AGRICULTURAL REHABILITATION

Although the Horn of Africa is viewed as a disaster zone where the land's productive capacity has been destroyed by drought and desertification, there is some potential for a recovery that could lift the region from its state of permanent emergency. Peace is a necessary precondition for a resuscitation of the Eritrean economy, but so is the provision of basic agricultural inputs that will allow the rural populations to reestablish themselves. Through its relief and rehabilitation programs, ERA sought to prevent depopulation and to establish conditions for repatriation. Food aid was needed, not just for emergency relief, but for the long process of recovery and attempts to establish self-sufficiency.

In 1985 ERA attempted to take advantage of resumed rainfall by developing the one-year Agricultural Rehabilitation Programme based on distribution of seeds, tools and oxen, as well as fertilizers and pesticides, to peasant farmers. The program was to be implemented jointly by ERA and the EPLF's Agriculture Commission. It had three objectives: to increase production, to stop refugee movements by providing the means by which farmers could remain in their villages, and to help peasants attain self-sufficiency. Extended to a three-year period, the program tried to replace the means of production lost because of war and drought. Specific aims included distributing tools to 275,000 households, providing 8,000 oxen to the poorest households, supplying seeds to plant 412,500 hectares of land and establishing 1,834 workshops for tool production, maintenance and repair.

Linked to the program were the provision of pesticides; soil and water management projects, such as terracing, planting cover crops, constructing small dams and reservoirs; and reforestation schemes involving plant protection efforts and tree-planting. ERA encouraged practical studies from specialists abroad on drought-resistant crops, plant diseases, soil surveys, crop variation, fertilizer and pesticide use, and so on. Based on its studies, ERA introduced new crops, such as sweet potatoes, and started raising chickens and rabbits for food. Although it recognized the necessity for research and long-term recovery programs, the continuing emergency forced ERA to concentrate on preventing immediate starvation.

ERA and the EPLF's Agriculture Commission established regional steering committees to collect information on the regions to be assisted, to administer the program, including allocating funds, ensuring that funds were spent on inputs, and reporting on the progress achieved. Need and regional equity determined distribution. Implementation was the responsibility of the beneficiaries themselves, who were organized in village committees and unions. Committees were responsible for purchasing inputs, ensuring that the poorest households, including those headed by women, were assisted and that oxen were maintained in good health. Village participation was good because benefits were direct and the beneficiaries were motivated to make the project succeed through their own efforts (Eritrean Relief Association 1989b). ERA noted some problems with distributing inputs where there was nepotism, and where an established hierarchy was able to manipulate the distribution to its own advantage. Proposed targets were not met because international support did not reach planned levels. Support varied annually, but, over the three-year period, only 54 percent of target funding was acquired. In some aspects, distribution of inputs exceeded the targets, as in the provision of oxen. Originally, ERA assumed that donors would not support this project and that costs would be prohibitive. However, donors recognized the importance of draft animals to agricultural rehabilitation. Originally, ERA attempted to provide oxen to communities for general use. However, Eritrean societies traditionally saw social welfare in terms of kinship relations, and EPLF's efforts to encourage new communal values were not always successful. For example, some oxen assigned to cooperatives died because they were overworked and not properly cared for. Rather than persisting with this procedure, ERA decided to provide one ox per household.

ERA distributed 9,850 tons of seeds in the period 1986–1988. Military activity restricted distribution, and there were problems with insects, floods and late rainfall, which required additional allotments to some areas. Pesticide acquisition went mainly towards the antilocust campaign. Tool distribution did not meet the target because of increased costs, a reordering of priorities and delays in shipment from Europe. Establishment of workshops was the least successful because of high costs of raw materials and because the program did nothing to benefit pastoralist groups.

War was the major factor in limiting rehabilitation. In 1988 there was significant displacement and military offensives were launched at the peak of the agricultural cycle. There was a drought in 1987, late rains the following year, and major pest infestations from 1986 to 1988. Despite these factors, lack of support, delays in shipment of materials and other problems, ERA estimated that 60 percent of its aims were met, that the program increased crop production to some extent and enabled many peasants to remain in their villages and work their land. Without the program many poorer peasants would have been forced into permanent dependency by borrowing enough money to plant their fields or would have become reliant on food aid. Displacement did occur, but was due to military attack rather than economic factors.

Based on partial success, the program was extended for another three-year period (1990–1992). The goals were to provide 15,000 oxen to needy households and 50,000 goats to pastoralists; distribute seeds and tools to 75,000 households; distribute cash to villages for community development work (including terracing, construction of wells, cisterns and embankments); and distribute forge sets for 500 workshops (Eritrean Relief Association 1989b). However, lack of rain in 1990–1991 reversed the progress. Much of the livestock supplied by the program died due to lack of water and grass. In the fall of 1990 50,000 livestock died in EPLF areas (Eritrean Relief Association in Canada 1990b). Pastoralist groups were hit particularly hard, but farmers also experienced a major setback. The second consecutive year of crop failure put more than two million people at risk; ERA appealed for 350,000 metric tons of food aid.

AFFORESTATION, SOIL AND WATER CONSERVATION

The Afforestation, Soil and Water Conservation Programme was linked to the Agricultural Rehabilitation Programme. Initiated in 1987, the aim was to conduct terracing for natural vegetation and tree-planting, introduce proper tilling practices, and construct small dams and reservoirs throughout Eritrea. By 1989 the program was supported only by Sweden. Most Western governments maintained their policy of supplying only limited amounts of relief aid to Eritrea through NGOs and banning any development activities for fear of antagonizing the *Derg*.

The program was to be conducted in the eastern escarpment of the highlands, but conflict delayed implementation until 1989. Main activities included identifying and collecting tree seeds, preparing seedlings in nurseries, preparing land, constructing dams, terracing and digging wells. Peasants who dug wells and ponds were paid in cash, as were those who watered seeds and supervised nurseries. Approximately 1,600 peasants received tools and were engaged in terracing (Eritrean Relief Association 1989a).

EDUCATION

ERA sought to assist thousands of children whose parents were dead, missing or too poor to care for them (Eritrean Relief Association 1984a). In 1978 a children's home was established in Keren to meet the nutritional, educational and emotional needs of 325 children, but war forced them to be moved, first to the EPLF-held area around Nakfa and then to the Solomuna refugee camp in the Sudan. Conditions were appalling; shelter was rudimentary, and refugees faced intense heat, water shortages and snakes. After thirty months, ERA opened another camp, New Solomuna, in northern Eritrea, where most of the refugees went in 1981. A kindergarten was established, but conditions were basic and the children suffered from a lack of educational facilities, clothing and toys. As they were under constant threat of aerial attack, their movements were limited, and the barren environment offered little stimulation. War and famine created growing numbers of new orphans; the staff were hard pressed to provide individual attention, so that many children were desperate for physical affection.

In 1976 the EPLF established a school in its base area and offered courses in seven grades. Schools were established throughout Eritrea when the liberation fronts advanced, but the strategic withdrawal in 1978 following Soviet intervention meant that many of these were shut down. Some continued to operate secretly and others reopened after the EPLF's victories since 1989. Zero School became the centre for a national school system that included 144 schools and more than 20,000 students (Eritrean Relief Association 1986). The EPLF printed textbooks in various languages. Educated Eritreans living abroad were encouraged to return to provide instruction. The EPLF initiated literacy campaigns and required literacy among its fighters, which probably increased their commitment (Firebrace and Holland 1985, 118). Literacy programs were established for adults, particularly women, who had an illiteracy rate of over 90 percent. Women were encouraged to take training courses in sewing and poultry production as well. The EPLF's Agriculture Commission provided short courses in soil and water conservation, horticulture, basic veterinary skills and tool repair. Students were chosen by village assemblies and, on completion, returned to their communities to share their knowledge. A technical school was established to provide instruction in mechanics and engine repair, carpentry, electronics and metal work. The aim was to provide a core of skilled workers for independent Eritrea.

The influx of Eritrean refugees had a major impact on the Sudan's educational system. Little was done to establish special schools for refugee children and, as a consequence, there was overcrowding, insufficient materials and competition for space. Refugee parents in Port Sudan established three primary schools for their children, but these had inadequate resources and untrained staff (Karadawi 1980). Retraining classes were established in Port Sudan for those wounded in the war, but these could not serve the needs of the refugee population as well.

ERA operated nine schools for refugees at three locations in Sudan. Despite recognition of its importance, opportunities for education remained limited for refugee children (Karadawi 1980). Refugees hoped to return home, so there was an emphasis on an Eritrean curriculum. Smock (1982) advised that gaps in the Sudanese educational system for refugees could be bridged by UNHCR aid to ERA. However, UNHCR provided no support for ERA's initiatives.

MEDICAL CARE

War and drought shaped the development of health care in Eritrea. Originally, EPLF medical units were small, mobile and focused on treating war wounds. From the mid-1970s, the emphasis was on training and providing medical care to the general population. Ongoing conflict required clinics to be mobile or camouflaged. As with educational and agricultural projects, the EPLF and ERA sought to secure popular support for medical programs.

ERA and the Eritrean Medical Association (formed among Eritrean doctors living in Europe and North America), contributed to the development of the Eritrean Public Health Care Programme. The centre of this network was "the longest hospital in the world," so named because it spread out along a valley floor in the mountains near Orota, and consisted of numerous buildings hidden underground or under a brush cover. The hospital had room for 1,200 patients and wings for ophthalmology, obstetrics, orthopaedics, dentistry, laboratories, an X-ray unit and an operating theatre where doctors performed sophisticated surgery in sterile conditions. There was also a special section for facial injuries and reconstruction. Most of the doctors were trained abroad and returned to live in these rugged conditions because of their humanitarian and political commitments. Medical specialists visited the hospital to train over 2,000 paramedics.

The network also included six smaller regional hospitals, eight health centres and fifty health stations. As well, "barefoot doctors" travelled by camel or donkey to remote areas to provide nomadic people with basic medical care and information. Students were selected by village assemblies and went through a three-year training program to learn how to cope with a wide variety of medical problems. The rocky valley also concealed a pharmacy where Eritrean technicians produced over forty types of drugs, including analgesics, antibiotics, chloroquine, and intravenous fluids.

In Port Sudan, a clinic was established for amputees and those with spinal injuries. The clinic emphasized rehabilitation and reintegration of the disabled. Many patients were wounded fighters, but the clinic also treated civilians who were injured by land mines or aerial bombing raids. The clinic reintegrated these people as technicians in various workshops or as teachers. One workshop produced artificial limbs and crutches.

TRANSFORMING THE ROLE OF WOMEN

Development entails social transformation. In Eritrea women were seen traditionally as inferior. Their status meant that they received less food, which made them particularly susceptible to diseases and malnutrition; they also suffered from dangerous practices, including clitoridectomy and infibulation, which created extremely high mortality rates during childbirth. Genital mutilation was abandoned within the EPLF, but still exists among some groups. ERA discouraged these practices through education.

ERA tried to incorporate useful traditional knowledge in health care; the power of traditional healers was recognized and ERA sought their support. One program for village midwives was to train 320 women annually and thereby improve health care for women in remote villages. By upgrading the role of traditional birth attendants and encouraging their participation in promoting social change, ERA and the National Union of Eritrean Women (NUEW) hoped to reduce risks involved with pregnancy and childbirth and reduce maternal mortality. In 1984, with NUEW support, a factory was established near Orota to produce sanitary pads for women. As part of a coordinated effort involving primary care and information, this was an important step in promoting women's health, although lack of raw materials limited the operation.

NUEW sought to improve the status of women by promoting literacy and training in agriculture, health and nontraditional occupations. In 1990 NUEW appealed for support for two women's centres that would assist one hundred women annually in programs such as leadership, food processing and bookkeeping. Other NUEW projects included establishing village flour mills and manufacturing household utensils.

REFUGEES, DEPENDENCY AND NATIONALISM

It is often assumed that aid creates dependency and that refugees are a helpless burden upon their hosts; this perception may be inaccurate (Kibreab 1990b; Harrell-Bond 1986). On the contrary, African refugees are very active and are attempting to improve their situation. Both ERA and the EPLF encouraged participation from refugees and the displaced population. Much of this was organized through appeals to nationalist sentiments.

While nationalism often involves negative sentiments of racism and xenophobia, it is clearly also a powerful tool for mobilizing support. In the context of revolutionary transformation, ERA achieved remarkable success in relief and rehabilitation efforts. Emphasis on self-reliance encouraged popular participation and commitment with impressive achievements, despite material limitations. Many observers commented favourably upon Eritrea's social revolution. Babu (1988, 56) found the EPLF's administration "far superior to many independent African countries." Similarly, Pateman (1990b) suggested that the egalitarian nature of the revolution and the commitment to voluntarism makes Eritrea a model for development.

Chambers (1983) stated that although rural development should be based on efforts to work with the poor, several factors worked against this. These included biases towards easily accessible areas where projects are already underway; concentration on those who are already users of services, which tended to include those who are relatively better off; a seasonal bias towards research and implementation in the dry season; a political aspect that tended to avoid giving offence to established powers; and a professional aspect that tended to confine work to areas of the outsider's specialization. All of these factors influenced relief and development activity in the Eritrean situation. However, the diplomatic factor was the most influential in preventing effective development assistance and solving the refugee crisis.

Donor governments and organizations, such as the United Nations, prefer to deal with governments of sovereign states. Although the EPLF was the de facto government in most of Eritrea, inconvenient realities went unrecognized. Donors supplied the most assistance to the *Derg*, although most of the famine-affected population lived in areas outside its control. Furthermore, there were many reports of the *Derg*'s misuse of food aid. Having helped to create famine, the *Derg* blocked efforts to alleviate it, forcing relief agencies to cease operations in Eritrea. Attacks on ERA food convoys were common. As a result, more refugees were forced into the Sudan. ICRC charged that Ethiopia was deliberately withholding food from those it considered its political enemies. There were many allegations that emergency aid was used to lure conscripts and to capture peasants in Tigray for "voluntary" resettlement. Many protested that food aid was being delivered to Ethiopian troops; Pateman (1990a) cited several instances.

Some former Ethiopian officials denied such charges (Wolde Giorgis 1989, 311); UN officials backed the denials (Jansson, Harris and Penrose 1987), as did Canadian government representatives. However, other Ethiopian defectors acknowledged that the charges were true. For example, in an April 1989 interview, Berhane Deressa, formerly deputy commissioner of Ethiopia's Relief and Rehabilitation Committee (RRC), said that he diverted food aid to the military. Former Ethiopian Foreign Minister Goshu Wolde confirmed that this was common. Both agreed that they had no choice in the situation, that the soldiers themselves were starving peasants who were conscripted, and that the military would have taken the food in any event.

These factors played a role in drawing assistance to Eritrea. Largely due to effective lobbying by Eritrean refugees abroad, a trickle of aid was provided through NGOs. However, while the *Derg*'s distribution of aid was not closely supervised, ERA's operations were subject to careful scrutiny. Whereas irregularities and losses were common in the government's distribution, "virtually every sack of grain" going into Eritrea through ERA was accounted for (Pateman 1990a, 199). There were no allegations of misuse of aid and ERA's efficiency and commitment were frequently praised. Nevertheless, political priorities meant that reports by independent monitors were ignored. OXFAM-Canada complained that Canadian officials refused to accept reports acknowledging ERA's effectiveness because the government was committed to the Ethiopian position.

Politics inhibited aid to Eritrea and exacerbated the refugee crisis. In addition to a preference among donors to deal with the sovereign state, external powers regarded the possibility of an independent Eritrea as not in their interest. Israel, for example, saw Eritrean nationalism as a movement linked with various Middle East states intent on turning the Red Sea into an "Arab lake." The U.S. opposed Eritrean independence, regarded the *Derg*'s alliance with the Soviet Union as temporary, and supported Ethiopia's "territorial integrity." Most OAU member states ignored Eritrea, fearing its independence would encourage secessionist movements elsewhere, despite the unique character of the Eritrean case, which is better seen as delayed decolonization rather than secessionism.

In 1985 it seemed that the U.S. might recognize ERA and the Relief Society of Tigray (REST) as effective channels of aid. However, politics outweighed humanitarian concern. The EPLF was ideologically unacceptable; many U.S. officials saw it as more Marxist than the *Derg*. It could not be equated with the contras or the mujahedeen and thus was ineligible for direct support. Nevertheless, Western strategists saw the usefulness of providing minimal humanitarian aid. Limited food aid would allow the war to continue and destabilize the *Derg*, but would not permit the Eritreans to win a decisive victory. The *Derg* blocked aid to Eritrea and protested against international efforts to help refugees. In Britain Ethiopian diplomats warned NGOs working in Eritrea about violating the Charities Act (Harrell-Bond 1986, 17). Similarly, Wolde Giorgis (1989, 316) criticized the international relief effort as an infringement on Ethiopian sovereignty; he attacked UNHCR for providing relief to refugees while ignoring internally displaced people, claiming this was a politically motivated effort to draw refugees to Sudan and embarrass the *Derg*. He insisted that refugees went to Sudan rather than to Ethiopian distribution centres because of propaganda by the liberation movements.

> [UNHCR] should have played a neutral humanitarian role, but proved to be a political instrument of those seeking to discredit our government. The UNHCR called those seeking food within our borders "displaced persons"; only when they crossed the frontiers were they called "refugees" and considered eligible for UNHCR assistance. Then the UNHCR became very interested, providing millions of dollars and sending the relief items that these same people had been denied on our side of the border. The massive influx of people into the Sudan would not have been anywhere near as great without this pull factor.

Wolde Giorgis charged that UNHCR refugee camps were centres of subversive activity, where sophisticated weaponry circulated freely and antigovernment forces were recruited and trained.

Ethiopian protests and Western strategic interests combined to limit aid to Eritrea. Other factors played a role. For example, Canada's former ambassador to Ethiopia, David MacDonald, told me that Canada would not assist Eritrea because it might "set a bad example for Quebec." Canadian NGOs that spoke out on Eritrea were warned that they could have their charitable status revoked for being too political. Yet working with the *Derg* had deadly consequences for the famine-affected population of Eritrea. Canada's response provides a good example.

In 1984 Canada responded generously, if belatedly, to the famine. However, the government insisted on sending most aid through the *Derg*, which was attacking Eritrea's civilian population. The Canadian International Development Agency (CIDA) refused to provide rehabilitation or development aid to EPLF-held areas, despite ERA's predictions that famine would recur if such measures were not taken. The government would not work directly with ERA in Canada and only provided minimal amounts of emergency aid through other NGOs, slowing the process and reducing direct benefits to those who were starving in Eritrea.

In 1989 Canada suddenly halved its estimate of those in need and reduced its aid provisions proportionally. According to one NGO representative, CIDA officials refused to reveal the source of their information, but CIDA apparently accepted only information provided by the *Derg* and the UN, which relied on the same source. CIDA rejected information supplied by ERA or Canadian NGOs with projects in Eritrea. During 1989–1990, most Canadian allocations went to government-held areas, although all of Tigray was under the control of the Tigrayan People's Liberation Front (TPLF) and the *Derg* held only a few towns in Eritrea (Canadian Council for International Cooperation 1990). Approximately 80 percent of the affected population were beyond the *Derg*'s reach. Rather than sending aid through ERA, Canada supported an expensive airlift to Ethiopian officials barricaded in Asmara, despite charges that food was being delivered to the army while civilians starved.

AID DELIVERY THROUGH MASSAWA

In January 1991 the EPLF opened Massawa. Under the auspices of the World Food Programme, aid was to be divided equally between ERA and the RRC. This arrangement ignored the fact that ERA had access to more people and RRC's distribution was limited to urban areas. While reopening Massawa was an important step in providing aid to areas around Asmara and southeastern Eritrea, the cross-border route remained crucial for delivery to northern and western regions. There were no direct roads from Massawa to these areas and delivery required transport by a circuitous route with delays, higher costs and without the benefit of the service infrastructure that was established along the route from Port Sudan. Furthermore, facilities at Massawa were not fully operational, reducing the intake capacity to 30,000 metric tons per month. ERA's share of this was sufficient to meet only half the monthly requirements. ERA expressed concern about Ethiopian attacks on the relief operation. Ethiopia had consistently targeted the civilian population and ERA convoys in the past. The Ethiopian assault on Massawa was particularly brutal, using cluster bombs that killed many civilians. For these reasons, continued use of the cross-border route seemed a sensible option. However, donor support to the operation declined and there was insufficient response to ERA's appeals in 1991. Whereas ERA required 18,000–19,000 metric tons monthly through the cross-border route, pledged food amounted to only 17,654 metric tons over several months (Eritrean Relief Association in Canada 1991a).

In a letter dated February 4, 1991, MP Dorothy Dobbie defended Canada's contributions as sufficient because there was "no significant starvation" in Eritrea and Tigray. The implication was that ERA and REST had exaggerated the levels of need. However, ERA interpreted the situation differently: "The vicious cycle continues unbroken. The famine affected people have been getting only below subsistence levels, just enough to keep them alive half-starved, but not enough to regain their vitality in productive work" (1990, 10). In March 1991 the Eritrean Relief Association in Canada (ERAC) reported a rapid decline of nutritional level, starvation and population movements that indicated all survival strategies were exhausted. ERA reported that 12,000 people had moved into EPLF zones from the Ethiopian-controlled parts of Hamassien and Seraye because of lack of food and expected that more would follow. Refugees were moving out of Sahel and into the Sudan because they had no water. Some of ERA's hospitals and camps for the displaced had to be moved due to water shortages.

CONCLUSIONS: HUMAN RIGHTS AND NATIONAL SOVEREIGNTY

In the Eritrean case, as elsewhere, the refugee problem required negotiation of the political issues that were the basis of conflict. Yet evasion of political issues behind refugee crises remains the norm. The idea that humanitarian aid can be nonpolitical in such situations is a bizarre fiction.

Practical steps could have been taken to prevent further refugee movements. The first of these would have been to recognize the reality of the situation. This would have entailed official recognition of ERA's effectiveness. Many NGOs testified to this. Brodhead (1986, 876) stated that ERA played a central role in the relief effort, although its work remained unrecognized. Hendrie (1989) also noted that ERA was effective yet unknown. Médecins Sans Frontières describes ERA as "the only [organization] in the whole region of the Horn with which one feels confident to leave alone with their distribution network ... it always reaches the affected people wherever they are." Even Wolde Giorgis (1989, 325), who tried to block support to ERA and REST while heading Ethiopia's RRC (Pateman

1990a, 192), later acknowledged the efforts of those organizations to assist the famine-affected population.

Recognition by the UN and Western governments was not forthcoming. UN Assistant Secretary General for Emergency Operations in Africa, Kurt Jansson, ignored ERA in his account of the relief operation (Jansson, Harris and Penrose 1987). The Canadian government refused to accept information provided by ERA and consistently relied on Ethiopian sources. Although the U.S. and Norway sent observers to monitor ERA's operations, Canada refused to do so and dismissed NGO reports (Canadian Council for International Cooperation 1990). However, one parliamentary report suggested that monitors should verify data in the areas served by ERA and REST and, to a limited extent, acknowledged that both organizations were significant in relief operations. The report recommended that the definition of humanitarian assistance be extended to include famine-prevention activities, such as providing agricultural inputs, medical programs and education (Parliamentary Delegation to Ethiopia and Sudan 1991), but it remains to be seen whether this recommendation will be implemented in other cases.

By the time the EPLF gained control of Massawa, an effective response would have been to acknowledge that the EPLF controlled most of Eritrea and that, therefore, aid distribution should be proportional. It was argued that this would infringe upon Ethiopian sovereignty. Yet the sovereignty of any state must be based not on repression but on claims to protect the rights of its members, including the right to food. Furthermore, Ethiopia's claims to sovereignty over Eritrea had been contested for three decades. There were convincing arguments that the federation was improper to begin with, but that Ethiopia's abrogation of it violated international law (Bereket 1989; Fenet 1988; Permanent Peoples' Tribunal 1984; Serapiao 1987; Semere 1987). Defending this sovereignty that was both morally and legally questionable was scarcely a principled course, and Canada's stand on Eritrea was contradicted by its position on annexation of the Baltic states. In any case, Ethiopian "sovereignty" was already violated by providing small amounts of aid through the cross-border operation. Ethiopia was fully aware of this and must also have recognized the strategy behind maintaining such operations at a minimal level.

Denunciations of the *Derg* and the liberation fronts for political use of food aid lose much of their moral tone when one examines how Western governments sought to achieve their political goals by withholding aid or utilizing certain channels for delivery. Providing food aid through the cross-border operation was not strictly a humanitarian gesture by Western governments but was intended to serve political objectives. In a manner reminiscent of the manipulation of the Iraqi Kurds in 1972, enough food was provided to keep the Eritrean nationalists active as a counter to the *Derg*, although the U.S. never intended that they actually succeed in establishing independence. Indeed, in 1991 as the EPLF appeared close to its goal, the U.S. threatened to cut off all food aid through the cross-border operation. The argument that relief is apolitical and that development aid could not be provided because it would have implied support to the EPLF is a facile one. Food aid is political and emphasizing Ethiopian government channels was not a neutral act. The assumption that "food-aid is a non-political input in conflict situations is widespread ... however, it does not necessarily bear scrutiny... Food-aid can be easily monetized or applied to non-humanitarian purposes, while, conversely, agricultural rehabilitation inputs have little military application. Thus the distinction between what constitutes political and non-political aid in the context of war is largely an externally-manufactured one" (Hendrie 1989, 359).

Furthermore, it is questionable whether the so-called "principle" of sovereignty ought to take precedence over human rights, including the right to food. While we have become accustomed to thinking in terms of security of states, we ought to think in terms of security of people. "States are less and less convincing in their claims to offer the security that partly legitimizes their power and authority" (Walker 1990). This is particularly so where a state continually shows brutal disregard for its population. The Ethiopian state insisted on maintaining its questionable "territorial integrity" through murder and terror operations against Eritrean civilians, creating disaster for its own people as well. On a practical, legal and moral basis then, one can argue that increased support to ERA would have been an effective means of preventing further crises in the refugee situation.

At present, the EPLF has established a provisional government and intends to proceed with a referendum on independence, although this already appears to have been achieved in fact if not yet in name. ERA's structure will no doubt change if independence is declared in the near future, but its experience will ensure that it can serve as an effective channel for implementing refugee repatriation and for development in Eritrea.

REFERENCES

Araia, Tseggai. 1986. "Historical Analysis of Infrastructural Development in Italian-Eritrea: 1885–1941." *Journal of Eritrean Studies* I (1): 19–33.

———. 1987. "Historical Analysis of Infrastructural Development in Italian-Eritrea: 1885–1941 (Part Two)." *Journal of Eritrean Studies*. I (2): 10–25.

Babu, Abdulrahman Mohammed. 1988. "The Eritrean Question in the Context of African Conflicts and Superpower Rivalries." In *The Long Struggle of Eritrea for Independence and Constructive Peace*, edited by Lionel Cliffe and Basil Davidson, 47–63. Trenton: Red Sea Press.

Bascom, Johnathan. 1983. "The Nature of Refugee Resettlement Patterns in Africa." MA thesis, Department of Geography, Kansas State University. Unpublished.

Bereket, Habte Selassie. 1989. *Eritrea and the United Nations*. Trenton: Red Sea Press.

Bondestam, Lars, Lionel Cliffe, and Philip White. 1988. "Eritrea Food and Agriculture Assessment Study Final Report." Leeds: Centre of Development Studies, Agriculture and Rural Development Unit, University of Leeds.

Brodhead, Tim. 1986. "If Africa Is the Question, Is NGO the Answer?" *International Journal* XLI (4): 869–81.

Bulcha, Mekuria. 1988. *Flight and Integration: Causes of Mass Exodus from Ethiopia and Problems of Integration in the Sudan*. Uppsala: Scandinavian Institute of African Studies.

Canadian Council for International Cooperation. 1990. "Discounting Famine." Ottawa: Canadian Council for International Cooperation.

Chambers, Robert. 1983. *Rural Development*. London: Longman. Eritrean Relief Association. 1983. "Eritrea: Drought Report 1983." Khartoum: ERA.

———. 1984a. "Children and the War." *Eritrea in Relief* (July-September).

———. 1984b. "Emergency Relief Budget Request for Eritrean Drought Victims." Khartoum: ERA.

———. 1984c. "Eritrea: Nutritional Survey." Khartoum: ERA.

———. 1984d. "Report on Drought and Famine in Eritrea." Khartoum: ERA.

———. 1986. "Zero School's Anniversary: Ten Years of Innovative Educational Programmes." *Eritrea in Relief* (September).

———. 1989a. "Afforestation, Soil and Water Conservation Programme: Semi-Annual Progress Report." Khartoum: ERA.

———. 1989b. "Agricultural Rehabilitation Programme Evaluation Report 1986–1988." Khartoum: ERA.

———. 1989c. "Agricultural Rehabilitation Programme in Eritrea: A Proposal to Extend the Programme Up to 1992." Khartoum: ERA.

———. 1989d. "Emergency Relief Budget: A Preliminary Request for 1990." Khartoum: ERA.

———. 1989e. "ERA's Transportation Capacity." Khartoum: ERA.

———. 1989f. "Food Crisis in Eritrea: Drought Situation and Requests, A Summary." Khartoum: ERA.

———. 1989g. "An Urgent Appeal for Emergency Transportation Aid." Khartoum: ERA.

———. 1989h. "Food Crisis in Eritrea: Drought Situation and Requests, A Summary." Khartoum: ERA.

———. 1990. "A Preliminary Assessment: Relief Needs in Eritrea." Khartoum: ERA.

Eritrean Relief Association in Canada. 1984. "Famine Situation in Eritrea." Toronto: ERAC.

———. 1988a. "Press Release: Battles of Life and Death in Eritrea." Toronto: ERAC.

———. 1988b. "Revised Emergency Relief Budget Request." Toronto: ERAC.

———. 1990a. "Program Proposal: Plant A Tree in Eritrea." Toronto: ERAC.

———. 1990b. "2 Million Placed at Risk of Famine." *Eritrean Newsletter* Number 20 (Fall): 1.

———. 1991a. "Eritrea News Update."

———. 1991b. "Eritrea News Update."

Eritrean Relief Committee. 1984. "Urgent Appeal: Drought Continues in Eritrea: Over 1.25 Million People Need Immediate Assistance." New York: ERC.

———. 1985. "Annual Report." New York: Eritrean Relief Committee.

———. 1986. "Update: Human Rights of Eritrean Civilians Violated by Ethiopian Military." New York: ERC.

Fenet, Alain. 1988. "The Right of the Eritrean People to Self-Determination." In *The Long Struggle of Eritrea for Independence and Constructive Peace,* edited by Lionel Cliffe and Basil Davidson, 33–45. Trenton: Red Sea Press.

Firebrace, James, and Stuart Holland. 1985. *Never Kneel Down.* Trenton: Red Sea Press.

Girmai, Abraham. 1989. "Political Will, Self-Reliance and Economic Development: The Eritrean Experience." *Journal of Eritrean Studies* III (2): 25–40.

Harrell-Bond, Barbara E. 1986. *Imposing Aid: Emergency Relief to Refugees.* Oxford: Oxford University Press.

Hendrie, Barbara. 1989. "Cross-Border Relief Operations in Eritrea and Tigray." *Disasters* 13 (4): 351–60.

Henze, Paul. 1985. *Rebels and Separatists in Ethiopia: Regional Resistance to a Marxist Regime.* Santa Monica: Rand Corporation.

Ingram, James. 1988. "Sustaining Refugees' Human Dignity: International Responsibility and Practical Reality." Lecture at University of Oxford, November 30.

International Commission of Jurists. 1981. "Eritrea's Claim to Self-Determination." *The Review* 26: 8–14.

Jansson, Kurt, Michael Harris and Angela Penrose. 1987. *The Ethiopian Famine.* London: Zed Books.

Jordan, Gebre-Medhin. 1989. *Peasants and Nationalism in Eritrea.* Trenton: Red Sea Press.

Karadawi, Ahmad. 1980. "Urban Refugees in the Sudan." Khartoum: Office of the Commissioner for Refugees.

Kibreab, Gaim. 1987. *Refugees and Development in Africa: The Case of Eritrea.* Trenton: Red Sea Press.

———. 1990a. "Host Governments and Refugee Perspectives on Settlement and Repatriation in Africa." A paper presented at the Institute of Social Studies, The Hague, August 27–29.

————. 1990b. "The State of the Art Review of Refugee Studies in Africa." A paper presented at the International Seminar on Refugees in Africa, sponsored by the International Development Research Centre, Arusha, Tanzania, July 30–August 3.

Korn, David A. 1986. *Ethiopia, the United States and the Soviet Union*. London: Croom Helm.

Kozlowski, Anthony J. 1982. "Refugees and Development in Africa." A paper presented to the Refugee Seminar, Khartoum, Sudan, September 11–14.

Kuhlman, Tom. 1990. *Burden Or Boon? A Study of Eritrean Refugees in the Sudan*. Amsterdam: Free University Press.

OXFAM-Canada. 1984. "Mission to Ethiopia / Tigray / Eritrea" (November / December).

Parliamentary Delegation to Ethiopia and Sudan. 1991. "Report of the Parliamentary Delegation to Ethiopia and Sudan." Ottawa: Parliamentary Delegation to Ethiopia and Sudan.

Pateman, Roy. 1990a. *Even the Stones Are Burning*. Trenton: Red Sea Press.

————. 1990b. "Liberté, Egalité, Fraternité: Aspects of the Eritrean Revolution." *The Journal of Modern African Studies* 28 (3): 457–72.

Permanent Peoples' Tribunal of the International League for the Rights and Liberation of Peoples. 1984. *The Eritrean Case*. Rome: Research and Information Centre on Eritrea.

Pike Report. 1977. Nottingham: Spokesman.

Refugee Policy Group. 1988. "Increasing the Rights of Longer-Term Refugees in Africa." Washington: Refugee Policy Group.

Rogge, John R. 1977. "A Geography of Refugees: Some Illustrations from Africa." *The Professional Geographer* XXIX, no. 2:186–93.

Semere, Haile. 1987. "The Origins and Demise of the Ethiopia-Eritrea Federation." *Issue* XV:9–17.

Serapiao, Luis B. 1987. "International Law and Self-Determination: The Case of Eritrea." *Issue* XV:3–8.

Smock, David R. 1982. "Eritrean Refugees in the Sudan." *The Journal of Modern African Studies* 20 (3): 451–65.

Tesfatsion, Medhanie. 1986. *Eritrea: Dynamics of a National Question*. Amsterdam: B.R. Gruner.

Tieleman, H. J., and T. Kuhlman, ed. 1990. *Enduring Crisis*. Leiden: African Studies Centre.

Walker, R.B.J. 1990. "Security, Sovereignty, and the Challenge of World Politics." *Alternatives* XV:3–27.

Wolde Giorgis, Dawit. 1989. *Red Tears: War, Famine and Revolution in Ethiopia*. Trenton: Red Sea Press.

PART THREE

Traditional Solutions:
Integration and Repatriation

5

Refugee Settlement
and Repatriation in Africa:
Development Prospects and Constraints

Peter H. Koehn

The so-called "durable solutions" to refugee flows are permanent acceptance and integration in the country of first asylum, third-country resettlement and voluntary repatriation.[1] In Africa, voluntary repatriation is the
preferred answer to the problem of external population displacement
among receiving countries and the international community. Although
secure repatriation is the most preferable solution, it is usually the most
difficult to arrange.[2]

This chapter examines the "inherent, stubborn structural barriers"[3] to
homeland return confronted by refugees living in neighbouring African
countries of asylum, along with the preconditions needed to encourage
return migration. It will also explore, with particular reference to refugee
populations in the Horn, the development implications of long-term resettlement for poor receiving countries. This chapter will also consider the
implications of and alternatives to repatriation.

REFUGEE REPATRIATION

The termination of exile depends upon changes in the forces and conditions
that prompted flight.[4] The principle obstacles to widespread return migration in Africa are: (1) the continuation of the regime responsible for creating
conditions that provoked the decision to flee; (2) continuous or intermittent
armed conflict and/or lack of resolution of the underlying bases for
nationality or internation struggle; and (3) the absence of acceptable homeland-readaptation opportunities. The first two barriers can operate inde-
pendently of each other, but both require attractive repatriation conditions
in order to provide sufficient motivation for return. On the other hand,
readaptation opportunities alone are not likely to induce the widespread
repatriation of postrevolution refugees.

REGIME CHANGE

The continuation of a colonial or postrevolution regime in Africa has constituted the most serious obstacle to refugee repatriation. Thus, repeated declarations of amnesty by Mengistu Haile Mariam have convinced few Ethiopians to return home.[5] As Leon Gordenker points out, "governments which oppress certain groups or individuals so heavily that they choose to leave the country will not readily take up initiatives leading to the return of emigrants."[6] From the refugee's perspective, moreover, a change in political authorities without fundamental alterations in the nature of the regime usually will not suffice to induce return migration.[7]

While most exiles agree on the need to witness a regime change, there is typically no consensus on the exact type of replacement that would inspire repatriation. In the short run, moreover, regime change is likely to provoke additional conflict and a small new refugee outflow.[8]

Homeland regime change has a greater chance of resulting in the mass repatriation of refugees from neighbouring countries of first asylum—who are usually the vast majority of the externally displaced population—than it does among those who have secured third-country resettlement. Refugees in camp settlements are typically not integrated into the host society. Those who live in close proximity to their homeland are able to maintain their cultural identity.

In the case of refugees who are resettled in Western countries, economic adjustment and social adaptation can override the strong desire to return to the country of origin. Some of the most thoughtful and objective of these refugees seriously question whether many of their exiled compatriots, who have adopted acquisitive values and individualistic lifestyles shaped by years of residence in a technologically-based society, *ought* to return to the home country.

Neither the outside forces that assist a repressive regime nor those that attempt to terminate it through destabilization measures generally succeed in achieving their objectives. Instead, the outcome tends to be prolonged conflict, exacerbated economic crisis and perpetual population outflows. Exile organizations in the North are usually too far removed from local action to exert much impact on regime change. In addition, opposition groups rarely overcome their fragmentation in exile.[9] Thus, while they have the potential to overthrow an unpopular regime, it is more probable that fragmented overseas support mobilization will perpetuate an inconclusive struggle.

Regime transformation and its replacement by a legitimate political system are fundamentally matters determined by the outcome of *internal* struggle and negotiation.

CONFLICT RESOLUTION

Perpetual political violence in the cities and armed struggle in the country-side constitute the second major obstacle to voluntary repatriation. Most exiles do not want to return to a situation where their lives and the lives of their immediate families would be in danger.

Political activists who are devoted to the goals of a liberation movement often form refugee-warrior communities on the borders of the sending country. Exiles committed to armed struggle train an eager and readily available pool of young fighters to sustain the movement's ideological fervour and to fight against the home country's military. The struggle of guerrilla forces against the homeland regime is frequently fuelled by nationality or religious objectives and supported by external powers.[10] In such situations, mass repatriation awaits resolution of the underlying sources of the conflict, as well as settlement of the current dispute. Among the refugees interviewed in Sudan by Mekuria Bulcha, for instance, "those who identified with the liberation movements, particularly the ELF [Eritrean Liberation Front], EPLF [Eritrean People's Liberation Front] and the OLF [Oromo Liberation Front], often gave the independence of their territories as a precondition to repatriation."[11] From the refugee's perspective, as Jeffrey Crisp points out, "voluntary repatriation means going 'home', and not going to a regime or to a political entity...."[12]

Refugee repatriation also can be blocked by war or unresolved territorial conflicts. The limited repatriation to Ethiopia from Djibouti and Somalia in the years immediately following the end of the 1978 war between Ethiopia and Somalia suggests that failure to resolve the underlying sources of conflict between nations, along with refugees' distrust of ruling political authorities, constitute formidable barriers to voluntary return.[13]

Cessation of armed hostilities and vastly diminished prospects for renewed conflict are the prerequisites for repatriation among most exiles who were primarily affected by intergroup violence and/or motivated by nationality or religious objectives.[14] It is likely that regime change, or at least a new set of political authorities, will be a necessary first step in order to clear the way for conflict resolution. Only a popular and legitimate regime is in a position to negotiate and enforce a durable settlement to violent conflicts.

The recent historical record offers little room for optimism regarding the resolution of deep and long-standing social conflicts in Africa. Neither intranational, regional nor superpower-sponsored efforts have been effective in removing the underlying bases for nationality and religious strife. Nonetheless, one can discern, in general terms, the most promising path to the long-term resolution of such conflicts. First and foremost, an agreement that will secure the interests of the local populations—particularly the most

impoverished—must be developed and implemented. Mass empowerment and local self-determination are essential.[15] All sides must be convinced that the benefits of peace outweigh the possible gains of armed
struggle. Refugee warriors must disarm as a condition for national
reintegration, external military support must be terminated, and the sale of
weapons must be effectively curtailed. Conflict resolution efforts should
also involve the most effective diplomatic skills of international negotiators,
preferably including widely respected exiles.

HOMELAND-READAPTATION OPPORTUNITIES

The fact that most contemporary refugees have lived in exile for a decade or
longer suggests that substantial individual readjustment to the home
country will be necessary in order for repatriation to succeed. In a reference
to economic migrants in the industrialized world that also applies to many
political exiles, Michael Piore maintains that "returnees are tied to their
home area by nostalgia rather than by realistic experience. They often have
problems of cultural assimilation which are as extreme as those of other
foreigners...."[16] The novelist Nuruddin Farah confirms that "even if I
returned, I would still be in exile because Somalia can't contain the experiences that I have been exposed to through living in so many different
countries and continents."[17] This situation requires that the original sending
country pay serious attention to issues of refugee readaptation in the
homeland.

My study of individual repatriation motives among exiles from Ethiopia
who were interviewed in Washington, D.C., reveals that professional
opportunities to participate in a meaningful way in rebuilding the homeland would be a powerful incentive among certain refugees, including
many of those who have settled in the North. About one-third of the
Ethiopian exiles in the sample, for instance, ranked the ability to help their
compatriots in Ethiopia, and concomitantly to use their education and
practise their profession, as one the foremost considerations that would
influence their repatriation decision. This also turned out to be a decisive
factor for several respondents who had already decided to return.[18] Three
additional homeland-readaptation measures are likely to be instrumental
in promoting refugee repatriation: (1) responsiveness to the educational
and social needs of children who may never have lived in their parents'
country of birth;[19] (2) involvement of refugees themselves in the planning
and preparation of readaptation; and (3) the establishment of culturally
sensitive and economically viable rehabilitation projects. In particular, the
opportunity to participate in promising local development projects sponsored by dynamic government agencies and/or by nongovernmental or-

ganizations, or to invest in small business operations, would be attractive to exiles who reside in the North.[20] For many exiles living in neighbouring countries of first asylum, however, the home country's investment in sustainable rural development projects and in the reconstruction of areas destroyed or disrupted by fighting is the most appealing rehabilitation strategy.[21]

In light of changes that occur while refugees are in exile, repatriation as a durable solution "involves more than a return to a place and a people; it is a process of creating a new home and new conditions which fulfil [sic] promises and expectations of a secure and prosperous future."[22] Adequate living conditions, appropriate employment and educational opportunities, and attention to basic human needs are essential ingredients in an effective economic readjustment approach. Reintegration is likely to demand creative solutions and considerable cultural sensitivity.

PROBABILITY AND VIABILITY

For the individual refugee, repatriation is a move with high stakes attached. The political and economic obstacles that must be overcome, both domestic and international, are deeply embedded and often reinforced by the prevailing norms that shape international relations, regional interaction and local politics. Consequently, "success in repatriation has been and probably will remain patchy."[23]

Nevertheless, voluntary repatriation—even by exiles who have resettled in the United States—remains a viable future option if the preconditions and postchange protections discussed in this chapter are brought into place. Regime change and resolution of the underlying sources of nationality and class conflicts present the most formidable obstacles to return migration in contemporary Africa. The 1991 overthrow of Mengistu Haile Mariam's regime in the face of coordinated actions by the Eritrean People's Liberation Front and the Tigrayan People's Liberation Front, combined with widespread opposition to brutal dictatorial rule, offered the rare prospect that both regime barriers and nationality conflicts might be overcome simultaneously.[24]

REFUGEE SETTLEMENT STRATEGIES: DEVELOPMENT IMPLICATIONS

In ways that often closely resemble economic migration, the South-North movement of refugees exerts considerable impact on Third World sending countries. The flight of talented, highly trained and committed individuals constitutes an obvious loss to postrevolution societies.[25] On the other hand, political migration promises some relief from employment pressures and demands for educational and other public services. It also offers the prospect of obtaining substantial hard-currency remittances from expatriates,[26] who send money to personal contacts in the home country. Although remittances have improved the economic standing of families who receive money from relatives abroad, they generally have not had a major positive impact on indigenous development. Most remittances are invested in land, housing and consumer goods. Such investments distort the real estate market and result in increasing pressures to import foreign luxury products.[27]

The burdens of first asylum are heavy for poor Third World countries that receive large numbers of political migrants from neighbouring lands and that host most of the world's refugee-camp populations.[28] In addition to overwhelming the administrative capacity of the host government to serve mass needs over the short and/or long term, refugees tax limited local resources and, at times, cause irreparable damage to the surrounding environment.[29] Moreover, the selective admission process employed by northern nations often removes the few skilled refugees who are prepared to perform vital community-development roles in first-asylum countries.[30]

The United Nations High Commissioner for Refugees (UNHCR) currently concentrates its attention and resources on feeding and accommodating refugees in receiving countries of first asylum.[31] Adequate relief assistance is essential to satisfy basic needs "so that any decisions the refugees reach about whether or not to repatriate will be based on their assessment of conditions in their home country, rather than on a lack of resources in their country of refuge."[32]

However, holding dislocated populations indefinitely in externally supported camps constitutes the least desirable method of assisting refugee populations.[33] When the prospects for repatriation are remote, immediate assistance programs must be replaced by permanent settlement and national integration.[34] This effort is necessary for the well-being of the refugees and the receiving society, even though "investment in one solution, for example, local integration, may make another solution, such as repatriation, appear less attractive by comparison."[35]

UNHCR endeavours to replace emergency relief operations with projects that directly incorporate refugees into the host country's economy and development process "on an equal footing with the surrounding population...."[36] This approach requires cooperation with international and bilateral donor agencies, as well as with NGOs.[37] UNHCR attempts to catalyse and coordinate such ventures, but avoids performing the functions of a development agency. Thus far, the results have been limited as the idea of linking refugee aid to development projects "has not yet been generally accepted by the donor community."[38]

Additional constraints, including host country resistance, limit the application of an integrated, development-oriented approach to refugee assistance in first-asylum countries.[39] First, efforts at integration are greatly complicated by the massive numbers of externally displaced persons who overload settlement areas. The level of U.S. and voluntary agency assistance has been particularly inadequate in several African contexts and by 1990 UNHCR only had half as much funding available on a per capita basis than it possessed a decade earlier.[40] Large numbers of desperate refugees place stresses on fragile natural resources in the reception zone. Externally-sponsored refugee assistance efforts frequently ignore local development plans and priorities and fail to address long-term maintenance costs. Furthermore, the success of highly motivated refugee communities that are supported by donor assistance commonly breeds resentment among the surrounding population.[41] As a result of these and other concerns, some governments oppose the use of urgently needed and limited development funds on refugee-oriented projects.[42] In addition, any assistance that excludes poor host communities exacerbates the hostility, tension and insecurity experienced by refugees.[43]

Two approaches to refugee settlement promise to reduce prevailing constraints on development. They are the provision of impacted-area assistance and an emphasis on community participation in development projects. As Mekuria Bulcha points out, "local integration efforts cannot be effective unless they are carried out simultaneously with the economic and infrastructural development of the regions in question."[44]

When linking refugee aid with self-reliant development, the strategy for involving the local migrant community requires careful attention. In the past, refugees have been excluded from participation in project planning, staffing and decision making. They have frequently been subjected to the imposition of "solutions" by patronizing agency staff.[45] The consequences are increased powerlessness, diminished self-confidence and greater dependency. Therefore, refugees and the local poor must be centrally involved from the start in project initiation and selection, budgeting and fund-raising, supervision, implementation, decision making, evaluation and monitoring.[46]

REPATRIATION AND DEVELOPMENT IMPLICATIONS

Little attention has been devoted to the development implications for the homeland when there is mass repatriation from neighbouring countries. The returning population could pose an additional burden of dependency for an impoverished receiving country. For instance, as Sidney Waldron points out with particular reference to refugees from Ethiopia living in

Somalia, children brought up in a dependent "refugee-camp culture" will find reverting to pastoral or agricultural activity especially difficult.[47]

On the other hand, refugees who mastered life in spontaneous settlements in neighbouring African countries are likely to return with new skills and attributes of industriousness that are conducive to sustainable development. In this case, the primary challenge will be reintegrating the returning population within the authority structure at the local government and cooperative levels.

There are potential drawbacks to national reabsorption of refugees who have resided for a lengthy period of time in the North. Members of this group are likely to have lost touch with the aspirations of those who remained behind, to have acquired Western values and imported tastes that are expensive for the home country to sustain, and to encounter difficulty in readjusting to a lifestyle devoid of multiple technological conveniences. Moreover, the jobs that refugees fill abroad and the skills and work norms that they acquire overseas are often inappropriate and even counterproductive for the home country's needs.[48]

On the positive side, many exiles living in industrialized nations have acquired educational attainments and professional skills that are desperately needed in their homelands. The level of commitment to the homeland, as distinct from the postrevolution regime, also remains strong among African exile communities. Returning refugees will retain business and other contacts in the North that could prove useful in a development context. Finally, the resourcefulness of successful refugees, along with their proven abilities to survive and often prosper in a foreign Western culture, augur well for readaptation in the homeland.

Impoverished African countries are in no position to undertake the required readjustment projects without substantial foreign assistance. Furthermore, "people who have stayed on through the fall of one regime and the emergence of another may be antagonistic towards the expenditure of scarce resources on those who fled."[49] Provided that it is responsive to indigenous needs, external support for rehabilitation ventures can help overcome such attitudes.[50] In order to promote peaceful reintegration, poor members of the sending society who did not leave must be given access to equivalent development opportunities. One way to avoid giving preferential treatment to returnees and provoking resistance among those who remained behind is by allocating "development aid to a returnee-affected *area*" on a long-term basis.[51] Donor aid and internal investment must be accompanied by drastic reductions in the level of domestic military spending. As an incentive, external creditors could match progress in cutting military budgets with significant debt-relief measures.

THE NEED FOR A MULTIDIMENSIONAL APPROACH

As their burdens increase, African countries are less willing to accept refugees from the region.[52] In most cases, this reluctance is quite understandable. The United States would need to admit fifteen million refugees in a year, for instance, to equal the per capita population burden placed upon Malawi by the exodus of refugees from Mozambique in 1988.[53]

The North's resources, as well as the contributions made by certain industrialized states to refugee-producing conditions in the Third World,[54] underline the obligation of wealthy nations to assume a major share of the global asylum burden.[55] This responsibility needs to be pursued simultaneously in tested and new ways.

Most political asylum seekers prefer to reside in their region of origin. Given that the vast majority of refugees will remain in the South, expanded support for permanent local integration and for development efforts that promote the well-being of refugee and host populations in the Third World is a vital element in an integrated global approach.[56]

Industrialized nations must also accept a more equitable share of the world's refugees.[57] James Silk accurately notes that "any failure of developed countries to provide asylum offers a strong justification for others to curtail their hospitality toward refugees."[58] In short, the world's wealthy nations cannot buy themselves out of a refugee-settlement role through financial assistance to impoverished first-asylum countries.[59]

Furthermore, major bilateral foreign policy changes are essential because, as Jonathan Moore admits, "the same nation-states which are providing significant humanitarian assistance to refugees may, at the same time, be pursuing policies that have the effect of generating refugees."[60] In particular, the lack of effective concern for human rights in U.S. foreign policy actions continues to exacerbate the conditions that push Third World citizens to head north.

The international political community needs to respond in a creative, coordinated and prevention-oriented way to challenges affecting refugee policy. In other words, "the resilience of the uprooted must be matched by ingenuity on the part of policy makers...."[61] In which specific policy directions should the global refugee regime look for promising approaches to managing cross-national political migration?

THIRD-COUNTRY RESETTLEMENT POLICY

African refugees are seldom resettled securely in neighbouring countries of first asylum. Local integration rarely occurs "because the countries of asylum do not have the resources, particularly arable land, necessary to make it politically feasible to absorb the increased population."[62] As part of a multidimensional approach that considers the interests of all affected parties, therefore, there should be an agreement on an expanded, UNHCR-operated quota system of refugee admissions to industrialized countries. Zolberg, Suhrke and Aguayo suggest that "for the asylee, a quota system means less uncertainty regarding the future; for the country of final settlement, it means greater control in the admission process; and for the first asylum country, it means that asylum can be extended with some assurance that the refugee burden will eventually be shared."[63] At present, the United States assumes responsibility for roughly half of all refugees resettled each year. However, it ranks behind Australia, Canada, Sweden and Denmark in its refugee-to-host population ratio.[64]

The new reception scheme should be based on equitable sharing of the resettlement burden according to each receiving country's population and should involve all industrialized countries, including Japan and Russia. Broad agreement on an expanded UNHCR-administered quota would result in a decline in the number of political migrants who are turned away at regional destination points. The prevailing alternative of attempting to deter asylum seekers merely diverts refugee flows without resulting in a long-term reduction in total numbers.[65]

INTERNATIONAL REFUGEE CORPS

The international community must respond in a proactive way to the twin challenges of appropriate refugee employment and sustainable indigenous development. One vehicle for this effort is establishing an International Refugee Corps (IRC) within UNHCR or the United Nations Development Programme (UNDP) and providing ample project funds.

IRC participants would be recruited from refugee-camp populations and from exile communities in the North. Program headquarters would be staffed and managed almost exclusively by refugees. Widely advertised employment opportunities would attract technical and professional men and women in all fields of expertise related to development and cultural change, experienced and well-informed agriculturalists (including former peasant farmers), and willing labourers. Resources also should be made available to fund scholarships for refugees who are willing to retrain in skill areas that are in short supply.

Projects would be conceptualized, identified, selected and budgeted for by refugees themselves, in consultation with host-country planners, donor agencies and NGOs. Most IRC personnel would be assigned to poor, refugee-impacted countries in the South, although useful projects in the

North would also be eligible for support. For some African refugees, the IRC would offer an opportunity to return to the home country strictly in a service capacity with diplomatic protection.

The IRC would also honour the position of exiles who are willing to serve on the continent, but elect not to return to their country of origin. Assignments would be of short-term as well as long-term duration in order to accommodate currently employed exiles.[66] Most initial work tours will be on a volunteer (expenses only) basis; subsequent assignments would be salaried. The IRC would also gradually develop a small career service that would be integrated into UNHCR or UNDP.

IRC's in-country objectives would include initiating small-scale, self-sufficient projects that benefit the local population—particularly, but not exclusively, in refugee-impacted areas. For the refugees themselves, participation in IRC might occasionally result in repatriation. The principal goal, however, is encouraging and promoting the productive application of refugees' expertise on the continent of their origin on a short-term or long-term basis. Thus, sustainable development experience with IRC might facilitate entry into other aid-giving agencies and NGOs, or participation in the Return of Talent Programme (or the Selective Migration to Latin America Programme).[67] A program that promotes continental repatriation would be particularly appropriate for highly educated exiles whose skills are less essential and often less appreciated in the North.[68]

TACKLING ROOT CAUSES

To date, "the international refugee regime has been largely ineffective in dealing with the root causes of refugee problems."[69] It is time, therefore, that international cooperation "be directed primarily towards the prevention of refugee movements and towards return."[70] There are internal and external factors associated with refugee generation in the South. The external forces that the international community must address include the arms race and defects in the global economic system.[71] Until this type of involvement by external powers is recognized as an important source of political migration and precluded through concerted diplomatic action, "little headway will be made towards a resolution of refugee problems."[72] Similarly, effective dispute-settling techniques must be used to avert international conflicts that provoke refugee flows.

International agencies traditionally have refrained from dealing directly with the factors that produce internal refugees. Deference to national sovereignty has kept UN institutions from acting to prevent human rights abuses and from sanctioning those in positions of authority who are responsible for them. They have reacted only after flight occurs.[73] From a humanitarian perspective that affirms human rights and concerns for states of refuge and the international community as a whole, a more proactive approach is both feasible and essential if the roots of the refugee crisis are to be addressed.

A more assertive approach requires willingness to focus on internal conditions in potential sending countries. One step in this direction would be the adoption of international conventions that address human rights obligations in the country of origin and the individual right of return to one's homeland. In fact, commitment to protecting human rights should underlie all aspects of international refugee policy.[74]

ENFORCING A PREVENTION-ORIENTED APPROACH

Enforcement is the most challenging aspect of preventing refugee situations. Prospective tools of enforcement include careful investigation into local conditions, in-country educational efforts based upon national values and self-interest, the glare of international publicity, the withholding of foreign assistance and "a system of international order which disciplines governments failing to meet their obligations to humanity."[75] On the latter score, Ved Nanda calls for enforcing an international instrument that specifies the liability of officials "who permit and encourage mass expulsions."[76] Daniel Derby shows that there are other available deterrents. They include holding states that engage in persecution and officials who participate in forced displacement responsible for international crimes, "assisting refugees in obtaining compensation from their home states for property losses resulting from their flight," and requiring that asylum countries be compensated by the governments of sending countries "for expenses incurred in accommodating refugees."[77]

UNHCR should play the leading role in the refugee-prevention effort. This means that the treatment of adverse conditions in sending countries should be considered within the scope of its mandate.[78] The guiding principle should be "the avoidance or the remedy of conditions which, if left unchecked, would cause people to leave their country and to seek refuge elsewhere."[79]

UNHCR's efforts should focus on constructing agreements and policy measures that are designed by indigenous forces and have widespread internal support. In the interest of securing locally accepted and durable solutions that will reduce or end refugee outflows, the international political community must refrain from engaging in "humanitarian" military interventions.

FACILITATING SECURE REPATRIATION

In postrevolution societies, the conditions responsible for refugee exodus are likely to remain operative for long periods of time. Under such circumstances, it is unconscionable for northern governments or the UNHCR to push repatriation.[80]

In the period following transformation of a refugee-generating political system, the durable and safe return of exile populations depends upon the availability of certain key protections. In the first place, there must be independent verification that the requisite changes have actually occurred.[81] It is particularly important that this step involve advance fact-finding visits to the country of origin by refugee representatives.[82] Concomitantly, it is necessary that the agencies involved in facilitating the return-migration process "evaluate and confirm the voluntary character of the decision to repatriate."[83]

The fundamental human rights of the returning population also must be guaranteed. International negotiations with authorities in the country of origin can play a vital role in securing formal human rights guarantees following regime change.[84] Firm assurances of free political expression and association are likely to be instrumental for the successful repatriation of former exiles. Returnees must be individually identified, accepted and available for follow-up contacts by representatives of respected international resettlement organizations. The new regime's willingness to allow public scrutiny and independent monitoring and auditing of its human rights record in all areas of resettlement would go a long way towards overcoming any lingering hesitation to return to the homeland. UNHCR must be granted unhindered, long-term access to returnees in order to ensure that they are not mistreated,[85] that their rights to political participation are protected, and that rehabilitation efforts and objectives are not subverted—in short, "to monitor fulfilment of such guarantees as may have encouraged them to repatriate."[86] Finally, the international donor community must provide considerable external resources to support reconstruction efforts and sustainable development projects that will meet the basic needs of the returning population.[87]

Although the international community has an important role to play in focusing attention on the underlying factors that promote refugee formation and in overseeing secure repatriation, "what governments do of their own accord or with their eye on other governments will have the greatest effect in encouraging or obviating forced migration."[88] In the end, "if states want their people to return, *they* must create conditions which are conducive."[89]

NOTES

1. Astri Suhrke, "Global Refugee Movements and Strategies of Response," in *U.S. Immigration and Refugee Policy: Global and Domestic Issues*, edited by Mary M. Kritz (Lexington: D.C. Heath and Company, 1983), 167; Jeffrey Crisp, ed., *Refugees: The Dynamics of Displacement* (London: Zed Books, 1986), 57.

2. See Sheila A. McLean, "International Institutional Mechanisms for Refugees," in *U.S. Immigration and Refugee Policy: Global and Domestic Issues*, edited by Mary M. Kritz (Lexington: D.C. Heath and Company, 1983), 180; Barry N. Stein, "ICARA II: Burden Sharing and Durable Solutions," in *Refugees: A Third World Dilemma*, edited by John R. Rogge (Totowa: Rowman & Littlefield, 1987), 56. The policy goals set forth in the UNHCR's budget "are typically repatriation in Africa and resettlement from Asia." Shelley Pitterman, "International Responses to Refugee Situations: The United Nations High Commissioner for Refugees," in *Refugees and World Politics*, edited by Elizabeth G. Ferris (New York: Praeger, 1985), 52.

3. Leon Gordenker, *Refugees in International Politics* (New York: Columbia University Press, 1987), 128.

4. Guy S. Goodwin-Gill, "Refugees: The Functions and Limits of the Existing Protection System," in *Human Rights and the Protection of Refugees under International Law*, edited by Alan E. Nash (Halifax: Institute for Research on Public Policy, 1988), 163; Norman L. Zucker and Naomi F. Zucker, *The Guarded Gate: The Reality of American Refugee Policy* (San Diego: Harcourt Brace Jovanovich, Publishers, 1987), 49.

5. Mekuria Bulcha, *Flight and Integration: Causes of Mass Exodus from Ethiopia and Problems of Integration in the Sudan* (Uppsala: Scandinavian Institute of African Studies, 1988), 21, 128. On the other hand, thousands of exiles returned to Namibia during and after the United Nations-supervised transition to independence and majority rule. See Ngila R.L. Mwase, "The Repatriation, Rehabilitation and Resettlement of Namibian Refugees at Independence," *Community Development Journal* 25, no. 2 (April 1990): 113–20.

6. Gordenker, *Refugees*, 128. See also Gervase Coles, "Approaching the Refugee Problem Today," in *Refugees and International Relations*, edited by Gil Loescher and Laila Monahan (Oxford: Oxford University Press, 1989), 404.

7. The return of African National Congress and other exiles to South Africa in 1990 and 1991 is an exceptional development. See *Christian Science Monitor*, October 10, 1990; *Washington Post*, October 9, 1990; *New York Times*, March 12, 1991.

8. Jacques Cuénod, "Refugees: Development or Relief?" in *Refugees and International Relations*, edited by Gil Loescher and Laila Monahan (Oxford: Oxford University Press, 1989), 242.

9. See Annabell Sreberny-Mohammadi, "Iranian Opposition in Exile: A Study in Political Communication." A paper presented at the Joint Meeting of the African Studies Association and the Middle Eastern Studies Association, New Orleans, Louisiana, November 24, 1985.

10. See Aristide R. Zolberg, Astri Suhrke and Sergio Aguayo, *Escape from Violence: Conflict and the Refugee Crisis in the Developing World* (Oxford: Oxford University Press, 1989), 152–54, 169, 218, 275–77.

11. Bulcha, *Flight*, 128. See also Peter Koehn, *Refugees from Revolution: U.S. Policy and Third World Migration* (Boulder: Westview Press, 1991), Chapter 8.

12. Jeffrey Crisp, "Somalia: Solutions in Sight," *Refugees* (December 1989): 62. For some exiles, "home" in this context would include a secure liberated area behind the battlefront.

13. See Gordenker, *Refugees*, 128–29; Peter J. Schraeder, "Involuntary Migration in Somalia: The Politics of Resettlement," *Journal of Modern African Studies* 24, no. 4 (1986): 649, 659–60; Hiram Ruiz, *Beyond the Headlines: Refugees in the Horn of Africa* (Washington: U.S. Committee for Refugees, 1988): 28–29. After the governments of Somalia and Ethiopia resumed diplomatic relations and demilitarized their border, some refugee-initiated repatriation ensued. See Crisp, "Somalia," 8.

14. See also Bulcha, *Flight*, 129.

15. For one proposal regarding the struggle in Eritrea, see Asmarom Legesse, "Eritrea and Ethiopia: The Prospects for a New Political Framework." A paper presented at the United States Institute of Peace Seminar, August 11, 1989, 9–10.

16. Michael Piore, *Birds of Passage: Migrant Labor* (Cambridge: Cambridge University Press), 119. Also see Barbara E. Harrell-Bond, "Repatriation: Under What Conditions Is It the Most Desirable Solution for Refugees? An Agenda for Research," *African Studies Review* 32, no. 1 (1989): 42. Robert Bach adds that international agencies also "construct idyllic images of 'home,' based on conditions that only existed prior to the crises that spawned the outflow." Robert L. Bach, "Third Country Resettlement," in *Refugees and International Relations*, edited by Gil Loescher and Laila Monahan (Oxford: Oxford University Press, 1989), 313–14.

17. Interview in Maggie Jonas, "Refugee Voices," *Journal of Refugee Studies* 1, no. 1 (1988): 75.

18. See Koehn, *Refugees from Revolution*, Chapter 8.

19. See Piore, *Birds of Passage*, 118.

20. On the former, see Peter H. Koehn, *Public Policy and Administration in Africa: Lessons from Nigeria* (Boulder: Westview Press, 1990), 290–95. On past experience with returning economic migrants, see Piore, *Birds of Passage*, 117, 189.

21. See Cuénod, "Refugees," 243; Crisp, *Refugees*, 59. On the rehabilitation approach that UNHCR provided for returning Ethiopian refugees from Djibouti, see Guy Goodwin-Gill, "Voluntary Repatriation: Legal and Policy Issues," in *Refugees and International Relations*, edited by Gil Loescher and Laila Monahan (Oxford: Oxford University Press, 1989), 267–70.

22. Bach, "Third Country Resettlement," 314.

23. Gordenker, *Refugees*, 131. Also see Stein, "ICARA II," 56.

24. *New York Times,* March 23, 1991, A1.

25. Dawit Wolde Giorgis writes that there are reportedly "more Ethiopian physicians in the United States than in Ethiopia, and more still in Europe." Dawit Wolde Giorgis, *Red Tears: War, Famine and Revolution in Ethiopia* (Trenton: Red Sea Press, 1989), 357. In the long run, however, "trained people flee, but new generations—initially with less training, but with a much different and higher level of consciousness—step into the breach." Richard R. Fagen, Carmen D. Deere and José L. Coraggio, Introduction to *Transition and Development: Problems of Third World Socialism* (New York: Monthly Review Press, 1986), 16.

26. See Elsa M. Chaney, "Migrant Workers and National Boundaries: The Basis for Rights and Protections," in *Boundaries: National Autonomy and Its Limits,* edited by Peter G. Brown and Henry Shue (Totowa: Rowman & Littlefield, 1981), 57; Michael S. Teitelbaum, "Immigration, Refugees, and Foreign Policy," *International Organization* 38, no. 3 (Summer 1984): 447.

27. See Demetrios G. Papademetriou, "International Migration in a Changing World," *International Social Science Journal* 36, no. 3 (1984): 418, 423; Mark J. Miller and Demetrios G. Papademetriou, "Immigration and U.S. Foreign Policy," in *The Unavoidable Issues: U.S. Immigration Policy in the 1980s,* edited by Demetrios G. Papademetriou and Mark J. Miller (Philadelphia: Institute for the Study of Human Issues, 1983), 174–75.

28. Zolberg et al., *Escape from Violence,* 231; Crisp, *Refugees,* 16; *World Refugee Survey: 1988 in Review* (Washington: U.S. Committee for Refugees, 1989), 35.

29. See W.R. Smyser, "Refugees: A Never-Ending Story," *Foreign Affairs* 64, no. 1 (Fall 1985): 160; Alan J. Simmance, "The Impact of Large-Scale Refugee Movements and the Role of UNHCR," in *Refugees: A Third World Dilemma,* edited by John R. Rogge (Totowa: Rowman & Littlefield, 1987), 12–13; Crisp, *Refugees,* 16; Crisp, "Somalia," 7.

30. See Beverly G. Hawk, "Africans and the 1965 U.S. Immigration Law." Ph.D. dissertation, University of Wisconsin, Madison, Wisconsin, 1988, 122–23; John R. Rogge, "When Is Self-Sufficiency Achieved? The Case of Rural Settlements in Sudan," in *Refugees: A Third World Dilemma,* edited by John R. Rogge (Totowa: Rowman & Littlefield, 1987), 97; "Conference and Symposia Reports," *Journal of Refugee Studies* 1, no. 1 (1988): 83; Howard Adelman, "Refuge Or Asylum: A Philosophical Perspective," *Journal of Refugee Studies* 1, no. 1 (1988): 8.

31. Cuénod, "Refugees," 219.

32. Hiram A. Ruiz and Bill Frelick, "Africa's Uprooted People: Shaping a Humanitarian Response," *Issue* 18, no. 1 (Winter 1989): 34.

33. John R. Rogge, Introduction to *Refugees: A Third World Dilemma,* edited by John R. Rogge (Totowa: Rowman & Littlefield, 1987), 45; Cuénod, "Refugees," 240.

34. See, for instance, Jonathan Moore, "Refugees Worldwide and U.S. Foreign Policy: Reciprocal Impacts," *Current Policy,* 1036 (November 1987): 2; Joseph Cerquone, *Refugees from Laos: In Harm's Way* (Washington: U.S. Committee for Refugees, 1986), 17. In light of the competitive implications of permanent

integration for poor host communities, local authorities often prefer to refer to this process as a "lengthy prelude to return." Gordenker, *Refugees*, 135.

35. Suhrke, "Global Refugee Movements," 167.

36. UNHCR informal report of 1986, cited in Cuénod, "Refugees," 229–31; *New York Times*, May 29, 1989, A3.

37. Ved P. Nanda, "The Challenge: Averting Flows of Refugees and Providing Effective Protection and Durable Solutions," in *Refugee Law and Policy: International and U.S. Responses*, edited by Ved P. Nanda (New York: Greenwood Press, 1989), 204–5.

38. Cuénod, "Refugees," 231, 234, 245. Also see Gordenker, *Refugees*, 136; Harrell-Bond, "Repatriation," 51.

39. Stein, "ICARA II," 57; Sadruddin Aga Khan and Hassan bin Talal, Foreword to *Refugees: The Dynamics of Displacement—A Report for the Independent Commission on International Humanitarian Issues*, edited by Jeffery Crisp (London: Zed Books, 1986), xv. On the lack of self-sufficiency and integration among refugees from Ethiopia living in Sudan, especially those inhabiting organized settlements, see Bulcha, *Flight*, 170, 178–79.

40. Gordenker, *Refugees*, 132, 147–48; Roger P. Winter, "Ending Exile: Promoting Successful Reintegration of African Refugees and Displaced People," in this volume. According to Crisp (1986, 65), an estimated 60 percent "of the refugees in Africa remain outside the international aid umbrella."

41. Eritrean refugees in eastern Sudan offer an example of this point. See Gordenker, *Refugees*, 134.

42. Cuénod, "Refugees," 229; Stein, "ICARA II," 57.

43. Harrell-Bond, "Repatriation," 51; Bulcha, *Flight*, 193; Crisp, *Refugees*, 16.

44. Bulcha, *Flight*, 24.

45. Bulcha, *Flight*, 187; Robert E. Mazur, "Refugees in Africa: The Role of Sociological Analysis and Praxis," *Current Sociology* 36, no. 2 (1988): 54, 59; Rogge, "When Is Self-Sufficiency Achieved?" 97.

46. Also see Mazur, "Refugees in Africa," 59; Robert E. Mazur, "Linking Popular Initiative and Aid Agencies: The Case of Refugees," *Development and Change* 18 (1987): 451–52. For additional recommendations, see Maxine E. Olson, "Refugees As a Special Case of Population Redistribution," in *Population Redistribution: Patterns, Policies, and Prospects* (New York: United Nations Fund for Population Activities, 1979), 147. Sidney Waldron adds the important point that "without some culturally informed, socially sensitive research on the facts of life of the refugees, the direction of planning and administration will continue to be from the top down." Sidney R. Waldron, "Working in the Dark: Why Anthropologists Are Essential in Refugee Relief." A paper presented at the American Anthropological Association Annual Meeting, Philadelphia, Pennsylvania, December 1986, 9.

47. Sidney R. Waldron, "Somali Refugee Background Characteristics: Preliminary Results from the Qoriooley Camps," mimeo, 1983, 6. Also see Crisp, "Somalia," 7.

48. See Piore, *Birds of Passage*, 116–19. In addition, some talented exiles have opted to work at unskilled jobs in industrialized societies for immediate monetary gain and consumer gratification.

49. Dennis Gallagher, Susan F. Martin and Patricia W. Fagen, "Temporary Safe Haven: The Need for North American-European Responses," in *Refugees and International Relations*, edited by Gil Loescher and Laila Monahan (Oxford: Oxford University Press, 1989), 352.

50. UNHCR currently provides rehabilitation aid, but normally places a one-year limit on direct assistance to returnees. Cuénod, "Refugees," 243; Crisp, *Refugees*, 59; Harrell-Bond, "Repatriation," 56, 58.

51. Cuénod, "Refugees," 243; Crisp, *Refugees*, 59–61.

52. Hawk, "Africans," 277; Jonathan Moore, "Refugees and Foreign Policy: Immediate Needs and Durable Solutions," *Current Policy* 945 (April 1987): 3.

53. Ruiz and Frelick, "Africa's Uprooted People," 34.

54. See Koehn, *Refugees from Revolution*.

55. On this point, also see Zolberg et al., *Escape from Violence*, 279.

56. Zolberg et al., *Escape from Violence*, 282. For examples of promising projects in Sudan, see *Refugees* 80 (November 1990): 27, 36.

57. The former UNHCR High Commissioner, Jean-Paul Hocké, forcefully argued this position. See Gallagher et al., "Temporary Safe Haven," 340. Also see James Silk, *Despite a Generous Spirit: Denying Asylum in the United States* (Washington: U.S. Committee for Refugees, 1986), 34.

58. Silk, *Denying Asylum*, 2, 7.

59. Zolberg et al., *Escape from Violence*, 279.

60. Moore, "Refugees and Foreign Policy," 3.

61. Aga Khan and Talal, Foreword, xv.

62. Ruiz, *Beyond the Headlines*, 4; also see Crisp, "Somalia," 7. Poverty-stricken Third World countries rarely offer citizenship to political migrants from neighbouring areas. Michel Moussalli, "Refugees in the World Today: Main Characteristics and Outlook for the Future," *Courier* 121 (May/June 1990): 70. On the exceptional case of Rwandan refugees in Tanzania, see Winter's contribution to this volume.

63. Zolberg et al., *Escape from Violence*, 281.

64. See *World Refugee Survey: 1988 in Review*, 36; Jewel S. Lafontant, "Refugees and Conflict Victims: Meeting Their Critical Needs," *Current Policy* 1252 (February 1990): 1.

65. Crisp, *Refugees*, 41.

66. Eritrean exiles from the North currently are contributing their services for periods of six to eighteen months in EPLF-held areas. Dan Connell, "Eritrean Rebels Prepare for Life After War—and After Marxism," *Christian Science Monitor*, November 15, 1990.

67. On these two programs, see Freda Hawkins, *Critical Years in Immigration: Canada and Australia Compared* (Kingston and Montreal: McGill-Queen's University Press, 1989), 160.

68. See also Tina Wallace, "Research into the Employment of Educated Refugees: A Case Study on Refugees from the Horn of Africa." Unpublished paper (London: World University Service, May 1984, 17–18.

69. Gil Loescher, "Introduction: Refugee Issues in International Relations," in *Refugees and International Relations*, edited by Gil Loescher and Laila Monahan (Oxford: Oxford University Press, 1989), 18.

70. Coles, "Refugee Problem," 392.

71. Harrell-Bond, "Repatriation," 63.

72. Loescher, "Introduction: Refugee Issues in International Relations," 19; Aristide Zolberg, Astri Suhrke and Sergio Aguayo, "International Factors in the Formation of Refugee Movements," *International Migration Review* 22, no. 2 (Summer 1986): 167. On the 1983 Contadora Initiative for Central America, see Zolberg et al., *Escape from Violence*, 266.

73. Loescher, "Introduction: Refugee Issues in International Relations," 18, 19.

74. Coles, "Approach the Refugee Problem Today," 389–90, 395; Nanda, "The Challenge," 204.

75. Stephen B. Young, "Who Is a Refugee? A Theory of Persecution," in *In Defense of the Alien* (Vol. V), edited by Lydio F. Tomasi (Staten Island: Center for Migration Studies, 1983), 52.

76. Nanda, "The Challenge," 204.

77. Daniel H. Derby, "Deterring Refugee-Generating Conduct," in *Refugee Law and Policy: International and U.S. Responses*, edited by Ved P. Nanda (New York: Greenwood Press, 1989), 44–45, 47–52. Derby points out that "increased deterrence through criminal law can be achieved only if more states enact statutory proscriptions against such conduct and also make them enforceable against conduct beyond their territory. The most logical extension of such proscriptions would be their application to conduct abroad that causes a local influx of refugees" (1989, 51).

78. Coles, "Approaching the Refugee Problem Today," 394. Also see Nanda, "The Challenge," 205.

79. This conception of prevention specifically excludes measures designed to block transfrontier movement. Coles, "Approaching the Refugee Problem Today," 395, 404.

80. Harrell-Bond, "Repatriation," 62.

81. Goodwin-Gill, "Protection System," 163–64; Ruiz, *Beyond the Headlines,* 40.

82. Guy Goodwin-Gill, "Voluntary Repatriation," 264.

83. This recommendation stems from UNHCR's controversial experience with repatriation from Djibouti to Ethiopia. See Goodwin-Gill, "Voluntary Repatriation," 278–79, 284; Harrell-Bond, "Repatriation," 56.

84. Gordenker, *Refugees,* 127.

85. In this regard, there is a need to develop "practical and effective methods of monitoring the security of those returning." Goodwin-Gill, "Voluntary Repatriation," 285.

86. Goodwin-Gill, "Protection System," 163–64; Bach, "Third Country Resettlement," 314.

87. Durable repatriation efforts are costly and might be required on a massive scale in the future. See Winter, "Ending Exile."

88. Gordenker, *Refugees,* 178.

89. Harrell-Bond, "Repatriation," 61.

6

Organized Versus Spontaneous Settlement of Refugees in Africa

Tom Kuhlman

In the quest for what are called durable solutions to Africa's refugee problems, most attention is focused on refugee integration in the country of first asylum. As is well known, three such solutions are recognized by the United Nations High Commissioner for Refugees (UNHCR): voluntary repatriation, integration in the country of first asylum and resettlement in a third country. The first is the preferred option, and millions of African refugees have repatriated voluntarily during the past two decades (Rogge and Akol 1989). However, this depends entirely on improvement of the situation in the refugees' country of origin; it is thus largely outside the perspective of observers and policy makers concerned with assisting refugees in the country of asylum. Attempts to stimulate it in the absence of such improvement are unlikely to meet with success—worse, they risk violating the principle of *nonrefoulement* (Harrell-Bond 1989).

Third-country resettlement is considered the least desirable option: it is expensive and the social problems of integration are, if anything, even more intractable than in the country of first asylum, where the cultural setting is often at least somewhat familiar to the refugees. In the current international climate, it is an option available only to a fortunate minority of better-educated refugees.[1] Moreover, by depriving the refugee community of precisely those elements that may constitute indigenous leadership and by fostering the hope of moving to a better place, the limited availability of this option may frustrate rather than enhance the success of local integration. Given the impotence of the international community in promoting the first durable solution and its unwillingness with regard to the third, integration in the country of first asylum becomes—if only by default—the most feasible option in all cases where a solution for the root cause of flight is not immediately in sight.

Two questions may then be asked: what constitutes such integration, and how is it to be achieved or, more modestly, promoted? As for the latter question, there are two alternative policies: either the refugees are allowed to settle freely among the local populace, or special settlement schemes are devised for them by the host country government in cooperation with UNHCR (a combination of the two is, of course, also possible). These alternatives are usually referred to as spontaneous and organized settlement, respectively. The term "spontaneous" is somewhat inadequate: there is little spontaneity in refugee movements, which tend to be governed by necessity rather than free choice. Instead, I shall often use the terms "self-settled refugees" and "settlements," meaning organized settlements.

This chapter proposes a definition of integration, formulated with a view to its convenience for policies and programs concerned with refugees. The focus is on economic integration, which is a crucial aspect for the refugees themselves and for the agencies that are spending funds on them. I review the debate on organized versus spontaneous settlement, as well as the policies that have been its outcome. Armed with the concept of economic integration, I evaluate the relative merits of organized and spontaneous settlement on the basis of empirical evidence. Most of this evidence comes from the case of Eritrean refugees in the eastern Sudan, among whom I have conducted research (Kok 1989; Kuhlman 1990); however, I have drawn also from literature on refugee integration elsewhere in Africa.

In assessing the influence of the type of settlement policy on economic integration, this chapter deals with only one aspect—albeit a crucial one—of those policies. It attempts to determine which type is the more conducive to economic integration. There are many reasons for adopting one policy or the other; while I shall comment on these reasons, it is not my purpose to prove wrong those policies that are actually followed by host country governments and by international agencies. My only concern is that those policies that are detrimental to economic integration are shown to be so, and that any argument in favour of such policies must be based on different grounds. Another point is that the chapter is concerned only with what have been termed the rehabilitation and the development phases of refugee assistance, not with the phase of emergency relief. Settlements are quite different from relief camps, and arguments concerning the one are not valid for the other.

WHAT IS ECONOMIC INTEGRATION?

Whereas integration is often hailed as the goal of refugee assistance, there has been little effort to define it with the precision necessary to ascertain whether it is being achieved. Of course, integration can be seen as a process rather than a goal, but even then it is necessary to state the intended direction. Thus, a UNHCR publication describes integration as "the process by which the refugee is assimilated into the social and economic life of a new national community" (United Nations High Commissioner for Refugees undated, 5). This definition is clearly unsatisfactory: it is tautological in merely replacing the term to be defined by another word.

A useful definition should reflect the purpose of a policy. The purpose of refugee assistance can be summarized as making itself superfluous—achieving a situation where assistance can be withdrawn. Thus, integration might be defined as a situation where the refugees no longer require external assistance. However, for that case I prefer the term self-sufficiency. Refugees are self-sufficient when they acquire an income (in cash or in kind), so that they do not need relief in the form of basic necessities. This is called *family self-sufficiency*. At that stage, aid for services—such as education, health and water supplies—may still be necessary. A situation where the refugees are also able to finance community services themselves (whether communally or through taxation) is called *community self-sufficiency*.[2]

Self-sufficiency of either type can be a useful objective for organized settlements. The concept has no meaning, however, in the context of self-settled refugees who survive without aid anyway and are therefore self-sufficient by definition. As they often live in abject poverty, however, it would be quite inappropriate to call them integrated. Therefore, integration should reflect a situation where the problems resulting from flight are solved.[3] Integration subsumes the concept of self-sufficiency without being identical to it.

These problems concern not only refugees but also the population of the host country, which bears the burden of their presence. Therefore, a definition of integration should include the effects of that burden. This element is reflected in Harrell-Bond's tentative definition "a situation in which host and refugee communities are able to co-exist, sharing the same resources—both economic and social—with no greater mutual conflict than that which exists within the host community" (Harrell-Bond 1986, 7). However, she immediately rejects this definition as too simple: access to resources may be unequal, one group may be exploited by another, and conflict within the host society may have increased due to the pressure of the refugees' presence (Harrell-Bond 1986, 7). Yet her definition has at least the merit that it looks at integration as something that happens not only to refugees but also to the host society.

Bulcha (1988, 85) uses a definition formulated by W.S. Bernard in connection with migrants in general: "integration is achieved when migrants become a working part of their adopted society, take on many of its attitudes and behaviour patterns and participate freely in its activities, but at the same time retain a measure of their original cultural identity and ethnicity." Bulcha thinks that this definition describes reality in Africa better than do concepts such as assimilation or absorption, in view of the plural nature of most African societies. Assimilation means that the migrants give up their former group identity and adopt the culture of the host society, but in a multicultural society migrants are likely to maintain their identity just like everyone else. In Bulcha's words, integration "implies a mutual 'live and let live' attitude based on tolerance of differences, solidarity and positive interaction. This is not to suggest a harmonious equilibrium or a static balance between the different groups. Conflict is naturally part of the relationship" (Bulcha 1988, 86). This may well describe what happens to refugees in Africa, but how are we to *measure* integration in this sense? To what can it be opposed? Bulcha (1988, 86) contrasts "integration" with "marginalization," the latter meaning "withdrawal of the minority group into certain occupations, separate areas of residence or an inferior status"; it also involves "a limited degree of tolerance and acceptance ... towards the minority ... [which] must learn to survive under extreme social stress." However, the concept of marginality—as is clear from Bulcha's own account—is the opposite of assimilation, not integration: he quotes sociologists such as Park, Stonequist and Merton, who all refer to "marginal man" as an individual who fails to become a member of the community into which he has migrated.[4]

Bulcha's own formulation of the concept of integration is vague and contradictory: there may be solidarity and positive interaction, but also disequilibrium and conflict. When is a refugee integrated and when is a refugee marginalized? Bulcha (1988, 86) seems to suggest that the former applies to refugees in Africa and the latter to migrants from Third World countries in Europe, but this is too facile: in Europe migrants *can* be marginalized because they could also be assimilated, whereas in plural societies there is nothing they could assimilate to—there is no common culture, nor any common standard of behaviour or well-being to which they could adhere or from which they could be said to deviate. Surely many refugees in Africa also "withdraw into certain occupations," suffer from "an inferior status" as well as from "extreme social stress."

Because of this vagueness, Bulcha's definition cannot be operationalized, nor does it take into account the refugees' impact on the host society—a reflection of the fact that refugee studies and refugee policies tend to be concerned with refugees only (cf. Chambers 1986). On the other hand, the distinction between assimilation and integration is a useful one, especially in an African context. Obviously, a practical definition of integration in a plural society[5] must recognize the existence of a social stratification correlated with ethnicity. This means, for instance, that income differences between refugees and nationals do not automatically indicate a lack of integration: they may reflect existing differences between ethnic groups within the host society. Similarly, social distance or antagonism between refugees and nationals may not be higher than between different groups of nationals.

Instead, I propose the following criteria: if refugees are able to participate in the host economy in ways commensurate with their skills and compatible with their cultural values; if they attain a standard of living that satisfies culturally determined minimum requirements;[6] if the sociocultural change they undergo permits them to maintain an identity of their own and to adjust psychologically to their new situation; if standards of living and economic opportunities for members of the host society have not deteriorated due to the influx of refugees; if friction between the host population and refugees is not worse than among the host population itself; and if the refugees do not encounter more discrimination than what exists between groups previously settled within the host society, then refugees are truly integrated. A durable solution to the problems arising from flight can be said to have been achieved. This may seem a paradisiacal achievement that is seldom if ever attained in practice. What matters, however, is that it gives us a yardstick for measuring progress and comparing the effects of alternative policies.

Integration itself is then defined as the process of change caused by the settlement of migrants in a plural society, if that process is evaluated in terms of the above criteria. It has many dimensions, each of which is the proper field of a particular science. We are concerned here with one dimension only: the economic, loosely defined as those aspects of social life that have to do with attaining material welfare through the optimal allocation of resources that are scarce and alternatively applicable.[7] Stated more simply, we are concerned with how incomes are acquired, how high they are and what standard of living they provide. Standard of living is taken here as meaning not only income (in cash or in kind) from economic activities, but also access to amenities such as housing, public utilities, health services and education.

The question with which this chapter is concerned can now be restated as follows: what are the differences between organized and spontaneous settlement in terms of (1) the participation of refugees in economic activities (both proportionally and in relation to their skills); (2) the incomes acquired; (3) their access to amenities; (4) the effects on the host population in terms of employment, incomes and access to amenities? In other words, which of the two settlement forms is likely to provide the refugees with satisfactory employment and a minimally acceptable standard of living, and which has the least negative effects on the host population?

In attempting to answer these questions, attention has to be paid to three issues: (1) the position of different socio-economic groups within both the refugee and host populations, rather than considering only the aggregate; (2) the distinction between short-term and long-term effects; and (3) the conditions that govern the effects of each settlement form: some effects depend not on the settlement form as such, but on changeable conditions in a particular case.

ORGANIZED VERSUS SPONTANEOUS SETTLEMENT: THE DEBATE

Whenever African governments have recognized the existence of a refugee problem, they have favoured organized settlement,[8] and in this they have been supported mostly by UNHCR. There are several sound reasons for such a policy,[9] especially when seen from the institutional interests of the state. In the first place, refugees always pose a security hazard to the state that gives them asylum, as its territory could be used as a launching pad by militant refugees for subversive action against their country of origin.[10] In order to avoid such a predicament, the 1969 OAU Convention prescribes that refugees should be settled at a reasonable distance from the border (Nobel 1982, 15). Putting refugees into settlements is the easiest way to achieve this and to control them.

A second reason for preferring organized settlement is that it is much easier to obtain foreign aid when the refugees are concentrated in a few locations where they are clearly visible than when they are dispersed among the local population. Spontaneously settled refugees are difficult to identify, their needs are not easily assessed, and the extent of the burden they impose on the host country is open to question. Refugees in camps, by contrast, pose a demonstrable and quantifiable burden, and thereby present a clear case for aid before the international community.

Aid organizations also have good reasons to support organized settlements. Their aim is to provide aid, and in order to get the necessary funds, they must be able to show their constituents the need for them. As is the case for the host country, settlements make it easy to demonstrate and quantify this need. With self-settled refugees, it would be very difficult to distinguish between aid provided for them and aid provided to the local population. These two are target groups for different aid organizations, and confusing them would raise all sorts of thorny issues regarding the competence of agencies and earmarking of funds.

Given the institutional context in which governments and aid organizations operate (see Kent 1987), these motivations are valid and realistic. Decision makers do not readily admit them, however, and therefore they are often justified by invoking other arguments. The most important of these arguments are that: (1) settlements would provide better economic conditions for refugees, and (2) by settling refugees separately from the local population, preferably in undeveloped areas and with external financing, the burden on the host country's economy would be minimized. These arguments, it will be recognized, deal with the question of economic integration as defined above, and it is with these that I shall take issue in this chapter. Other more doubtful arguments are sometimes advanced:

- There can be many reasons why governments wish to keep refugees separate from nationals (Holborn 1975, 1:306–7): sometimes the refugees augment the numbers of a particular group in the host country, upsetting a precarious balance (cf. Karadawi 1983, 540).
- In some host countries there is fear that a large number of self-settled refugees could lead to an increased crime rate. Such fears are rarely expressed in international fora, but they are frequently stated privately (and in domestic political debate, publicly as well). Regardless of its validity, this motivation must be recognized when examining the preference for organized settlement.
- Settlements would permit the refugees to live in their own communities under their own leaders.

Rogge (1981, 200) mentions some further points: (1) aid can be more concentrated and thus cheaper in settlements; by keeping refugees together, their eventual repatriation is facilitated; (3) governments want to keep refugees out of cities, where they would add to urban problems.

None of these arguments can, I think, be considered valid. While concern about changing proportions of ethnic groups is perhaps understandable, it hardly deserves support. The fear of alien criminals is inspired by xenophobia rather than by evidence; if there is higher delinquency among refugees, it is likely to be due to restrictions imposed on their legal economic activities.

As for the supposed autonomy of settlements, they are highly artificial communities. Established not by the refugees but by others, more often than not joining people from diverse social and cultural backgrounds whose original leadership structure may have collapsed, and controlled by a bureaucracy of camp authorities, settlements do not necessarily permit refugees more autonomy than do self-settled circumstances (cf. Harrell-Bond 1986, 87–104). As for the arguments quoted by Rogge, setting up and maintaining settlements is more expensive than assisting self-settled refugees to achieve the same standard of living as enjoyed by those in the settlements, as will be demonstrated later in this chapter. When mentioning the argument on repatriation, Rogge must have had forced repatriation in mind; if the conditions are favourable to voluntary repatriation, refugees will return home without having to be herded into trucks. The final argument depends on whether one is talking about keeping rural people out of the cities by force (a policy that is doomed to fail) or about rural development in order to make the rural areas more attractive. In the latter case, the argument is the same as the first argument that asserts that economic integration is more easily achieved in organized settlement. That argument is, of course, the one with which this chapter is primarily concerned.

Whatever the arguments in its favour, the policy of organized settlement has not been a success: most refugees in Africa are spontaneously settled. In the early 1970s, less than 20 percent were in organized settlements (Gould 1974, 423). A recent source gives the proportion as 25 percent (Cuénod 1989, 8). There are two possible reasons: either governments and UNHCR are unable to accommodate the refugees or the latter are unwilling to be accommodated in the settlements earmarked for them. As a matter of fact, both reasons apply. UNHCR's budget is already strained by the burden of supporting Africa's refugees, and settling four times as many would be quite beyond its present resources. As for host country governments, the potential for settling more refugees depends on what type of settlement one chooses. These types are discussed later in this chapter. However, resource limitations are not the sole reason for the failure of settlement policies. Many host governments (including the Sudan) attempt to draw more refugees into the settlements, but most refugees are apparently reluctant. They seem to prefer the hard struggle for survival as underprivileged aliens among the local population to the settlements where supposedly their subsistence is guaranteed, where social services such as education, health and water are provided, and where they are expertly assisted in becoming self-sufficient. A curious phenomenon indeed.

Naturally, this has given rise to considerable debate on the issue. A problem was that very little was known about the spontaneously settled refugees. One of the pioneers in this respect was the anthropologist Art Hansen, who studied spontaneously settled Angolan refugees and those in government settlements in Zambia from 1966 onwards. He concluded that refugees were reluctant to live in government settlements because they wanted to maintain control over their own lives, which was worth more to them than the higher living standard prevailing in the settlement (Hansen 1981, 31). Furthermore, they feared forcible repatriation. Thus, one reason why governments favour organized settlement is the very reason why refugees might dislike it: Hansen's Angolans were eager to repatriate, but only when *they* thought conditions had improved sufficiently, not when the Zambian government deemed it convenient.

At the International Seminar on Refugees in Africa held in Arusha, Tanzania, it was concluded that "non-organized settlements have a better chance of developing self-reliance and self-management while avoiding the dependence mentality which has often been found in organized settlements" (Kibreab 1985, 100, quoted by Wijbrandi 1986, 10). However, the recommendations of the Arusha seminar did not result in a change of policy. Several students of refugee issues criticized Hansen's view: the burden of refugees on the host country needed more attention (Betts 1981; Chambers 1986); self-settled refugees were often extremely poor and economically insecure, and organized settlements were improving their performance (Wijbrandi 1986, 10–11).

Wijbrandi concludes that "there is a growing consensus among scholars, governments and international and voluntary organizations that organized settlement of refugees should be given preference to self-settlement" (Wijbrandi 1986, 12). However, he adds that this conclusion is not definitive, as there is a need for further research on spontaneous settlement. He and his colleagues carried out such research, and further fieldwork was done by the team of which I was a member. This allows a closer look at burdens on the host and the economic situation of the refugees. Based partly on Wijbrandi's work, and partly on other studies, some further statements on the potential of organized settlements can also be made.

ECONOMIC CONDITIONS FOR REFUGEES: SOME EMPIRICAL EVIDENCE

Wijbrandi's team made two comparisons between a location with self-settled refugees and an organized refugee settlement in the Gedaref region of eastern Sudan. In both cases the locations were chosen in such a way that the principal differences between self-settled refugees and those in settlements could be ascribed to the settlement type, other relevant conditions being similar. The first study (in 1983) was concerned with the little town of Doka and the nearby settlement of Umrakoba; this is a so-called land settlement, where plots of land are issued to refugees by the Sudanese government. On the whole, living conditions of refugees appeared to be better in the settlement: 67 percent of households attained an income considered sufficient for basic needs, compared to 52 percent among the self-settled; moreover, those in the settlement were better housed and did not have to pay rent, and they also had wider access to education and health facilities.

From a social and a legal point of view, the situation of the refugees in the settlement was considered preferable. In both locations, however, the economic position of refugees was much below that of the Sudanese population, due to their limited access to means of production and the various restrictions imposed on them (Wijbrandi 1984).[11] The second part of the field research, undertaken six months later, compared refugees and

Sudanese in the town of Wad el-Hilew and in the settlement of Abuda. In this case, conditions among self-settled refugees were notably better: in Wad el-Hilew 61 percent of the refugees had an income above Wijbrandi's poverty line, compared to only 13 percent in Abuda. As in the previous case, housing and health services were better in the settlement, but the percentage of refugee schoolchildren was higher among the self-settled (Wijbrandi 1985).

From these findings, Wijbrandi concluded that the settlement type itself is not a decisive factor in economic integration: in one case the refugees in the settlement were better off, in the other case the self-settled had the advantages (1986, 123). This conclusion, however, may be challenged. In the first place, the differences in the latter case are far larger than in the former. Taken together, the two samples indicate that 57 percent of self-settled households attain an income above the minimum compared to 40 percent in the settlements.

The economic situation had worsened during the time elapsed between the two studies; this would have increased the number below the minimum, but one would have expected that this effect would be most pronounced among the self-settled who did not have access to the relief food given to those in settlements.

Secondly, and more importantly, even if the proportion below the poverty line in settlements were equal to that among the self-settled, this would only mean that the vast amounts of aid provided both for relief and for making the refugees self-sufficient have resulted in a living standard not notably higher—and quite possibly lower—than that of refugees who remained entirely outside the aid network and who had to cope with enormous odds.

TABLE 6.1: **Length of Employment by Type of Settlement (%)**

| | Settlement Type | |
Months	Organized	Spontaneous
0-3	25	14
4-8	33	17
9-12	42	69
Total %	100	100
N	280	133

Source: Based on M. Bulcha, *Flight and Integration: Causes of Mass Exodus from Ethiopia and Problems of Integration in the Sudan* (Uppsala: Scandinavian Institute of African Studies, 1988), 157.

Therefore, I think Wijbrandi's research supports quite a different conclusion: that the settlement policy has utterly failed to enhance the economic integration of refugees. Apart from Wijbrandi's study, there is scant other evidence comparing economic conditions in the two settlement forms. Bulcha (1988), who did research in three settlements and three locations among self-settled refugees, compared the length of employment during 1982 (See Table 6.1).

From Table 6.1, it appears that the self-settled have a more secure livelihood than the refugees living in settlements. Table 6.2 presents a different picture regarding incomes: in urban areas the self-settled are better off, but in the rural areas the reverse seems to be the case, with 92 percent far below the minimum necessary for subsistence (given by Bulcha as £625 per year for rural areas and £825 for urban areas). It is difficult to understand how those 92 percent can survive, considering that they do not receive any aid. However, the representativity and statistical significance of these figures may be doubted, in view of the very small number of interviews. Where the average of rural and urban refugees is taken, the picture is again favourable to the self-settled (Bulcha 1988, 167).

TABLE 6.2 Income Distribution by Type of Settlement

| Income (£S) | Settlement Type | | | |
	Organized Rural	Spontaneous Rural	Organized Urban	Spontaneous Urban
0	26	24	19	18
1–299	13	68	10	3
300–599	30	6	25	7
600–899	16	0	32	13
900–1,199	7	2	3	12
1,200–1,499	4	0	7	25
>1,500	4	0	4	22
Total %	100	100	100	100
N	134	54	93	60

Source: Calculated from Bulcha (1988, 162).

The oldest settlement scheme in the eastern Sudan, Qala en Nahal, may have achieved self-sufficiency at family level, after many years of failures. However, the costly water supply and tractor schemes may have to be subsidized indefinitely (Rogge 1985, 106–7)—in other words, community self-sufficiency was not remotely in sight in 1985, after sixteen years of operation.

Why is it so difficult to achieve a high level of self-sufficiency in settlements? One important reason is that there was insufficient land for refugees. The official allotment is 10 *feddans* (a *feddan* is about an acre) per family, but Wijbrandi reports that in Umrakoba and Abuda refugees in practice received only 5 *feddans*; according to data he received from the authorities, 39 percent of all households in Umrakoba were issued such allotments; in his sample, however, only 9 percent of households were actually given land (1984, 93). In Abuda the situation was better: 77 percent were provided with a plot (Wijbrandi 1985, 58). In Qala en Nahal, the survey mentioned above found that 90 percent of the refugees received no land at all, and of the remainder, 15 percent received less than the stipulated acreage (Betts 1982, 92). Cree (1983, 3) reported that land allocation was also a problem at the settlement of Um Ali. Abuda is regarded by Jonsson and Cree (1982, 22–23) as having relatively favourable prospects of attaining at least self-sufficiency in staple food. However, this is on the basis of 10 *feddans* per family, which—as Wijbrandi says—"stands in shrill contrast to the actual situation in Abuda" (1985, 58).

It is not that the Sudanese government is unwilling to grant land to the settlers; rather, it found it more difficult to do so than it had anticipated (this difficulty is covered in the next section). Instead, since the late 1970s the government has opted for two alternative settlement forms in addition to the land settlement: the wage-earning rural settlement and the peri-urban settlement. The Sudan has large areas of commercial farming, where the labour supply is a principal bottleneck. Most of the labourers in commercial farming are peasants, who subsist for part of the year on their own meagre farms and for another part on casual work on the large estates. It was thought that by locating refugee settlements in areas of large-scale agriculture, the refugees would not need land, but could earn a living as agricultural labourers, thereby making a positive contribution to the Sudanese economy.[12] The peri-urban settlement was intended to accommodate those refugees now self-settled in towns: a settlement near the town would be created for them with external financing, which would permit them to continue their income-generating activities while removing the pressure they exert on the urban infrastructure.

A UNHCR consultant studied the economic viability of five wage-earning settlements (four rural and one urban). Judging an annual income of about £500 to be the minimum for satisfying basic needs, he estimated actual income per household in the four rural settlements at slightly below £300, and potential income (assuming eight months of available employment and optimal refugee participation) at less than £400 per year. In other words, the outlook for economic self-sufficiency even at household level was bleak, and income levels were actually worse than in the land settlements. Among

Sudanese villagers in the same area, only 1 to 14 percent of households had incomes below £500 (quoting a International Labour Organisation and United Nations High Commissioner for Refugees survey). The report concluded that three of the four rural settlements were not actually or potentially viable, while the fourth was marginally viable (Purcell 1983, 55–61). The main difficulty with these settlements is the seasonal nature of agricultural employment, which does not permit the labourers to earn wages throughout the year. Unlike the Sudanese "semiproletarians," they do not have plots of their own with which to supplement their wages.

The viability of peri- or semiurban settlements appears to be somewhat better. For the Ethiopian refugees in the Sudan, only two have been created: one at Khashm el-Girba, the other, called Towawa, just outside the large town of Gedaref. In both of these semiurban settlements, refugees are better off than in the rural settlements of either type (International Labour Organisation and United Nations High Commissioner for Refugees 1984, 83). Khashm el-Girba is regarded by Purcell (1983, 61) as having an acceptable economic base. Towawa, however, shows lower incomes than among the urban self-settled (Table 6.2). This is confirmed by Post (1985, 73, 118). The greater distance to the work sites is undoubtedly a major reason: most inhabitants of Towawa depend on economic activities within the settlement itself, which is poor (Post 1985, 81). External assistance for income-generating activities has been given, but it has failed to provide the refugees in settlements with an income equal to that of the self-settled. As the ILO and UNHCR documents point out, "The activities supported by voluntary agencies are heavily supported financially and administratively. Most of the projects could be considered as social welfare schemes rather than socially and economically viable activities, and it is doubtful that these activities would survive the withdrawal of the support" (1984, 141).

A fairly good case can be made that, in spite of massive aid to settlements for Ethiopian and Eritrean refugees in the eastern Sudan, the refugees settled there are no better off—and frequently worse off—than the self-settled who survive largely without aid. Harrell-Bond (1986, 351–55) provides circumstantial evidence suggesting the same conclusion for Ugandan refugees in the southern Sudan.

These cases are not sufficient, of course, to prove that settlements cannot be beneficial to refugees. Other countries may have had more successful experiences with them. Tanzania has been regarded as a country where organized settlement has been quite successful (Daley 1984; Gasarasi 1987). Unfortunately, there has been no systematic comparison with the conditions of the self-settled. Even in Tanzania, many refugees prefer to be self-settled and attempts have been made to move them forcibly to the settlements (Daley 1984, 111). Armstrong (1987, 89) suggests that self-settled refugees are worse off than those in settlements, but not worse than the local population. He also remarks that there "seems to be a recurring trend" of refugees leaving older settlements where aid has been withdrawn (1987, 100). Apparently, lasting community self-sufficiency was not achieved. In Zambia's Mehaba settlement for Angolan refugees, Hansen regarded material living conditions for refugees as better than those for the self-settled, yet very few refugees went there voluntarily (Hansen 1982, 30).

Whereas the record of settlements is not encouraging as far as income-generating activities are concerned, in most cases social services, such as health and education, are better than those among the self-settled. The same is often true for housing and sometimes for water. Of course, the same result could have been achieved if the aid spent on them had been used to assist self-settled refugees. On the whole, the aid spent on refugees in settlements cannot be shown to have had a positive impact on their economic well-being.

There are, however, two points that must be raised against this conclusion. First, it is likely that the so-called vulnerable groups—disabled and elderly people, single-parent households, orphans (cf. Pankhurst 1984)—tend to be more heavily represented in settlements; such groups have greater difficulty in earning a living, which reduces the settlements' potential for becoming self-sufficient. Indeed, it may be part of some refugees' survival strategy to let relatives who are less capable of fending for themselves live in a settlement where they can depend on aid. In this way, the existence of settlements contributes to the economic integration of the self-settled. Second, while organized settlement might not be the best solution for refugees, it may still be preferable because it minimizes the burden imposed by the refugee influx on the host country. The latter point is taken up in the next section; the former I shall discuss presently.

All ordered societies have mechanisms for providing for those who are unable to fend for themselves. Some are better at this than others, depending on the level of economic development, the prevailing ideology and the nature of the disaster that the society has to cope with. Refugees have faced a significant disaster and do not constitute an ordered society. Relief is extended to them in the initial stages in relief camps; those who are able to fend for themselves gradually drift out of the camps, while those who are not remain behind and are eventually transported to permanent settlements. The availability of this option, combined with the extreme difficulties faced by the self-settled in surviving economically, make it unfeasible for the latter to care for vulnerable persons in their midst. If the funds now spent on settlements were used to assist the self-settled, and if existing restrictions on their integration imposed by the host government were removed, they would probably be able to look after destitute members of their communities themselves.[13] If not, and if no better way can be found to assist the vulnerable, settlements might continue to have a role to play in the economic integration of refugees, but their goals would have to be quite different from what they are now.

THE BURDEN OF REFUGEES

If settlements are not good for refugees, might they not be good for the host country because they avoid the burden that the self-settled impose on the population? The impact of a large influx of refugees on the region where they settle was the principal object of the study in which I participated in 1986–1987, in the region of Kassala in the eastern Sudan (Kuhlman 1990). The impact of refugees turns out to be a highly complex matter that is very difficult to quantify. The region one studies is likely to be subject to many factors causing social and economic change, of which the refugee influx is only one. Moreover, the effects of a mass influx of refugees differ by economic class and, in a plural society such as the Sudan, also by ethnicity. However, the results of the study do permit some general conclusions.

While the influx of refugees did constitute a burden, its impact was by no means uniformly negative to the host population. In the town, they had contributed to an expansion of the economy, in demand as well as in the supply of labour. Commercial horticulture near Kassala and mechanized agriculture throughout the southern part of the Eastern Region benefited enormously from the influx of cheap labour; many among the former labourer class of West African origin have not been unemployed as a result, but have achieved better economic positions, thanks to the general expansion of the economy. Since 1978 the Sudan has been in an economic crisis, which has caused declining real incomes for most, but this decline does not appear to be any worse in Kassala than in less refugee-affected areas such as the Central Region.

The only sector that was clearly negatively affected by the influx of refugees is that of small-scale rainfed agriculture, where their numbers severely tax the limited natural resources and where ecological degradation due to population pressure is clearly in evidence. Overgrazing and, in some places, overcultivation are causing accelerated erosion. Water resources are quite possibly insufficient to support a settled population. Deforestation makes the decreasing firewood supply an ever greater problem. Ironically, the villages of that zone have the least complaints against refugees. This is because the refugees who have settled there belong to the same ethnic groups as the local Sudanese.

Both were nomads until recently, and the villages are the result of a settlement process that is still continuing. What difference does it make whether someone was forced to settle because of the economic decline of nomadism on one side of the border or because of political violence on the other?

To be sure, a region's absorptive capacity may be severely taxed by rapid population growth, such as a mass influx of refugees. Indeed, at the time of the research it was too early to assess the full impact of the drought from which the Kassala region was recovering, and which also brought a renewed large flow of refugees. But the large and steady flow from 1967 to the early 1980s did not result in an overall deterioration of either incomes or employment among the host population, except for the small farmers in the rainfed sector. So much for the refugees' impact on employment and incomes. However, we must also consider the effects on other aspects of the economy.

The water supply in Kassala town is under pressure from population growth (caused by natural growth and by rural-urban migration, as well as by refugee influx); however, water resources are adequate and the fact that they are not yet adequately harnessed is due to the general economic situation, not to the refugee influx. Housing has become more congested since the arrival of the refugees (there is 19 percent less space per person than twenty years previously), but curiously enough rents have not increased relative to the general price level. Instead, many Sudanese responded to demands for rented housing by either building houses or renting out part of their own homes.

Education and health services must cope with increased demand due to the refugee influx, but this increase is much less than the number of refugees would lead one to suppose. In the case of education, the refugees' access is restricted, and in the cases of both education and health, there are facilities that have been created especially for refugees and that partly compensate for the burden. In 1986 the proportion of refugees among the pupils in government primary schools in the research area was 12 percent, while they made up 20.5 percent of the total population in the area; in secondary schools the proportion of refugee pupils was 10 percent. In the health sector, there are no statistics that show the number of refugee patients. Sudanese and refugees are treated without discrimination, and no patient is asked to which group he or she belongs. The proportions are likely to reflect those among the population as a whole, with the understanding that facilities for refugees also cater to the Sudanese.

Thus, the overall burden is less than proportional to the number of refugees, but it is a burden nevertheless. However, one may legitimately ask why this burden could not be borne by the host country. If the refugees contribute to a higher regional income from which these services are financed, why could the state not finance the necessary expansion in them? The answer is, of course, that social services are at present not adequately financed in the Sudan because of the economic crisis and the crisis of the state, but refugees cannot be blamed for that. It is a fact that the expansion in social services over the last twenty years has lagged far behind the increase in population. This means that the burden of refugees is expressed in deteriorating services rather than in increased government expenditure.

Self-settled refugees suffer many disadvantages because of their lack of legal status: they are subject to travel restrictions, they are liable to be detained by police at any time (a frequent occurrence, especially in Khartoum), they cannot obtain business licences from local authorities, and because most do not have a work permit, they are at the mercy of their employers' whims—which make them a docile and cheap labour force, undercutting their Sudanese colleagues. In view of the positive effects that they have had on several sectors of the regional economy, the observer may wonder whether less restrictions on refugees' economic activities would have greater positive effects. Higher aggregate regional incomes can also be taxed to provide the necessary financing for expanding social services. While special aid to these services is necessary to cope with the initial shock of a mass influx, in the long term the need for such aid must disappear, provided the refugees are able to acquire adequate incomes.

Thus, the burden of self-settled refugees needs to be qualified: in most respects it is far less than one would think from just adding more beneficiaries to a fixed amount of resources, and there are significant positive effects to compensate for part of it. Moreover, with more enlightened policies the positive effects might have been enhanced and the burden would have been lighter, yet a burden it unquestionably remains. But what about the impact of the settlements? Whereas the financial costs for setting up and running the settlements is borne by foreign donors (mainly UNHCR),[14] the host country provides the land. In the Sudan it was thought at first that giving land to refugees would be a boon rather than a burden to the country. The country is large and thinly populated, with much of its land resources unused or underused. The settlement refugees could help to realize the Sudan's potential for agricultural development. In economic terms, the cost of land was regarded as small, yet as we saw in the previous section, the government finds it difficult to make sufficient land available to refugees.

The degree to which land may be under- or overutilized is not a given quantity because it depends on the technology applied. Land may be thinly populated, yet utilized to the full or even overexploited with the technology available to the users. Land that is not cultivated at a particular time may yet play an essential role in the local production system: it may be used as pasture, as a reserve of forest products or left fallow as part of a shifting cultivation system. If part of such land is expropriated for refugee settlement, the balance of the existing agrarian system may be upset. The local

population will either resist such encroachment or, seeing that with investment the potential of the land is raised, attempt to benefit from the increase
in value themselves.

We saw the results of the former case in the previous section, while the
latter is exemplified by the scheme at Qala en Nahal. The area is fertile, but
it suffers from two problems: there is no permanent water supply, and the
soil is too heavy to cultivate efficiently without the aid of tractors. Hence, it
was little used and considered a suitable area for refugee settlement—with
the appropriate investments in tractors and water supply. Once these were
available, however, Sudanese nationals also became interested in the land
and by 1980 a survey by the agency ACORD found that 45 percent of the area
under crops was cultivated by Sudanese farmers (Betts 1982, 91). The
Sudanese government had clearly been too optimistic in its estimates of the
amounts of land that could actually be issued to refugees.

Obviously, if it is so difficult to make land available to refugees, the cost
of organized settlements to the host country must be substantial. The initial
optimism was probably due to the fact that the government simply appro-
priated land from the rural population.[15] It could afford to believe that the
opportunity cost of the land was low because it let others pay that cost. The
cost of wage-earning and peri-urban organized settlements is lower, of
course, as land needs to be provided only for residential purposes; in rural
wage-earning organized settlements, however, self-sufficiency is even
more difficult to achieve than in the land settlements. Only the peri-urban
settlements might be considered justifiable, in the sense that the cost to the
host country is relatively low and the potential for self-sufficiency reasonable—which is not to say that they are, on balance, preferable to spontaneous organized settlement in urban areas.

In fact, wage-earning settlements entail a different and seldom noticed
cost to the host country. The food aid given to those settlements without
family self-sufficiency serves in effect to subsidize the Sudanese commercial farmers: they enable refugees to work for wages below those on which
Sudanese workers could subsist. In this way, they undercut not only wage
opportunities but also wage levels and working conditions for the Sudanese.

CONCLUSIONS

It is not possible to make a definitive conclusion as to which of the two major
alternatives for the settlement of refugees in Africa performs better in terms
of economic integration as I have defined it—much less to state which is
preferable, all things considered. For that the data at our disposal are too
crude and too few. Nevertheless, the evidence strongly suggests that: (1) the
massive external intervention necessitated by the policy of organized

settlement has—at least in the case of Ethiopian and Eritrean refugees in the Sudan—failed to make the refugees self-sufficient or even to make them better off than the self-settled, and (2) that it is not as effective in lessening the economic burden of refugees on the host country as had been thought, partly because the burden of the self-settled is not an unmitigated one, and partly because the cost of organized settlements is substantial not only to the international community but to the host country as well.

The experience in other cases of refugees in Africa may be different, of course. This is difficult to evaluate, as there is a lack of empirical data on self-settled refugees and on the impact of both the self-settled and those in settlements on the host country. The reported success of Tanzania's settlements must be due to a large extent to the generosity with which land was made available (either because there really was plenty of unused land or because the government was able to overcome resistance among the local population). This generosity has also been expressed by the way the Tanzanian government treated refugees equally with nationals, even in that the latter were also subject to enforced resettlement under the *Ujamaa* ideology (Rogge 1981, 206–9). Tanzania has even granted naturalization to refugees, something rarely done elsewhere in Africa. The common reluctance of refugees to be resettled, while due to several reasons, is at least in part a reflection on unattractive economic conditions in the organized settlements.

This is not to say that the self-settled tend to be well integrated economically. On the contrary, their standard of living is usually lower than that of even the more disadvantaged groups of nationals, nor is the burden they impose on the host population to be minimized. What I am suggesting is that policies could be designed to enhance economic integration among the self-settled, which would stand a much better chance of success than the prevalent policy of favouring organized settlement. Whereas even under present conditions economic integration among the self-settled appears to be better than in the organized settlements, appropriate policies could do much to improve it with regard to the economic situation of the refugees themselves and with regard to the burden they impose on the host country. At present, this integration is hampered by the restrictions imposed on refugees by host country governments, and aid agencies appear to be less willing to share the burden where the self-settled are concerned. If those institutional constraints could be overcome, and if host country governments could face their responsibilities more squarely, both the refugees and the host populations would be better off.

Host countries could lift restrictions on the refugees' participation in the national economy. First and foremost, this would mean legalizing the status of the self-settled and thereby removing any threat to relocate them forcibly to settlements. Such a simple stroke of the pen would—in the Sudan—automatically mean that refugees would be entitled to work permits. Other important restrictions are those on travel within the country and on conducting business activities. Removing them would enable the host country to utilize the refugees' potential to the full. This does not necessarily mean that there would be no restrictions applying to refugees at all. In the Sudan, for instance, the Regulation of Asylum Act (1974) states that the minister of the interior will determine where the refugees may reside. The policy of organized settlement is based on this clause, but it could also be interpreted as signifying that the minister may denote certain regions for refugee settlement. Even while refugees may travel freely, their work permits will state where they live and they may be required to justify a sojourn in a different area.

The international community would have to commit its financial support to programs designed for assisting self-settled refugees and for helping the host country to cope with the burden they impose. This would require the removal of present institutional barriers that prevent aid agencies from contributing to programs for both refugees and host populations, and agencies concerned with development aid from helping refugees. Research has an important role to play in identifying those socio-economic groups that are most in need of assistance and in outlining the ways in which assistance could most effectively be used. In the Kassala research study it was found that such target groups would at the same time include the majority of the refugees and those among the nationals that were most severely affected by the refugee burden. Such assistance programs would be concerned with income-generating activities. Outside this domain, there are other specific forms of assistance to refugee-affected areas that will be useful, such as assistance to social services and infrastructure, in order to compensate for the initial adjustment to a large increase of population, and assistance in soil and water conservation and reforestation to cope with the environmental impact of refugees, which is one of the most notable aspects of the refugee burden in eastern Sudan.

Of course, as pointed out in the introduction, economic integration is only one consideration in refugee policy. It is important in that it is often used as justification for a policy and, as I have argued, wrongly so. While it may be impossible to sustain such justification, there may still be compelling reasons for not adopting a policy appropriate to economic integration. These reasons have to do with the institutional interests of those who make those policies. While this is perhaps only to be expected, it often leads to a misperception of the refugee condition and to a failure of those policies to achieve their stated objectives. Refugees are seen not only as people in need, but as people in need of those things that aid organizations want to provide:

certain goods and certain kinds of know-how. Host governments only define persons who have fled from a neighbouring country as refugees, want to settle them in camps and have them provided with those things that donors are eager to provide. Perhaps the country of asylum wishes to embarrass the country of origin by publicizing its domestic problems, or because it fears that the refugees might upset the local balance of power and should therefore be isolated in a remote area,[16] or because it is faced with a crisis such as a mass influx, which it cannot handle without external support. In a sense, people become refugees because the host government sees fit to capture them under the aid umbrella.[17]

NOTES

1. For example, in 1986 only a few thousand Ethiopian refugees were able to leave the Sudan for resettlement, out of a total of over 650,000 (Neuwirth 1988, 31).

2. A somewhat different terminology is used by Rogge (1987, 87): self-support means independence from food hand-outs, self-reliance means producing almost all daily needs, and self-sufficiency is complete independence from any external help. The latter two are equivalent to family and community self-sufficiency, respectively.

3. These are not the problems that *caused* flight. Some authors (e.g., Zolberg et al. 1989, 263–68; Bulcha 1988, 235; Wijbrandi 1986, 128) rightly stress that a true solution to the problems of refugees can only be achieved by addressing the root causes of flight. However, this chapter is concerned with the question of what can be done in the absence of such a fundamental solution by those who have little power to address the root cause, such as host governments and UNHCR (cf. Aga Khan and Bin Talal 1986, 57; Stein 1986, 267).

4. The distinctions between integration, assimilation, marginalization and segregation have been cast into a model by the psychologist John W. Berry (1988, 45). All four may be considered as modes of acculturation, a process in which there are two basic dimensions: the degree of contact between migrants and natives and the extent to which the former maintain their own cultural identity. No contact and maintaining one's own identity means segregation or separation, whereas intensive contact and loss of identity results in assimilation. It may also happen that the group withdraws into itself, yet its culture is destroyed—this is what Berry calls marginalization, and examples are provided by many American Indian groups and the Australian aborigines. Finally, a combination of intensive contact with the dominant society while also maintaining one's own culture is termed integration.

    I disagree with Berry in that I think his two dimensions are not logically independent of one another: maintaining one's own cultural identity has to go together with intensive social relations within one's cultural group, and this means less contacts outside. Yet, as a midway compromise between full segregation and total loss of cultural identity, his concept is elucidating and highly suited to a plural society.

5. A plural society is defined as one in which ethnic groups not only coexist, but where each group occupies its own niche in the economy. As economic role tends to be strongly correlated with power, income and status, this means that social stratification has a strong ethnic bias. This does not necessarily mean that socio-economic position is totally determined by ethnicity: it is sufficient that the two are correlated. The term originates with J.S. Furnivall (1939) in a work on colonial Indonesia.

6. Each culture has its own criteria of what constitutes an acceptable minimum standard of living. This is the only valid approach to a "poverty line": general criteria such as those proposed in Dudley Seers's famous definition of development (Seers 1969) cannot be universally applied, much less specified. The minimum requirements for physiological survival (another possible approach) are far below what human beings consider a life worth living; and moreover, in many if not all cultures, some values are placed even above the biological survival of the individual, as even the most doctrinaire neo-classical economist must admit. On this issue, see the discussion in Sen (1981, 12–18).

7. This meaning of the word "economics" combines elements of Lionel Robbins's famous definition of economics (1932) and Polanyi's "substantive" definition (1958).

8. There are a few exceptions, notably the case of the refugees from Portuguese Guinea who fled to Senegal during the war of independence in the 1960s and early 1970s. The Senegalese government took no measures to settle them in camps, but encouraged them to settle among the local population (Rogge 1981, 200). There are other cases where people fled their country because of oppression, but were never recognized as refugees because the host country government did not find it politically opportune to advertise the existence of a problem or to invite foreign involvement in its relations with a neighbouring state (cf. Zolberg et al. 1989, 37, 58).

9. Most of the arguments that follow are listed in Wijbrandi (1986, 11–12). However, my treatment of them is quite different from his.

10. However, it would be wrong to suppose that most refugees are revolutionaries bent on overthrowing the regime in their home country, while the host government is filled with the most peaceful intentions towards its neighbour. In the case of Eritrean refugees in the Sudan, the majority are not engaged in any political activity against Ethiopia; the Sudanese government, on the other hand, actively supports the Eritrean guerrillas, as Ethiopia does for the southern Sudanese rebels.

11. It must, however, be pointed out that the sample of refugees in Doka was drawn from one particular group of Ethiopian refugees, namely, those who could be easily identified. This means a certain ethnic bias, as those refugees who belong to the Beni Amer tribe (found on both sides of the border) were left outside the sample. As the latter integrate more easily, the sample probably erred in ascribing too low average incomes to the self-settled.

12. Wage labour is also a factor in the incomes of refugees in land settlements.

13. It must be admitted that this does not necessarily mean that the vulnerable will be cared for adequately. However, inadequacies common in poor countries and cannot be ascribed to refugee status.

14. Some help is also given to compensate for the burden of self-settled refugees. In the case of Kassala, UNHCR provides some assistance to the departments of health and education in the region, and special projects have been designed after the second International Conference on Assistance to Refugees in Africa (ICARA II) in 1984, such as extension of electricity and water supplies, and a credit scheme for the rural areas.

15. In the Sudan, land that has not been specifically recognized as freehold is by law the property of the state. This means virtually all land, with the exception of some large estates that belong to a few rich families.

16. This was clearly a consideration in moving the first wave of Eritrean refugees to Qala en Nahal (Karadawi 1983).

17. This is a central theme in Barbara Harrell-Bond's *Imposing Aid: Emergency Relief to Refugees* (1986).

REFERENCES

Aga Khan, S., and H. Bin Talal. 1986. Foreword to *Refugees: The Dynamics of Displacement: A Report for the Independent Commission on Humanitarian Issues*, edited by Jeffrey Crisp. London: Zed Books.

Armstrong, A. 1987. "Refugee Settlement Schemes in Tanzania." *Land Reform* no. 1/2:83–108.

Berry, J.W. 1988. "Acculturation and Psychological Adaptation: A Conceptual Overview." In *Ethnic Psychology: Research and Practice with Immigrants, Refugees, Native Peoples, Ethnic Groups and Sojourners*, edited by J.W. Berry and R.C. Annis, 44–52. Amsterdam: Swets & Zeitlinger. Selected papers from a North American Regional Conference of the International Association for Cross-Cultural Psychology, held in Kingston, Ontario, August 16–21, 1987.

Betts, T.F. 1981. "Rural Refugees in Africa." *International Migration Review* 15, no. 1:213–18.

———. 1982. "Spontaneous Settlement of Rural Refugees in Africa, Part III: Sudan." London: Euro-Action ACORD. Unpublished.

Bulcha, Mekuria. 1988. *Flight and Integration: Causes of Mass Exodus from Ethiopia and Problems of Integration in the Sudan*. Uppsala: Scandinavian Institute of African Studies.

Chambers, R. 1986. "Hidden Losers? The Impact of Rural Refugees and Refugee Programs on Poorer Hosts." *International Migration Review* 20, no. 2:245–63.

Cree, T.J. 1983. "Agricultural Survey of Refugee Settlements in the Eastern Sudan." Report of a mission undertaken for UNHCR in collaboration with the Food and Agriculture Organization of the United Nations. Unpublished.

Cuénod, J. 1989. "EC Assistance to Regions with Large Numbers of Refugees." A paper presented at the International Conference on Refugees in the World: The European Community's Response, held at The Hague, Netherlands, December 7–8.

Daley, O.P. 1984. "The Rural Settlement of Refugees in Africa with Special Reference to Tanzania and the Sudan." MA thesis, London School of Oriental and African Studies. Unpublished.

Furnivall, J.S. 1939. *Netherlands India: A Study of Plural Economy*. Cambridge: Cambridge University Press.

Gasarasi, C.P. 1987. "The Tripartite Approach to the Resettlement and Integration of Rural Refugees in Tanzania." In *Refugees: A Third World Dilemma*, edited by J.R. Rogge, 99–114. Totowa: Rowman & Littlefield.

Gould, W.T.S. 1974. "Refugees in Tropical Africa." *International Migration Review* 8, no. 3:413–30.

Hansen, A. 1981. "Refugee Dynamics: Angolans in Zambia 1966 to 1972." *International Migration Review* 15, no. 1:175–94.

———. 1982. "Self-Settled Rural Refugees in Africa: The Case of Angolans in Zambian Villages." In *Involuntary Migration and Resettlement: The Problems and Responses of Dislocated People*, edited by Art Hansen and Anthony Oliver-Smith, 13–35. Boulder: Westview Press.

Harrell-Bond, Barbara E. 1986. *Imposing Aid: Emergency Relief to Refugees*. Oxford: Oxford University Press.

———. 1989. "Repatriation: Under What Conditions Is It the Most Desirable Solution for Refugees? An Agenda for Research." *African Studies Review* 32, no. 1:41–69.

Holborn, L. 1975. *Refugees, A Problem of Our Time: The Work of the United Nations High Commissioner for Refugees* (2 vols.). Metuchen: Scarecrow Press.

International Labour Organisation and United Nations High Commissioner for Refugees. 1984. *Towards Self-Reliance: A Programme of Action for Refugees in Eastern and Central Sudan*. Geneva: ILO and UNHCR.

Jonsson, L., and T.J. Cree. 1982. "Self-Reliance in Refugee Settlements in the Eastern Sudan. Memorandum to the Acting Representative of UNHCR, Khartoum." Unpublished.

Karadawi, A. 1983. "Constraints on Assistance to Refugees: Some Observations from the Sudan." *World Development* 11, no. 6:537–47.

Kent, R.C. 1987. *Anatomy of Disaster Relief*. London: Pinter Publishers Ltd.

Kok, W. 1989. "Self-Settled Refugees and the Socio-Economic Impact of Their Presence on Kassala, Eastern Sudan." *Journal of Refugee Studies* 2, no. 4:419–40.

Kuhlman, T. 1990. *Burden Or Boon? A Study of Eritrean Refugees in the Sudan*. Amsterdam: Free University Press.

Neuwirth, G. 1988. "Refugee Resettlement." *Current Sociology* 36, no. 2:27–41.

Nobel, P. 1982. "Refugee Law in the Sudan." Research Report No. 64. Uppsala: Scandinavian Institute of African Studies.

Pankhurst, A. 1984. "Vulnerable Groups." *Disasters* 8, no. 3:206–13.

Polanyi, K. 1958. "The Economy As Instituted Process." In *Trade and Markets in the Early Empires*, edited by K. Polanyi, C. Arensberg and H.W. Pearson, 243–70. Glencoe: The Free Press.

Post, J. 1985. *Ruimtelijke integratie of segregratie van urbane vluchtelingen. Deelnota 2: Verslag van een onderzoek naar de vestiging van vluchtelingen in Gedaref (Soedan)*. Amsterdam: Vrije Universiteit.

Purcell, R.A. 1983. "A Study of the Socio-Economic Viability of Five Wage-Earning Refugee Settlements in the Eastern Sudan." Report prepared for the Commission for Refugees, Government of Sudan. Unpublished.

Robbins, L. 1932. *An Essay on the Nature and Significance of Economic Science*. New York: St. Martin's Press/London: Macmillan.

Rogge, J.R. 1981. "Africa's Resettlement Strategies." *International Migration Review* 15, no. 1:195–212.

———. 1985. *Too Many, Too Long: Sudan's Twenty-Year Refugee Dilemma*. Totowa: Rowman & Allanheld.

———. 1987. "When Is Self-Sufficiency Achieved? The Case of Rural Settlements in Sudan." In *Refugees: A Third World Dilemma*, edited by John R. Rogge, 86–98. Totowa: Rowman & Littlefield.

Rogge, J.R., and J.O. Akol. 1989. "Repatriation: Its Role in Resolving Africa's Refugee Dilemma." *International Migration Review* 23, no. 2:184–200.

Seers, D. 1969. "The Meaning of Development." *International Development Review* 11, no. 4:2–6.

Sen, A.K. 1981. *Poverty and Famines: An Essay on Entitlement and Deprivation*. Oxford: Clarendon Press.

Stein, B.N. 1986. "Durable Solutions for Developing Country Refugees." *International Migration Review* 20, no. 2:264–82.

United Nations High Commissioner for Refugees. Undated. *The Integration of Refugees*. Geneva: UNHCR.

Wijbrandi, J.B. 1984. *Verslag van een onderzoek onder Ethiopische vluchtelingen in Doka en Um Rakoba (Oost-Soedan), ockober-november 1983*. Amsterdam: Vrije Universiteit, Onderzoeksprojekt Vluchtelingen in de Derde Wereld, interimrapport III.

———. 1985. *Verslag van een onderzeok onder Eritrese en Ethiopische vluchtelingen in Wad el-Hilew en Abuda (Oost-Soedan), april-mei 1984*. Amsterdam: Vrije Universiteit, Onderzoeksprojekt Vluchtelingen in de Derde Wereld, interimrapport III.

————. 1986. *Organized and Spontaneous Settlement in Eastern Sudan: Two Case Studies on Integration of Rural Refugees*. Amsterdam: Free University, Faculty of Economics, Department of Development Studies.

Zolberg, A.R., A. Suhrke and S. Aguayo. 1989. *Escape from Violence: Conflict and the Refugee Crisis in the Developing World*. New York: Oxford University Press.

7

Voluntary Repatriation by Force: The Case of Rwandan Refugees in Uganda

Edward Khiddu-Makubuya

In October 1990, the Rwandese Patriotic Front (RPF), consisting mainly of Rwandan refugees who were living in Uganda, launched an armed incursion into Rwanda. It seemed that the RPF's general aim was to ensure that Rwandan nationals who had for years lived as refugees in neighbouring countries and further afield could return to their motherland. It can be provisionally assumed that the RPF's rationale was that such refugees and exiles had no other way of reentering Rwanda except through force. The RPF achieved initial military successes against the Rwandan armed forces and even temporarily captured a few border towns. However, Belgium, Zaire and others went to Rwanda's aid, effectively stopping the RPF's advance. Diplomatic and other interventions led to a March 29, 1991 cease-fire agreement enabling the two sides to seek a peaceful resolution. However, this cease-fire was soon broken and fighting continued throughout 1992.

This chapter reviews the historical aspects of the phenomenon of Rwandan refugees crossing into Uganda and examines the application of relevant refugee instruments and norms to the Uganda-Rwanda situation and the involvement of the United Nations High Commissioner for Refugees (UNHCR). It considers the extent to which the usual solutions to the refugee problem could have been and were actually applied. Some attention is also directed to the invasion, to whether voluntary repatriation by force is a viable alternative, and to some lessons for the future.

BACKGROUND

There are three ethnic groups in Rwanda: the Hutu, the Tutsi and the Twa. The traditional social structure had two patterns: the chief-peasant arrangement based on peasants tilling the chief's land and giving him part of their harvest, and the patron-client arrangement in which cattle keeping was a key factor. The Tutsi were traditionally the minority as well as the rulers, while the Hutu majority were more or less their serfs. This arrangement did not endear the Tutsi to the Hutu.[1]

Pursuant to the Berlin Conference of 1884, Rwanda became a German colony, but after World War I it was handed over to Belgium as a mandate territory. Belgian colonial policy changed a number of things in Rwanda. Belgium established a cash economy in Rwanda, introducing crops like coffee, tea and pyrethrum. Poll tax and forced labour were used to get people to grow these crops.

Beginning in the 1920s, Belgian colonial policy led to mass exile of Rwandans fleeing from the colonial whip and other forms of human degradation. In 1910 Belgium (then ruling Rwanda) and Britain (then ruling Uganda) agreed to readjust the Berlin boundary. As a result, segments of the Hutu population who were residents in Rwanda became residents in Uganda's Kisoro subdistrict. In the 1920s Britain encouraged Rwandans to go to Uganda to boost the labour force there.

In the late 1950s and on the advent of independence in Rwanda, power slipped from the minority Tutsi to the majority Hutu, accompanied by violence and recrimination, forcing the Tutsi to flee to neighbouring countries, including Uganda. The flow of the Tutsi into Uganda continued into the 1960s. Once in Uganda, the Rwandan refugees were assigned to settlements—Oruchinga, Nakivale, Kyaka, Ibuga, Rwamanja and Kahunge—where they were taken care of by the UNHCR and also checked on by the relevant Ugandan authorities. The present Rwandan community in Uganda, which numbers about 1.3 million, is composed of several categories of people.

The arrival of Rwandans in Uganda prior to 1959 was essentially voluntary, and they moved freely back and forth across the border. [2] However, these Rwandans and any of their children who were born in Uganda could not become citizens of Uganda when the country attained independence on October 9, 1962 because they were not British-protected persons. This was approximately half of the total Rwandan community. About one-third of the Rwandans in Uganda are Ugandan nationals whose grandparents and parents found themselves inside Uganda after the Berlin boundary was readjusted. Between 200,000 and 500,000 of the community are refugees who arrived in Uganda in 1959 or after, or who were born there of refugee parents.[3]

LAW AND THE USUAL SOLUTIONS

Uganda acceded to the major international instruments governing the status of refugees, e.g., the United Nations Convention relating to the Status of Refugees (1951), the Protocol relating to the Status of Refugees (1967) and the Organization of African Unity (OAU) Convention governing the Specific Aspects of Refugee Problems in Africa (1969).

The Ugandan Constitution has been silent on refugees.[4] However, the Control of Alien Refugees Act (Chapter 64, Laws of Uganda: [1964]) sets out an elaborate regime for refugees. The Alien Refugees Act proclaims itself to be "an act to make provision for the proper control of alien refugees, for regulating their return to their country of residence and for making provision for their residence while in Uganda."

This Act defines a "refugee" as any person in a class of aliens who are declared by the minister by statutory instrument to be refugees for the purpose of that Act, but does not include any person who is ordinarily resident in Uganda, any person with diplomatic immunity, any agent or employee of any government who enters Uganda in the course of duty, or any person or class of person who is declared not to be a refugee by the minister by statutory instrument. The Act enables the minister to appoint a director of refugees who has the authority to establish refugee settlements anywhere in Uganda.

Refugees who entered Uganda after June 30, 1960 need a permit to remain in Uganda. They may be ordered by a competent authority to reside anywhere in Uganda. The Alien Refugees Act also gives the minister the power to detain a refugee if the minister is "satisfied" that a particular refugee is acting in a manner prejudicial to peace and good order in Uganda and any other government. The minister has the power to dispose of any animals imported into Uganda by any refugee. It is illegal for any person to harbour a refugee without the consent of the director of refugees.

The OAU definition of a refugee is broadly acceptable to a wide cross-section of people in the world today and therefore provides a common point of departure in dealing with refugee issues. The definition of a refugee in the municipal law of Uganda is subjective and highly restricted in terms of dates and target group. Leaving refugee matters to executive/ministerial discretion undermines the protection of refugees. In the case of Rwandan refugees in Uganda, legalistic arguments on the scope of municipal law have occasionally been used to restrict their basic human rights.

Ugandan law requires refugees to stay in gazetted settlements only, thus flatly contradicting Article 26 of the 1951 Convention, which requires every contracting state to accord refugees who are lawfully in its territory the right to choose their place of residence and to move freely. The Alien Refugees Act gives the minister unfettered power to detain a refugee on somewhat subjective considerations. Perhaps the biggest drawback in Uganda's refugee law is the overwhelming discretion vested in the executive without providing safeguards that a refugee could pursue before the courts of law.

While the municipal law appears formidable and restrictive with regard to refugees, Uganda has been generally very receptive and hospitable to foreigners and to refugees in particular. Despite the requirement for permits, etc., I have not heard of cases of *refoulement* at Uganda's borders. Refugees have usually had ample access to social amenities and facilities—not any less than the citizens.

The Ugandan government established refugee settlements for Rwandan refugees in several places in the southwest of the country at Oruchinga, Nakivale, Kyaka, Ibuga, Rwamanja and Kahunge, but these are open settlements rather than closed camps, and refugees have had de facto freedom to come and go—with remarkable social consequences.

Over the years, the UNHCR office in Uganda has been active with regard to Rwandan refugees in Uganda. It has supplied them with food, funds for education, health services and guidance and counselling services.

WHY THE RPF INVADED RWANDA ON OCTOBER 1, 1990

The Kenya Weekly Review of February 8, 1991, featured President Yoweri K. Museveni of Uganda as "a man to watch." It underscored the alleged views of President Museveni's colleagues in the region regarding the RPF's invasion of Rwanda in these terms:

> Museveni, reportedly under pressure from the Rwandan refugees, especially those who had served in the (National Resistance Army) and helped to bring him to power, later put pressure on the Rwandan government to take them back, without success; Rwanda believes that the refugees are Uganda's problem. A Rwandan government spokesman told journalists that most of the refugees had been born and brought up in Uganda, and had acquired Ugandan citizenship. The official Rwandan view seems to be that the refugees are actually Ugandans out to topple the Rwandan government with the support and approval of the Ugandan government.

According to a Kenyan foreign affairs official, Rwanda, Kenya and other neighbouring countries are nervous because Museveni seems to be using the same tactics that brought him to power to topple the Ugandan government and either install a puppet government or annex the country, a move that might not stop with Rwanda. "After Rwanda, it might be Burundi, then Zaire, then Tanzania and finally Kenya," said the Kenyan official.[5]

These speculations seem rather far-fetched. For years the exiled Rwandan community, including Rwandan refugees in Uganda, has been planning a return to Rwanda. The expansionist theory ignores the Rwandan refugees' genuine grievances with regard to Uganda as a receiving country and Rwanda as their motherland. To assert that all those involved in the RPF endeavour are Ugandan citizens is to oversimplify the situation and evade responsibility.

THE FAILURE OF THE USUAL SOLUTIONS

Temporary asylum has proved practically inapplicable to the case of Rwandan refugees in Uganda. There is nothing temporary about staying out of one's country for over thirty years (1959 to 1990) with no hope of either settling permanently in the host country or returning to the country of origin.

Resettlement in a third country has not worked in this case. Rwanda's neighbours other than Uganda, i.e., Burundi, Kenya, Sudan, Tanzania and Zaire, either already have sizeable numbers of Rwandan refugees or have peculiar socio-political circumstances that effectively prevent them from being countries of resettlement. Statistics are not readily available, but one senses that there have not been massive relocations of Rwandan refugees from Uganda to other countries—Europe or North America.

One may cite three explanations. First, the majority of Rwandan refugees in Uganda had little or no formal education. This must have been a major handicap against attempts to relocate in the West. Second, they were cattle keepers tied to their animals and to the land. In those circumstances, travel to places for resettlement would naturally be impractical for the majority. The second generation of refugees, who may have crossed the educational barrier while in Uganda and also detached themselves from cattle culture, probably felt little pressure to move out since they could prosper in the public and the private sector without too many hurdles. Third, the majority of the original Rwandan refugees were Tutsi, who are related to the Hima of Ankole in western Uganda. The Hima community provided aid and comfort to the refugees and encouraged them to stay. The general Ugandan society into which the original refugees arrived was less harried, more tolerant, accommodating and hospitable than in subsequent years.

Rwandan refugees have been integrated into the Ugandan community, but only to a limited extent. Rwandan refugee women have married male citizens of Uganda and, to a lesser extent, Rwandan refugee men have married female citizens of Uganda. This informal integration has been cemented partly by the phenomenon of the inclusive African family and the broad in-law network. In earlier times, informal integration was made easier by accommodating and hospitable Ugandan societies.

However, both informal and formal integration (naturalization) of Rwandan refugees into Ugandan society have, to some extent, been made difficult by certain harsh realities in Uganda. The Ugandan citizenship law tends to be rigid especially *vis-à-vis* prospective applicants for naturalization from non-Commonwealth countries. The same law insists that in matters of citizenship, a child of a refugee is in exactly the same position as the parent.

The Ugandan population has been increasing steadily from about five million people in 1959 to ten million in 1969 to about eighteen million in 1989. Over the years, facilities and the social infrastructure have become increasingly run down. Successive governments in the 1970s and 1980s ran down the Ugandan economy. Poverty, scarcity and want have become the order of the day for many people in Uganda. Violence, terror and violations of human rights prevailed over the same period. Amidst these social dynamics, the original generous hospitality and accommodation to refugees have correspondingly and gradually decreased, leading to resistance to the participation of Rwandan refugees in the economy and socio-political life of Uganda. There is no doubt that the traditional Ugandan hospitality for the Rwandan refugees in the 1960s has been progressively replaced by resistance and outright hostility.

Two incidents since the National Resistance Movement (NRM) came to power in Uganda in 1986 dramatically illustrate this change in attitude towards Rwandan refugees. In 1988 the government enacted the Penal Code Act (Amendment) Statute 1988 (Statute No. 9 of 1988), which introduces Section 42A into the Uganda Penal Code. Section 42A provides as follows:

1. A person who prints, publishes, makes or utters any statement or does any act which is likely to:
   (a) degrade, revile or expose to hatred or contempt;
   (b) create alienation or despondency;
   (c) raise discontent or disaffection among; or
   (d) promote, in any other way, feelings of ill-will or hostility among or against, any group or body of person on account of religion, tribe or ethnic or regional origin, commits an offence and shall be liable, on conviction, to imprisonment for a term not exceeding five years.

2. It shall be a defence to a charge under subsection (1) of this section if the statement was printed, published, made or uttered, or the act was done with a view to exposing, discouraging or eliminating matters which promote or have a tendency to promote sectarianism.

These provisions were enacted ostensibly to prevent the propagation and/or spread of sectarian ideology or tendencies. However, the bulk of the parliamentary debate on the bill, as well as public comments in the press or elsewhere, suggested cynically that the whole intent of the law was to prevent the Ugandan public from discussing Rwandan refugee issues.

The other incident is related to government ranches. In the 1960s and 1970s, the Ugandan government established five ranching schemes: Ankole Ranching Scheme (fifty ranches), Masaka Ranching Scheme (fifty-nine ranches), Buruli Ranching Scheme (twenty-seven ranches) and Bunyoro Ranching Scheme (thirty-seven ranches). Large tracts of land were allocated for these ranches. Many ranches in the Ankole and Masaka schemes were underutilized. Other cattle keepers moved in with their animals and settled on the ranches, often with the consent of the rancher to whom the new-comer, popularly called a "squatter," would pay rent in the form of one cow per year.

In 1990 relations between ranchers and the squatters turned sour, espe-cially in the counties of Mawogola and Kabula (part of the Masaka Ranching Scheme). The squatters apparently wanted a more secure arrangement. The squatters or their children had engaged themselves in Uganda's civil wars. Some were heavily armed and demanded a share of the land. Some ranches were looted, assets were destroyed, lives were lost and the situation threatened to turn into a blood bath.

In August 1990 the government convened a special three-day session of the National Resistance Council (Uganda's interim parliament) to discuss the issue. The NRC debate revealed deep-seated feelings among the Ugan-dan elite regarding the Rwandans. They felt that most of the squatters were Rwandans bent on taking over land to the detriment of nationals. The government set up a board to restructure the ranching scheme. The board has yet to report.

During the 1970s and the 1980s, resentment developed against Rwandan refugees in Uganda. They were accused of opportunism, craftiness, cun-ning and duplicity. Many refugees had left settlements and pursued educa-tion, business and other opportunities, often in disguise. Some joined the army and other security services, where the natives accused them of participating in murders and terrorism. All of this did not endear the Rwandan refugees to the Ugandans. One author noted the following:

> It is this education and success that distinguishes the Banyarwanda refu-gees from "Ugandan" Banyarwanda and migrants. Traditionally the latter two groups have had low status. They have been cattle keepers who, like most nomads, reject education; poor peasants with little land; labourers in town doing jobs no one else wants to do. In contrast, many of the refugees have been resourceful high achievers. This has earned them intense resent-ment from the local population. Refugee (S.M.) commented, "When we arrived, the nationals offered us jobs in their gardens. That's how we got food and made ends meet. But by 1972–73, we were employing them. That's why we are at loggerheads. They can't understand how we passed them."[7]

Despite their apparent success, the Rwandan refugees seem overwhelmed by feelings of rootlessness and loss. Many have had to disguise their Rwandan origins in order to achieve educational and material success.

Virginia Bond's recent empirical study of Rwandan refugee life in Uganda concludes that the Rwandan refugees are afflicted by an identity crisis of enormous proportions. Rwandan refugees in Uganda are unable to integrate their various statuses, roles and diverse experiences. They lack a sense of wholeness and integration and are not in a position to achieve a coherent sense of self.[8]

Other recent research on the Rwandan community in Uganda has revealed a wide range of problems.[9] Local resentment of Rwandans and their success exploded into ugly violence in October 1982 when Mbarara district officials and politicians in western Uganda embarked on an exercise of "chasing Banyarwanda" out of Uganda.[10] All sorts of allegations were brought up: (1) in the 1980 general elections they had supported the opposition Democratic Party and not the Uganda People's Congress (UPC), which was declared the winner and formed a government under M. Obote; (2) in 1971–1979 many Banyarwanda allegedly supported the dictator Idi Amin and were even involved in his killing machine, such as the State Research Bureau and Public Safety Unit, etc.; (3) they stole cattle and killed some UPC youth wingers who tried to trace the stolen cattle; (4) they allegedly supported Y.K. Museveni who was then in the bush conducting a guerrilla war against the government; (5) they allegedly grabbed land to the detriment and loss of the natives.

Local chiefs, UPC youth wingers and the paramilitary Special Force became actively involved in chasing the Banyarwanda. People were killed and properties were looted or destroyed while Rwandan refugees fled into refugee settlements or into Rwanda. There were numerous killings, maimings and rapes. It is estimated that 35,000 people were uprooted from their homes and fled to settlements; about 4,000 fled into Rwanda, while about 1,000 people were stranded at the Uganda-Rwanda border when Rwanda sealed its border against the influx.

The UNHCR office in Uganda became very involved in protecting those affected by the eviction exercise and brought their plight to the attention of the international community. The Ugandan government was irritated that the truth of the sordid operation was publicized to the international community and unceremoniously ordered the UNHCR country representative in Uganda, Tom Unwil, to leave the country. Finally, however, the UNHCR, the Ugandan government and the Rwandan government agreed to set up screening teams so that the legal status, nationality, etc., of all people directly affected by the eviction exercise could be more or less objectively established.[11]

As a result of the persecution the Rwandan refugees suffered at the hands of the UPC government in the early 1980s, a number of them joined Museveni's then antigovernment guerrilla group, the National Resistance

Army (NRA). Some believe Museveni must have promised to assist the Rwandan refugees in their effort to gain reentry into Rwanda. Indeed, the Ugandan government under Museveni, working closely with the Rwandan government, has attempted to find a solution to the problem of Rwandan refugees. However, some in the RPF thought that more could have been done by President Museveni's government to ensure repatriation of Rwandan refugees, at least in appreciation of their contribution to the NRA struggle.

Ordinary voluntary repatriation has not been available to Rwandan refugees in Uganda who have, over the years, wanted to return to Rwanda. One learns that "the origin of the invasion is that the government in Rwanda shut its borders for 30 years to about two million of its people. President Habyarimana categorically stated that Rwanda was too full to accommodate all its nationals, a statement which itched the minority Tutsi exiles. Habyarimana used the analogy of a glass full to the brim to describe the situation."[12]

Rwanda has thus been unwilling to open its doors to the mass return of its nationals living in Uganda or elsewhere. Rwanda proposed allowing a small number of Rwandan refugees to return to Rwanda; securing Ugandan citizenship for the majority of the Rwandan refugees in Uganda; and resettling a still larger number in third countries.[13] These proposals have proved inadequate and unacceptable to the Rwandan refugees.

Rwandan refugees in Uganda took the opportunity of the NRM/NRA to obtain military training and combat experience, which would stand them in good stead should they decide to return home by force. The October 1, 1990 invasion of Rwanda by the refugees from Uganda under the banner of the RPF was the refugees' answer to the resistance they were encountering inside Uganda and the intransigence of the Rwandan government. The exact figures are hard to come by, but the invasion force consisted of about 5,000 soldiers who had deserted *en masse* from the National Resistance Army of Uganda, taking their weapons, vehicles and other supplies.

From about 1979 to 1983, the RPF worked clandestinely to send many refugees into Museveni's guerrilla movement. By 1986, it was operating openly. It has an eight-point program, including national unity, democracy, building a self-sustaining economy, ending abuse and misuse of public office, providing social services, democratizing security forces, developing progressive foreign policy and ending the socio-economic system that generates refugees. The RPF seeks to overthrow the Habyarimana government and, at minimum, share power with the new government.[14]

After six months of inconclusive military campaigns on the part of the RPF and the Rwandan armed forces, and after intense international and regional diplomatic efforts, the RPF and the Rwandan government recently agreed to a cease-fire and negotiations to resolve the crisis without further military actions.[15] However, the cease-fire was abandoned, conflict resumed and there were killings and arrests of Tutsi people in Rwanda who were suspected of being RPF supporters.

REFLECTIONS ON THE FUTURE

Much of the literature on refugees recounts the atrocities, deprivations, pain and suffering that they endure. It more or less implicitly suggests that refugees always use nonviolent means to obtain redress from relevant authorities.[16] The RPF invasion of Rwanda on October 1, 1990 challenges this basic assumption. It is therefore necessary to address the legal issues surrounding the invasion. Regardless of whatever social justification and military opportunities the Rwandan refugees had in Uganda, was the RPF invasion of Rwanda a justified and lawful act?

One notes that Article 2(4) of the United Nations Charter generally prohibits resort to force in international relations. Article 2(4) directs that "All members shall refrain in their international relations from the threat of or use of force against the territorial integrity or political independence of any state, or in any other manner inconsistent with the Purposes of the United Nations." The Article 51 exception regarding self-defence has no relevance here.

It is a fact that the RPF is not a state. Still, the individual is a recognized subject as well as a beneficiary of contemporary international law. The RPF as a group of individuals is definitely caught by the general prohibition against the use of force.

The RPF invasion of Rwanda would also seem to be illegal under the legal regime established pursuant to the Organization of African Unity arrangements. A review of the RPF program shows that they were originally bent on removing the Habyarimana regime in Rwanda. Article II of the OAU Charter indicates that one of the purposes of the OAU is "To defend their sovereignty, their territorial integrity and their independence." The relevant principles of the OAU set out in Article III, 1, 3 and 5 are: (1) the sovereign equality of all member states; (3) respect for the sovereignty and territorial integrity of each state; and, (5) unreserved condemnation, in all its forms, of political assassination as well as of subversive activities on the part of neighbouring states or any other state.

Refugee law appears to make the RPF invasion of Rwanda illegal. According to Article 1 F(c) of the 1951 Convention relating to the Status of Refugees, the benefits conferred thereby do not apply to any person with respect to whom there are serious reasons for considering that "he has been guilty of acts contrary to the purposes and principles of the United Nations."

The invasion flatly contradicts the purposes and principles of the UN as set out in Article 1 of the UN Charter. In no way can the invasion be viewed as a contribution to maintaining international peace and security, nor can it be viewed as a contribution to promoting friendly relations among nations. As a consequence, the RPF combatants can no longer claim the benefits of refugee status.

This point is reinforced by Article III of the 1969 OAU Convention, of which both Uganda and Rwanda are signatories. Article III imposes certain duties on the refugee with regard to the host country; in particular, the refugee shall abstain from any subversive activities against any member state of the OAU. Article III also states that signatory states undertake to prohibit refugees residing in their respective territories from attacking any member state of the OAU, by any activity likely to cause tension between member states and in particular by use of arms, through the press or by radio.

Similarly, Article 23(2) of the 1981 African Charter on Human and People's Rights provides—for the purpose of strengthening peace, solidarity and friendly relations, states party to the present charter shall ensure that:

a. Any individual enjoying the right of asylum under Article 12 of the present charter shall not engage in subversive activities against his country of origin or any other state party to the present charter;
b. Their territories shall not be used as bases for subversive or terrorist activities against the people of any other state party to the present charter.

Despite vigorous denials at the highest level in Uganda that the Ugandan government had no prior knowledge of the RPF's plans, and that it does not support the RPF, the above provisions nevertheless would make Uganda responsible for the fact that the RPF came from Ugandan territory, having "stolen" arms, ammunition, uniforms and vehicles from the government forces there.

On the other hand, Article 15 of the Universal Declaration of Human Rights provides that everyone has a right to a nationality and that no one shall be arbitrarily deprived of his nationality or denied the right to change his nationality. At the same time, Article 13(2) of the Universal Declaration says that "Everyone has the right to leave any country, including his own, and to return to his country." Rwandan refugees were forced to flee from their country and that it has not been possible for them to acquire alternative nationality. They are entitled to return to Rwanda, but the Rwanadan authorities have insisted for years that there was no room for returnees since the "glass was already full to the brim." However, Article 29(3) of the Universal Declaration states that "These rights and freedoms may in no case be exercised contrary to the principles and purposes of the United Nations." In light of these provisions, one cannot readily identify a practical alternative to the RPF action.

Was the RPF invasion of Rwanda an exercise of the right to self-determination? The UN General Assembly declared in 1960 that "All peoples have the right to self-determination; by virtue of that right they freely determine their political status and freely pursue their economic, social and cultural development."[18] Cassese subsequently distinguished between external self-determination (i.e., decolonization) and internal self-determination (i.e., the choice of internal socio-economic and cultural systems for the country.[19] There are indeed many outstanding matters that would have to be analysed before a meaningful answer could be given. The right of self-determination is a collective rather than an individual right. Would Rwandan refugees in Uganda qualify as "people," even if they are by definition a minority in Uganda? Kiss suggests an alternative in the affirmative.[20] Wars of national liberation, i.e., those intended to end colonial rule, enjoy a semblance of legality in contemporary international law and combatants in such wars have POW status on capture.[21] But the RPF has not claimed that they are waging an anticolonial struggle. They are just Rwandan nationals who assert their legitimate right to return to their country. Since the majority of the Rwandan refugees are Tutsi, which is a minority nationality in Rwanda, the best claim they can make would be for protection of minority rights.

The RPF invasion of Rwanda also reawakens the issue of burden-sharing. The popular approach is to view the refugee "burden" to be shared as essentially or, indeed, exclusively economic. This is clearly evident from some leading authorities on refugee issues.[22] Taking economics first, is a country of origin justified in saying that it cannot take care of all its people and in regarding refugee life as a permanent "solution" for excess population? This is the substance of Rwanda's argument. When and to what extent should other members of the international community accept this argument? One acknowledges that Rwanda is a small, poor and overpopulated country, but Rwanda's neighbours are not necessarily any better. Each country must accept primary responsibility for its nationals.

The RPF considers that the bad government policies pursued in Rwanda since its independence in 1962 are far more responsible for generating refugees than the country's small size, poverty and overpopulation. These policies have included sectarianism, the tribal identity card system, official favouritism for Hutus and blatant discrimination, harassment, suppression and repression of the Tutsi.[23] Criteria would have to be established for evaluating the politics and economy of the country of origin before one can seriously talk of burden-sharing.

The economy of the receiving country also must be considered. Uganda is a poor, underdeveloped country. Refugees arrive without any warning, yet Uganda has a duty not to turn them away at the border. In this regard, the additional economic requirements the receiving country incurs in hosting refugees should certainly be shared.

However, burden-sharing with regard to refugees cannot be viewed only in economic terms. The psychological and cultural load involved in hosting refugees must be considered as well. A harassed, poor, undernourished, diseased and unprivileged people in the host country are being asked to put up with strangers who are often better provided for, thanks to UNHCR, than the nationals, and who may also view themselves as superior to the nationals. In Uganda, the situation has often been left to take care of itself with full confidence in the altruism and humanitarian feelings of Ugandans. This confidence is not entirely justified. People need to be properly prepared to share limited territorial space and to bear with rather unfamiliar customs. People in the host country will need to be educated on the refugee phenomenon and why it should not be viewed as "God's punishment for the refugees' sins." It will be easier for UNHCR and NGOs than for the host government to educate the Ugandan population. This certainly would seem to be the case in Uganda.

Another aspect of burden-sharing relates to the refugees' behaviour. The relevant instruments address the duties of refugees to the host country, but we have to deal with the actual dynamics of interaction between the refugees and the host population. Rules of good behaviour need to apply in this interaction if xenophobia in reaction to alleged misbehaviour is to be avoided.

On March 30, 1991 the Rwandese Patriotic Front and the government of Rwanda agreed to a cease-fire at the end of an intensive round of talks. Although both sides have accused each other of violating the cease-fire, the two sides have engaged in two subsequent rounds of negotiations. The second round of talks led to a Protocol of Understanding on arrangements for the Rule of Law in Rwanda. The third round of negotiations has been underway in Arusha, Tanzania, ever since July 1992. By mid-October 1992, sources close to the negotiations indicated that the Rwandese Patriotic Front and the Rwandan government were likely to reach agreement on power-sharing arrangements in a transitional government that would organize general elections and put in place long-term political arrangements for Rwanda. It is hoped that these Arusha peace talks will lead to a peaceful resolution of the Rwandan refugee crisis. Peaceful resolution of this is preferable to military confrontation. Indeed, this alone should be a major achievement by the RPF. Before the invasion, the international community rarely focused on the plight of Rwandan refugees in East Africa.

Shortly after the invasion, there was a flurry of diplomatic activity in East Africa that involved Belgium and the EEC. The peace talks in Arusha are the positive result of these diplomatic efforts. To focus this kind of attention at the height of the recent Gulf War has been a major achievement on the part of the RPF. Should the cease-fire and planned negotiations fail to resolve the serious Rwandan refugee crisis, then the following scenarios cannot be ruled out:

- A continuation of protracted military action by the RPF that may engulf Rwanda, Uganda and perhaps the entire region in a war.
- A change of government in Rwanda with a possible change in perspectives and policies on ethnic criteria in the allocation of scarce resources in Rwanda, and a change in Rwandan official perspectives and policies on Rwandan refugees, exiles and immigrants.
- A reconsideration of durable solutions to the refugee problem, including resettlement in third countries (initiated by UNHCR), integration into Ugandan society (initiated by the Ugandan government, UNHCR and NGOs) and some aspects of repatriation. Indeed, the Rwandan government released a document that was intended to show that it was doing everything possible to pursue this multifaceted approach.[24] While the particular constellation of facts that gave rise to the RPF and to the October 1, 1990 invasion of Rwanda are unlikely to recur elsewhere in a similar fashion, the refugee rights constituency must still think seriously about the strengths and weaknesses of durable solutions to the refugee problem and that if they fail to work satisfactorily, refugees may be left with no alternative but to resort to force in the manner of the Rwandese Patriotic Front.

NOTES

1. On this aspect of background, one may wish to consult R. Lemarchand, *Rwanda and Burundi* (London: Pall Mall Press, 1970). For centuries, the Tutsi minority dominated the Hutu, who comprise 90 percent of the population. A civil war broke out in 1959 and the Tutsi domination was ended. The monarchy was abolished in 1961, pursuant to a referendum calling for its abolition. Rwanda became independent from Belgium on July 1, 1962. Rwanda has a population of 6.5 million people in a total area of only 10,169 square miles. It is one of the most densely populated countries in Africa; see *The World Almanac and Book of Facts 1987* (New York: Newspaper Enterprises Association Inc., 1986): 607–8.

2. Pre-1962 Rwandan migration into Uganda and its socio-dynamics there have been covered in some detail by Audrey I. Richards, *Economic Development and Tribal Change: A Study of Immigrant Labour in Buganda* (Cambridge: Cambridge University Press, 1952).

3. The question of the actual number of Rwandan refugees in Uganda has been examined in some detail; C. Watson, *Exile from Rwanda: Background to an Invasion* (Washington: U.S. Committee for Refugees/American Council for Nationalities Service, 1991).

4. See Chapter 2 (Citizenship) of the Uganda Independence Constitution (1962) and Chapter 2 (Citizenship) of the Constitution of the Republic of Uganda (1967).

5. *Weekly Review* (February 1991): 20–21.

6. For details on the ranch-squatter issue, see *The Exposure*, no. 36 (October 1990).

7. Watson, *Exile from Rwanda*, 8.

8. Virginia Bond, "Identity Crisis: Banyarwanda Refugees in Uganda," MA dissertation, University of Edinburgh, 1988.

9. See, for example, R.G.M. Namusisi, "The Plight of Rwandese Refugees in Uganda," a paper submitted in partial fulfilment for the requirements of the degree of Bachelor of Laws, Makerere University, Kampala, Uganda, 1988; and R. Gureme, "Refugees in Uganda," a paper submitted in partial fulfilment of the requirements for the degree of Bachelor of Laws, Makerere University, Kampala, Uganda, 1988.

10. For details on the "chasing" of the Banyarwanda, see E. Hooper and L. Pirouet, "Uganda: The Minority Rights Group," Report no. 66 (London: Minority Rights Group, 1989) and Jason Clay, *The Eviction of Banyarwanda* (Cambridge: Cultural Survival, 1984).

11. T.S. Karuganrama, *The Screening Exercise in Uganda*, vols. 1–3 (Kampala: UNHCR, 1983).

12. See "Rwanda: What a Homecoming?" *Africa Events* 6, no. 11 (November 1990).

13. See "Towards Solving the Rwandese Problem in Uganda," *The Newsdesk* (March/April 1990).

14. See Karrim Essak, *Civil War in Rwanda* (Dar es Salaam: Newman Publishers, 1991).

15. *The New Vision* 6, no. 77 (April 2, 1991).

16. See, for example, G.S. Goodwin-Gill, *The Refugee in International Law* (Oxford: Clarendon Press, 1983).

17. See I. Brownlie, *Principles of Public International Law* (Oxford: English Language Book Society/Oxford University Press, 1979): 69 and 561.

18. See the Declaration on the Granting of Independence to Colonial Countries and Peoples, United Nations, General Assembly Resolution 1514 (XV) of December 14, 1960.

19. A. Cassese, "The Self-Determination of Peoples," in *The International Bill of Rights*, edited by L. Henkin (New York: Columbia University Press, 1981).

20. A. Kiss, "The Peoples' Right to Self-Determination," *Human Rights Law Journal* 7 (1986): 165–75.

21. See Article I, especially Article I(4) Protocol 1, Protocols Additional to the Geneva Conventions of August 12, 1949 (Geneva: United Nations, 1977).

22. For example, Yefime Zarjevski, *A Future Preserved: International Assistance to Refugees* (Oxford: Pergamon Press, 1986) and CIMADE, INODEP and MINK, *Africa's Refugee Crisis* (London: Zed Books, 1986).

23. Essak, *Civil War in Rwanda.*

24. The following joint communique, which was issued at the end of the third meeting of the Uganda/Rwanda joint ministerial committee on the problem of Rwandan refugees living in Uganda, is an extract from *The Exposure* 4, no. 37 (December 1990): 9–10:

    The purpose of the meeting was to discuss the recommendations made by the UNHCR Independent Committee of Experts within the framework of the mandate entrusted to UNHCR by the second meeting of the Uganda/Rwanda Joint Ministerial Committee and review a plan of action and timetable.

    The UNHCR informed the meeting that an Independent Committee of Experts had been established to carry out the survey on the refugees and had presented a number of recommendations to the two governments covering all aspects of the survey.

    The recommendations were discussed at the meeting and agreed on the following:

    • the independent Committee of Experts be enlarged to include a representative of the OAU

    • a quadripartite Commission be established composed of members of Uganda/Rwanda Joint Ministerial Committee, representatives of OAU and UNHCR to determine modalities of the exercise at all stages

    • prior to the survey, UNHCR should carry out an information campaign in order to disseminate all relevant information to the refugees

    • UNHCR is to determine the modalities of carrying out the survey and ensure impartiality and non-interference throughout the survey

    • the questionnaire to be completed by the refugees is to be finalized by UNHCR and submitted to the two governments for approval

    • a representative group of refugees accompanied by UNHCR is to visit Rwanda prior to the survey

    • an absorption capacity study in Rwanda is to be carried out by a credible and impartial body

    • the process of amending Uganda laws affecting refugees be continued.

8

Ending Exile: Promoting Successful Reintegration of African Refugees and Displaced People

Roger Winter

The 1980s produced an explosion in the number of refugees. As the decade began, the world's refugee count was about seven million. As the decade closed, it was over fifteen million.[1] Overwhelmingly, the increase in the number of refugees—and of internally displaced people, who are more difficult to document—occurred as a function of "regional conflicts," mostly in developing countries. To a great degree, these conflicts were civil wars, though Afghanistan became much more than that with the Soviet invasion in December 1979. Virtually all of these conflicts involved significant international intervention by Eastern and Western geopolitical blocs. Such international interventions had enormous impact on the nature and evolution of each conflict and on the societies and populations involved. Interventions also directly affected the lives of refugees and internally displaced people.

As superpower confrontation dissipated, opportunities have materialized in Africa and elsewhere for significant repatriation of refugees and the rerooting of internally displaced people. It is not at all clear, however, that the world community will take full advantage of these opportunities in order to ensure successful repatriation and reintegration. Although some time has already been lost, the next few years will still offer the international community the chance to help reconfigure a number of divided societies. Capturing the momentum that successful conflict resolution can generate to foster reconciliation and development can also contribute to reducing future conflict and thus future conflict-based population displacement.

INTERVENTION IN AFRICA'S WARS

Superpower politics and external intervention have been major factors in recent conflicts in Africa. High-profile examples during the 1980s include Angola, Ethiopia/Eritrea, Mozambique, Namibia, Somalia, South Africa and the Sudan. Others, like the conflicts in Chad and Western Sahara, are less well known. All of these examples differ in important ways in both dynamics and specifics; all, however, produced substantial, even enormous, numbers of refugees and internally displaced civilians.

While such attempts have their limitations, it is useful to examine themes that emerge from a review of these situations.

1. *All of these conflicts have roots that precede the 1980s and, in many senses, that precede even the geopolitical conflict that materialized after World War II.*

No generation has had a monopoly on human conflict or peace. Conflict has plagued human societies since the beginning and probably always will. In Africa, colonialism stunted and disfigured natural social evolution and imposed too many borders that were irrational in terms of indigenous human reality. In some cases, members of the same ethnic groups found themselves on opposite sides of a new international border, their traditional homeland split and governed from the "capital" of their new "country." Equally often, ethnic groups that for centuries were wary of or even hostile to one another were lumped into newly created "nationalities." Most often, decisions about these groupings and divisions were made in Europe without any consultation with or regard for the people directly affected by them. Those demarcations contribute substantially to social volatility in many locations even now.

But the pattern of conflict in much of Africa today stems from many other factors as well: levels of development and education of the masses; exploitative economic neo-colonialism; in some cases, the recency of independence (e.g., Angola, Mozambique); abusive styles of governance and lack of popular participation therein; ethnic hostilities. There are, of course, plenty of others.[2]

2. *Large external powers—and smaller ones—often, especially in the 1980s, had interests that caused them to intervene in indigenous, localized or otherwise limited conflicts in Africa, thus adding entirely new dynamics to those conflicts. Often, but certainly not primarily, a former colonizer intervened. More often, however, it was undertaken by or in association with the two major superpowers, the United States and the Soviet Union.*

Delineating the range and pursuit of external interests is beyond the scope of this chapter. Clearly, however, interests were pursued—by Libya and

France in Chad; by the United States, the Soviet Union and Cuba in Ethiopia and Somalia; by South Africa, the United States, the Soviet Union and Cuba in Angola. In some cases, intervention was military involvement that directly influenced the course or outcome of the conflict, as when Soviet and Cuban troops stepped in to help Ethiopia repel a Somali invasion in 1978. In other cases, the external powers stayed on the sidelines, directing and fuelling the conflicts by providing military advisers and the weapons needed to sustain or expand the conflict. The U.S. and Soviet roles in Angola are examples of this (although in that same situation, South African and Cuban troops directly participated in the conflict).

Intervention also took other forms, such as financial and diplomatic support to contending parties. At times, it even included the way in which "humanitarian aid" was provided to the civilian victims of those conflicts.[3] Although U.S. intervention did not begin with the Reagan administration, the Reagan Doctrine was a clear example of the conscious U.S. commitment to pursue such an interventionist policy; the Soviet Union obviously adopted the policy well before the Reagan years.[4] This intervention (by both blocs) was the prime cause of the explosion in the numbers of refugees and displaced people in the 1980s. The Reagan Doctrine sought to challenge what it held—often correctly—as Soviet intervention in Third World conflicts and thus to bleed the Soviet system to death. In geopolitical terms, the approach certainly had an impact. Civilian victims were, however, massively chewed up in the process. At a hearing of the Senate Subcommittee on Immigration and Refugee Affairs in 1987, Senator Edward Kennedy proposed that each policy decision to intervene in such situations, e.g., Angola, should be contingent on the results of a "refugee impact study."

3. *Such external interventions fuelled and prolonged those conflicts, rendering them irresolvable solely in the more indigenous or localized terms that may have initially lit the fuse.*

External intervention fuelled conflicts by increasing the supply and quality of the fire-power available for Africans to use to destroy each other. The old tools of war, such as spears and *pangas*, have been supplemented by readily available mines, napalm, helicopters, jet fighters, rockets, tanks and the ever-present Kalashnikov AK-47.[5] The number of noncombatant civilians who were killed, injured and maimed in these conflicts as a result of this fire-power staggers the imagination. The persistence of these weapons and their pervasive availability assure violence, instability and killing for years to come in many areas.

Intervention also prolonged conflicts because it multiplied the number of principal actors whose interests were at stake.[6] Local and external actors were "allied" to varying degrees, and such allies had to be consulted.

Important decisions bearing on Angola, for example, were made in Washington, Moscow, Havana and Pretoria. Aside from simply increasing the complexity of diplomatic and political dynamics, combatants who ran out of fire-power could be and were resupplied, perpetuating the fighting. It is no wonder that many of these disputes become widely viewed as proxies for the larger geopolitical confrontation, with local considerations almost entirely submerged.

4. *Intervention resulted in tragedy for civilians caught up in or otherwise affected by these conflicts. Hundreds of thousands have been killed in Mozambique and Angola, and, according to a 1989 United Nations Children's Fund (UNICEF) report, the deaths of an estimated 494,000 Mozambican and 331,000 Angolan children under five years of age are attributable to the conflicts in those countries. Another report says that Angola has the highest rate in the world of civilian casualties and amputees who were victims of land-mines.*

Obviously, large numbers of people died or were maimed; villages disappeared from the face of the earth; the capacities of future generations were permanently blighted through loss of education and, more basically, war-induced malnutrition; poor economies, geared to a war, were essentially bled to death. War-induced famine, perhaps the greatest killer of all, was another phenomenon facilitated by external intervention.

The ability to pursue scorched-earth policies—razing fields to prevent crops from being harvested, bombing or shelling the countryside to keep people from farming, disrupting food supply lines and controlling food distribution—in other words, the use of food as a weapon of war—has led to millions of deaths beyond those caused by direct military actions. In 1988 250,000 civilians died because of war-induced famine in the Sudan alone. In some regions, severe malnutrition among children has left whole generations disadvantaged.

The conflict in Africa in the 1980s also clearly affected the creation of refugees and internally displaced civilians and the nature of their predicaments. In general, compared to prior periods, the refugee of the 1980s was more typically a "long-stayer," or at least the refugee situations associated with such conflicts were themselves long-stayers.

Ethiopian refugees in Somalia, Mozambicans in Malawi and other neighbouring countries, Saharawis in Algeria and Angolans in Zambia and Zaire are just a few examples of these long-staying refugee populations. Millions of Sudanese, Mozambicans, Ethiopians and Angolans are among Africa's long-staying, internally displaced populations. With the exception of Namibia, conflicts in which there was significant external intervention just did not end in the 1980s.

Two situations clearly differ from this pattern of intense international intervention. One was the flight of 55,000 Hutu from Burundi in August 1988, which became a short-term exodus for most, an episode related to deeply-entrenched, long-term ethnic conflict. The other was the remarkable return of hundreds of thousands of Ugandan refugees from Rwanda, Sudan, Zaire and elsewhere, which was precipitated or facilitated by changes within Uganda, particularly the coming to power of the National Resistance Movement government, led by President Yoweri Museveni, in January 1986.

Meanwhile, refugee numbers increased dramatically during the 1980s throughout the world, with conflicts generally not ending, with long-staying refugee populations remaining in exile, and with externally fuelled violence enduring. Between 1980 and 1989, the number of refugees in Africa increased by 25 percent, from 3.6 to 4.5 million. From 1985 to 1989, refugee numbers increased worldwide by 50 percent, from ten to fifteen million. Internally displaced civilian numbers, though more difficult to document, appear to have increased even faster.

REFUGEES AND INTERNALLY DISPLACED PEOPLE

The two groups of uprooted people in Africa, refugees and the internally displaced, have often been forced from their homes by the same externally supported conflicts. In this sense, both have been driven into exile, and both groups will be able to return to their homes as the conflicts that displaced them are resolved. Although both groups face many similar difficulties, their situations differ markedly.

With respect to refugees, the demands upon the United Nations High Commissioner for Refugees (UNHCR), nongovernmental organizations (NGOs) and other entities that embody the international community's efforts to share the burden of dealing with refugees had by the turn of the decade strained those institutions, almost to the breaking point.[7] In many cases, critical refugee needs increasingly went unaddressed.UNHCR had, on a per capita basis, only half the resources available to meet refugee needs than it did a decade earlier. Even today, despite the crisis that has resulted, donor governments, such as the U.S.and those of western Europe, show little inclination to dramatically increase those resources.[8] They have other priorities. Standards of assistance have diminished everywhere; in some locations, they have plunged.[9]

The realities of this deteriorating situation can be seen in refugee camps throughout Africa. It has dramatic implications not only for health, survival and dependency, but also for refugee protection and host government attitudes. In some locations, insufficient levels of international assistance threaten to force refugees and local residents into increased competition for scarce resources, which is a recipe for conflict and undermines the institution of asylum.[10]

If the current situation for refugees in asylum in Africa is unacceptable, so too are most of the alternatives. Substantial resettlement from the continent to third countries is politically inconceivable. For a decade or more, European countries have been alarmed at the prospect of continued substantial migration from "the South" and have taken restrictive actions that affect not only migrants, but refugees and asylum seekers as well.[11] The United States too has always set a low ceiling for the intake of African refugees. Although that ceiling has been raised from 2,000 and 3,000 in recent years to 7,000 in the 1993 fiscal year, that still represents only a small percentage of the ceiling of 132,000 worldwide refugee admissions for the 1993 fiscal year. Also, the policy of the Organization of African Unity (OAU) is to discourage resettlement of African refugees outside of Africa[12] Obviously, some individual refugees—particularly bright young people—will continue to find their way to the developed countries of Europe and North America, but formal third-country resettlement of refugees from Africa has always been minimal. That is not likely to change.

Permanent integration within countries of asylum has also proven to be a limited solution in Africa, although it is potentially valuable in a few notable situations. Although African countries have by and large been generous in offering asylum—even for long periods—to refugees from neighbouring countries, few have been anxious to integrate the refugees permanently by offering them full citizenship. Tanzania is somewhat of an exception. A few years ago, it offered citizenship to some 21,000 Rwandan refugees, many of whom had been in Tanzania since 1959. Despite widespread antipathy towards the refugees, naturalization in Uganda of over 100,000 refugees "of Rwandese origin" who had been in exile for three decades was one likely outcome of an exercise implemented by UNHCR and the two involved governments when a desperate invasion of Rwanda by some of those exiles in October 1990 disrupted the procedure.[13] But integration possibilities are not at all the norm.

There is only one major solution for most refugees in Africa: informed voluntary repatriation when security permits it. Throughout the 1980s, voluntary repatriation seemed an unattainable ideal. The late 1980s' thaw in the Cold War changed that in the case of Namibia, a situation that once seemed intractable.

Following a U.S.-brokered agreement between the United States, South Africa, the Soviet Union and Cuba, Namibia was finally put on the road to independence (which it attained in March 1990), and more than 43,000 Namibian refugees returned home. The repatriation, carried out by UNHCR in conjunction with the Council of Churches of Namibia, was a largely successful exercise, but there were two major problems associated with it. First, it was very costly; in fact, it ran out of money before all those who sought repatriation could be accommodated, leaving many scattered around the world. Second, returnees received very limited reintegration assistance.

Because the numbers were relatively low, these problems in Namibia were surmountable. However, the actual end of the Cold War has changed the repatriation landscape. Other repatriations, some already underway, involve hundreds of thousands—or even millions—of people. In the absence of adequate resources, the problems to be confronted are much more troublesome indeed. They could spell disaster for those forces in the homeland seeking to foster stability, reconciliation and development. Nevertheless, just when geopolitical changes have proven favourable to substantial regional conflict resolution that would permit large-scale repatriation, Western donor governments—despite their rhetorical wish for such repatriation—are clearly looking elsewhere. The very end of Cold War competition that has enabled repatriation has, in its demise, cost refugees the political priority they once had among many donor governments.

Repatriation is underway in Angola and South Africa. Numerous other African conflicts, including those in Mozambique, are moving towards resolution and thus repatriation of refugees. There is a choice for the international community—for UNHCR, donor governments and home countries—to maximize the odds for successful repatriation, or to leave refugees essentially on their own in devastated wastelands with little or no assistance, running the risk that their return will further disrupt societies that are most desperately in need of stability and reconstruction.

In many ways, the situation for internally displaced people is parallel to that of refugees but much worse. The international community has, over time, developed a system for responding to the needs of refugees, i.e., people who cross international boundaries and who are in need of protection and assistance. At the core of that system is the UNHCR, supported by other international organizations, donor governments, private and voluntary aid agencies. However, there is no effective "full-service system" like UNHCR has been in the past to protect and assist the internally displaced—people similarly forced to flee their homes, but who have remained within the boundaries of their home countries—who often have not fully escaped the evil that uprooted them. The closest existing mechanism is the mandate of the International Committee of the Red Cross (ICRC), whose vital work sometimes is able to reach civilians in zones of conflict. But ICRC has access only if the government agrees and the opposing parties also permit it. And ICRC, too, has suffered at the hands of fickle donor governments in the developed world. For example, the U.S. contributed as much as 40 percent of ICRC's budget in the early 1980s, but less than 20 percent by the late 1980s. ICRC's ability to respond to the displaced and victims of violence has been significantly crippled by donor whim and donation level.

Even when refugees were receiving assistance more intensively than they do now, aid to the internally displaced was patchy and highly inadequate. In the few situations where home governments were willing to aid the displaced, e.g., in Mozambique, those governments had to depend on the generosity of donor governments and private and voluntary agencies to provide the needed assistance, but such cases were the exception. In most situations, internally displaced people were—and continue to be—viewed by their governments as, at best, suspect and, at worst, as enemies. In such cases, governments actively prevented aid from reaching the displaced.

As long as such people remain internally displaced, there is no third-country resettlement or even permanent settlement in a country of asylum. The only viable solution available to them is to go home—when the situation permits it. As with refugees, that may become increasingly possible due to the demise of the East-West conflict. But as with refugees, the international community's interest in assisting with the successful return and reintegration of internally displaced populations is limited and not a high priority for resources. The international community is not making adequate provision for the repatriation of refugees. It does not even seem to recognize the *need* for assisting the internally displaced to return home.

Resources—money—of course, is not the only means to promote successful repatriation. The recently created post of UN undersecretary-general for humanitarian affairs could be a new key factor in this task.

MOZAMBIQUE: A WORST-CASE SCENARIO

The specific problems associated with repatriating refugees and internally displaced people may vary from country to country, but the similarities outnumber the differences. It is possible, though, to visualize the situation of Mozambique—which has generated massive refugee and internally displaced populations—as a worst-case scenario.

Mozambique is a devastated country, raped by harsh colonialism, and then, since sudden independence, embroiled in seventeen years of the most brutal civil strife imaginable. A generation of young people has grown up knowing no other way of life. Violent acts, often entirely gratuitous, have been perpetrated on countless civilians; the infrastructure in huge portions of the country has been obliterated; people have been uprooted by the millions—nearly a million and a half are refugees (mostly in Malawi, but also in all contiguous countries), and nearly three million are internally displaced.[14]

Recently, the Mozambican government and the Mozambique National Resistance (RENAMO) have concluded a lengthy dialogue that could be the basis for ending this hellacious conflict. Since most repatriation is usually spontaneous, one could certainly imagine, if a bargain in fact were struck between the parties, four or more million people on the move within a short span of time, all wanting to return home. While this is clearly a desirable end, care must be taken to assure that such movement does not precipitate a repatriation emergency through lack of planning or inadequate resources. Maximizing repatriation success and minimizing the potential for a repatriation emergency are tasks that need work now.

UNHCR is the best repository for information on refugee repatriation practice. Institutionally, it has been directly involved in managing many repatriations for several decades. But UNHCR's approach to repatriation has been focused on protection, legal arrangements and logistics, as well as in reintegration assistance inside the home country; most often this has largely consisted of providing seeds and food to rural refugees and perhaps a limited number of infrastructure-oriented activities, such as restoration of water sources and the like. However, UNHCR's mandate in reintegration is no longer clear. During the last five years, donor governments have pushed that responsibility away from UNHCR and onto the United Nations Development Programme (UNDP).[15] UNDP does many things well, but functioning under emergency conditions is not at all a forte of that organization, as its role in the recent Somalia tragedy illustrates. Unfortunately, the international donor governments have blurred UN responsibility for repatriation and reintegration at just the time when a coherent approach is most needed.

The Mozambican government and UNHCR have both recognized the potential emergency that massive, spontaneous repatriation could present and have taken at least some steps to plan for it, but their appeals for funds to help plan for large-scale repatriations have yielded almost no response from donors. This irresponsible approach to repatriation prospects cannot continue without placing millions of the world's most vulnerable victims of conflict at further avoidable risk. Several tasks must be urgently pursued if we are to avoid tragedy and capitalize on opportunities.

Task One requires that the United Nations get its act together quickly in clarifying roles and responsibilities in the emerging external and internal repatriation arena. In an emergency outflow of refugees from their home country, the international community knows what to do. Not so with repatriations. There is no time to waste. A half dozen major repatriations are all either underway or likely to be within the next twenty-four months. There must be more clear accountable structure and less "ad hocracy" in responding to these as they materialize. And in each individual situation, it will be dysfunctional to approach the matter too narrowly. Conceptually, the definition of a needed response must take into full account the reality inside the home country and the needs of returning refugees, internally displaced people and other desperate locals. UNHCR and host governments cannot be preoccupied only with getting refugees back into the home country, while the home country's structure and capacity are only minimally able to cope or completely incapable of doing so. *Turning desperate refugees into desperate internally displaced people is not a solution, except to bureaucrats.*

A critical aspect of this task is for the UN secretary-general, perhaps acting through the new undersecretary-general for humanitarian affairs, to assume a much more central role in managing the UN's response to repatriations until more clearly defined systems are well established. As of now, there is no "full-service" UN agency for repatriations, nor has the undersecretary-general yet proven to be a valuable addition to the refugee response system. Unfortunately, we currently face the prospect of dealing with repatriation emergencies while the UN mandate for repatriation is in some flux.

Task Two is to apply the agreed-upon structure in a tailor-made fashion to each situation, with practical effectiveness as the primary determinant. Discussions should begin as early as possible with the parties in a given conflict (e.g., RENAMO and the Mozambican government) regarding repatriation. Of course, this will never be their priority while the conflict continues, but it *will be* the day after the conflict ends.

Most repatriations occur spontaneously. The point of prearrangements with the conflicting parties is to take spontaneous resettlement fully into account. Asylum governments need to be involved in a process that precludes unacceptable pressures on refugees to repatriate prematurely. The point of all of this is to make arrangements and plans in advance to help manage what could be a mammoth transition. Mozambique is no Namibia; in dimension it is Africa's Afghanistan. Namibia was, comparatively, a piece of cake.

Task Three is to arrange initial financing in advance. Despite the weakening impact of a continuing funding crisis, UNHCR obtains resources for repatriation by issuing appeals to donors for voluntary contributions. It has no way of knowing when or how generously donors will respond. And donors too often want to micromanage the way in which their particular contribution is applied to the existing needs. This unpredictability of resources is a recipe for disaster; as massive repatriation looms, it leaves UNHCR unable to manage effectively.

In fact, UNHCR already has been unable to generate what it determined are the needed funds for repatriation of Ethiopians from Somalia, Angolans from Zaire and, as noted earlier, even for some Namibians. In a situation like

Mozambique, where millions of people may be on the move spontaneously, UNHCR, UNDP and others will need to know more precisely what resources will actually be readily available. Prearrangements with NGOs to cooperate may be possible. It will not be feasible to wait months for the current voluntary donation mechanism to sort itself out, governed as it is by donor governments' budgeting processes and competing priorities. But right now, there is no reason to believe donor governments will be any more generous towards the needs of repatriating refugees in Africa than they are to those very same refugees while in asylum. This has to change.

One proposal is the creation of a Going Home Fund or funding strategy organized by the UN that would overcome the deficiencies of the current approach. This is a variation of the Durable Solutions Fund created by UNHCR in 1979. Such a fund must relate not only to the costs of the mechanics of repatriation but to the emergency aspects of reintegration as well.

However, negotiations to arrange funding in advance should also take into account long-term reintegration. The home governments involved, such as that of Mozambique, are in dire financial straits at the best of times. Setting them up for failure after repatriation is in no one's interest. There should be sufficient resources to build on the optimism repatriation normally engenders to promote reconstruction and help avoid conflict over inadequate resources in an emergency. Helping the home government gear for success will result in a durable solution.

When all is said and done and even without these steps being taken, it is likely that most refugees will still go home as soon as the conflict seems resolved. The result could well be massive suffering, substantial loss of human life and perhaps fostering of conflict within what might otherwise have been a more reconciled society. Such suffering may not touch the people in the donor countries of the North because most of the deaths will be out of our sight. And if, after repatriation, reconciliation fails and conflicts continue, even without the geopolitical and ideological implications that characterized regional conflicts of the 1980s, those continuing conflicts will likely appear, to Western eyes, to be increasingly irrelevant.

But repatriation can be done properly. We in the North can invest at least as much planning, diplomacy and resources in the rebuilding of fractured societies—in Africa and elsewhere—as we did in our interventions into the conflicts of the 1980s. If anyone deserves to benefit from peace in the 1990s, it is the victims of the conflicts we helped create in the last decade.

NOTES

1. U.S. Committee for Refugees, *The World Refugee Survey: 1989 in Review* (Washington: U.S. Committee for Refugees, 1990).

2. U.S. Committee for Refugees. *Human Rights and History: The Reasons for African Refugees and Displaced People* (Washington: U.S. Committee for Refugees, 1989).

3. The U.S. response to humanitarian needs of starving Sudanese civilians in the zone held by the rebel Sudan People's Liberation Army (SPLA) was significantly delayed for political reasons in 1988 as efforts were made to forge an international umbrella—or fig leaf—Operation Lifeline Sudan. The SPLA was seen as linked to Ethiopia, the major Soviet client in Africa above the equator.

   Conversely, no international umbrella was required when the U.S. provided "humanitarian"—and military—assistance to civilians associated with UNITA, the U.S.-linked Angolan rebel movement or to the Nicaraguan contras.

4. See, for example, Stephen S. Rosenfeld, "The Guns of July," *Foreign Affairs* (Spring 1986).

5. Mines, for example, have taken an incredible toll on civilians in Angola. *Children on the Frontline: The Impact of Apartheid, Destabilization and Warfare on Children in Southern and South Africa* (New York: UNICEF, 1989).

   In a 1990 example, Belgian and French troop intervention into Rwanda's civil war was preceded by substantial arms shipments. Many of the refugees I interviewed in November 1990 spoke of their villages being attacked by helicopters.

6. A more recent, nongeopolitical example is that of France's involvement in Rwanda's civil war, which almost all observers agree has been prolonged by that intervention.

7. In Dimma, a Sudanese refugee camp in western Ethiopia, the series of retrenchments in refugee services caused by shortfalls in UNHCR funding are tangibly evident in 1990. As a new maternity clinic was being built, the funding crisis hit. As budgets were revised downwards, the maternity clinic's plans were too. The entire foundation was laid, but walls were only put on half the foundation. Finally, the equipment couldn't be obtained due to new budget limitations. This deformed building stood empty when I visited Dimma in August 1990.

8. Although in the U.S., Congress forced on the administration meaningful increases in appropriations for overseas assistance for refugees for fiscal years 1992 and 1993, these actions were taken following intense lobbying by concerned nongovernmental organizations.

9. See "The International Refugee Funding Crisis," testimony of Roger P. Winter before the U.S. Senate Committee on Appropriations, Subcommittee on Foreign Operations, May 7, 1990.

10. In 1989–1990 major reductions in funds to service refugees in Malawi and Sudan caused both governments to contemplate some measures that would have compromised the quality of asylum offered to refugees.

11. Antiforeigner violence levels in Europe, notably in Germany but also elsewhere, are increasing. Since most European countries do not have a legal immigration program, many of those targeted by violence are refugees or asylum seekers.

12. United Nations High Commissioner for Refugees, *UNHCR Handbook for Social Services* (Geneva: UNHCR 1984).

13. United Nations High Commissioner for Refugees, Rwanda-Uganda: Durable Solutions for Rwandese Refugees, February 5–18, 1990.

14. U.S. Committee for Refugees, *Refugees from Mozambique: Shattered Land, Fragile Asylum* (Washington: U.S. Committee for Refugees, 1986). Updated version, 1988.

15. "UNHCR EXCOM Working Group: December 11 Meeting of Budget Task Force," unclassified State Department Cable 11432, December 1989, from the U.S. Mission in Geneva to the secretary of state.

PART FOUR

Refugees and Development

The ethnic conflicts created by arbitrarily-drawn colonial boundaries led to civil war in many of the new African states. In South Africa, the white minority regime with its ideology of apartheid was a major force in destabilizing neighbouring states and creating mass refugee movements in Angola and Mozambique (Mazur 1989). Throughout Africa, colonial rule transformed traditional relations and created new classes, new institutions and new rivalries for state power that shaped postindependence politics (Anthony 1991). Colonialism also transformed African economies, emphasizing the production of what was most immediately profitable, generally replacing food crops with cash crops for export. This strategy had both social and environmental impacts.

REFUGEES AFTER INDEPENDENCE

Independence for many of the former African colonies was achieved in name only. Many African countries became reliant on monocrop production, and by continuing policies from the colonial period, they became dangerously subject to fluctuations in world market prices and protectionist strategies. Demand for many of the raw materials produced in Africa has declined in recent decades. Furthermore, much of the continent's present impoverishment was created by inappropriate "development" programs, encouraged by Western experts and Western banks, which contributed to the further impoverishment of the poor while benefiting the elite. Generally, humanitarian goals have been secondary to the commercial objectives of foreign aid programs (Griffin 1991). Seen in this context, it is hardly surprising that international development aid to Africa has not been linked to effective programs to assist refugees. In the 1980s interest rates soared on loans for those development projects that received enthusiastic support; while drought afflicted much of the continent, Africa's debt was more than half of its GNP. As elsewhere, it is the poor who have suffered under the International Monetary Fund-imposed austerity plans when the loans were due to be repaid.

However, the legacy of colonialism is not the only factor that underlies Africa's contemporary refugee crisis. States such as Ethiopia, Mauritania and Morocco maintained their own expansionist ambitions, which created mass refugee movements from the former European colonies of Eritrea and Western Sahara. Lack of democracy, corruption, military dictatorship, ideological fanaticism and religious intolerance characterize many of the new African states. State terrorism, including assassination and torture, became a standard political tool in Africa and was responsible for increasing numbers of refugees. States such as Ethiopia have devoted most of their budgets to the acquisition of armaments while the poor starve. Both the former Soviet Union and the United States considered that their own interests would be served by supporting such brutal regimes. In South Africa, the racist regime maintained an impoverished labour force through repression and attacked neighbouring states.

Appeals by Africans for effective assistance have gone unheeded. At the UN in 1990, President Museveni of Uganda requested that developed nations increase their aid to the poorest countries, but this initiative was rebuffed by the United States. Within this context, there have been attempts to avoid providing assistance to African refugees. Some suggest that many African refugees are not fleeing political persecution but are moving in response to environmental or economic pressures. For example, while visiting Eritrean refugee camps in eastern Sudan in 1983, an adviser to former U.S. President Reagan considered the refugee influx to be of this nature and advised that UNHCR should take steps to halt such movements (Crisp 1984b, 20). Yet as the situation in Eritrea so clearly demonstrates, economic, environmental and political causes of refugee movements are interrelated in the African context. Nevertheless, donor governments in the developed countries may increasingly attempt to make such distinctions in the future in order to justify their lack of support for African refugees (Kibreab 1990). With the end of the Cold War, foreign aid will likely decline generally and the amount of aid to the poorest countries will be further reduced (Griffin 1991).

DEALING WITH THE REFUGEE CRISIS

Three well known alternatives have been proposed as solutions to refugee problems: repatriation, local integration or resettlement in a third country. The last option is usually dismissed as undesirable and unworkable. It is argued that most African refugees are from rural areas and would not easily be integrated into Western societies. Therefore, in contrast to the experience of other refugee populations, an extremely limited number of African refugees find asylum outside the continent. It is difficult to believe that, in addition to the anticommunist orientation noted by Matas (1989) and Whitaker (1987), racism does not influence Western immigration policies that place restrictive quotas on African refugees (Kibreab 1990). As Rogge (1986) notes, many Southeast Asian refugees have similar rural backgrounds or equally limited skills. In any case, the number of urban refugees in Africa has grown in recent years and these are the refugees who are most likely to find asylum in a third country. At the same time, these skilled refugees are the ones who may be most critically needed in Africa (Rogge 1986).

Repatriation is regarded as the preferred solution by both host govern-ments and many of the refugees themselves. Rather than seeking integra-tion into the host country, many refugees hope to return home as soon as possible. Successful repatriation of refugees did occur in the case of Alge-rians who fled during the war of independence, and throughout the 1970s UNHCR coordinated the return of refugees to the Sudan, Guinea-Bissau, Mozambique, Angola, Zaire, Uganda and Zimbabwe.

However, for many refugees a safe return to their home remains a remote possibility. Understandably, many refugees fear violence and persecution and are mistrustful of the regimes they fled, regardless of what assurances of safety are offered. Economic conditions may make repatriation imprac-tical or uninviting. Yet for host governments who must bear the burden of supporting refugees, there is an increasing temptation to encourage repa-triation, even if conditions for return are not safe. Although the 1967 Addis Ababa conference on refugees and the 1979 Arusha conference organized by the Organization for African Unity and the UN called for burden-sharing by other African governments, and ICARA II stressed the need for in-creased support from the developed countries, the response has been inadequate. Despite the magnitude of the problem, international support for African refugees has been less than half of what is provided to refugees elsewhere (CIMADE et al. 1986, 93).

REFUGEES AND DEVELOPMENT

Most of the refugee-receiving countries are among the least-developed states in Africa, characterized by widespread poverty, low employment rates, illiteracy, poor health and educational services and high mortality rates. To suddenly become the hosts to large numbers of unexpected refugees may constitute a considerable burden to such countries, particu-larly when international assistance is inadequate. In many areas, the sud-den influx of refugees places a strain on minimally developed social services. For example, in 1990 the government of Sierra Leone said that the arrival of over 125,000 refugees from Liberia raised housing and commodity prices and swamped the country's ability to provide basic services to its own people in the areas where refugees had settled; fearing that the economic and social disruptions caused by this population movement would create political instability, the government closed the country's borders and launched an appeal for international aid (U.S. Committee for Refugees 1991, 57). South Africa, which has one of the worst records on the continent in hosting refugees, has referred to the potentially destabilizing impact of such population movements as a justification for virtually barricading itself against refugees from Mozambique (U.S. Committee for Refugees 1991, 57).

However, determining the effect of refugee movements on host countries is not always a straightforward matter. Refugee influxes may affect various classes and regions differently within the host country (Kuhlman 1990). For example, while workers may be threatened by a drop in wages because of an increased available supply of labour, employers may benefit. As Kuhlman argues in this volume, the impact of refugees on the host country may not always be as it initially seems, and further research is required to accurately determine the positive or negative effect that refugees may have on their host country.

Furthermore, the effects of refugees on local people in the host country may be perceived differently according to a researcher's theoretical perspective. For example, Mijere (1990), while studying Angolan refugees in Zambia, reported that economists on the research team concluded that there were economic benefits for the local population from refugee involvement in agricultural and business endeavours, while social scientists were informed by respondents that there was no improvement in living standards for the locals as a result of refugee activities.

While many refugees undergo traumatic experiences when they are uprooted and plunged into a life of despair in grim settlement camps, it seems that migration and, in many cases, circumstances of desperate need can also spark their creative potential. In several cases refugees' hard work contributed to an increase in food production and stimulated economic activity (Kibreab 1985). It has been suggested that refugees can be assets to underdeveloped countries because of their labour power and skills, and because they provide a broader market and generate demands for certain goods. When comparing the settlement of refugees in Botswana, the Sudan and Tanzania, Rogge (1986) detected differing levels of success, but concluded that the impact of refugees was positive in all three cases. He maintained that refugees have labour resources that can benefit the host country, that refugee settlements can bring new areas under cultivation and remote regions into national development programs, and that providing services to refugees can lead to a general upgrading of rural facilities for all inhabitants of the region. In Rogge's view, the main constraints on refugee-related development are the numbers of refugees and limited land and resources.

On the other hand, Stein (1981) has dismissed the suggestion that refugee influxes constitute an opportunity for host countries because resources are too limited. As noted above, in countries where social services are already poorly developed, refugees may become a burden on educational systems and health care, as well as water supply. However, material resources are not the only key to the success or failure of refugee-related development. The case of Eritrean refugees and displaced people is one striking example in which impressive steps were taken under the most terrible conditions.

Large numbers of refugees may have an impact on fragile African environments and thus pose additional problems for development. Substantial population growth for Africa has been noted and this, in combination with commercialization of agriculture, has placed increasing pressure on marginal lands (Lewis and Berry 1988). In some cases, the expansion of cash crop production has restricted pastoralists to limited areas, resulting in overgrazing, desertification and famine (Franke and Chasin 1980). Refugee movements also have an effect upon the environment. Settlement camps for refugees may be established on marginal lands, particularly in densely populated countries where citizens are already competing for limited fertile land. This means that the opportunities for refugees to become self-supporting are limited and that the settlement camps will create further environmental problems. Typically, areas in the immediate vicinity of refugee camps are stripped of vegetation cover because wood is needed for cooking and shelter. This alters soil and water balances and leads to erosion, soil depletion and decreased productivity. Water resources in Africa are limited and refugee populations draw heavily on existing supplies. Environmental changes in Africa will contribute to increased population movements in the future.

Whatever the real effect of refugee influxes, refugees are often perceived as burdens on the host society. For example, refugees in the Sudan were blamed for water shortages in 1982 and 1983 even though the problems were technical and unrelated to their presence (Bulcha 1988, 192). Providing aid to refugees may create conflict if the host population is deprived of similar assistance; this is one negative result of a failure to develop an integrated strategy that would consider refugees as a factor in development (Kibreab 1985, 99).

Refugees frequently find themselves blamed for creating political instability in the host country. Furthermore, if refugee camps are established along border areas (as is frequently the case with self-settled refugees), this may present a security threat to the host country since the state from which the refugees fled may launch raids against the camps or may pressure the host government to deny refugees permission to remain (United Nations 1979). In such situations, governments may target refugees and, directly or indirectly, force repatriation.

In Djibouti, for example, despite the provision of aid, refugees from Ethiopia strained an already overburdened infrastructure that was further weakened by drought. In addition, an influx of Issa refugees exacerbated existing ethnic tensions and provoked increased violence from the rival

Afar group. In 1982 the government responded to this situation by forcing the repatriation of refugees, many of whom were executed in Ethiopia. Unfortunately, UNHCR did not defend the rights of refugees but instead collaborated with the governments of Djibouti and Ethiopia in forcing repatriation (Crisp 1984a). In 1986 the government of Djibouti launched another widely criticized repatriation drive in which UNHCR violated the basic rights of the refugees it was supposed to be protecting (Harrell-Bond 1986).

Problems with repatriation have been noted elsewhere. Repatriation programs for Ugandan refugees in the early 1980s were characterized by poor planning and lack of coordination, including a lack of reception facilities and rehabilitation procedures (Crisp 1986). In some cases refugees were simply abandoned by UNHCR rather than returned to their villages. Violence and intimidation were reported, as were political favouritism and corruption in the distribution of food and seeds to returnees. Furthermore, repatriation was less than "voluntary" in that UNHCR collaborated with the Ugandan government in "pushing" refugees to return by reducing aid in the Sudan and endorsing exaggerated claims of safety and security.

Where voluntary repatriation has taken place, returning refugees may sometimes be able to bring home new skills they acquired in the country of asylum and thus may contribute to development at home. Akol's (1986) study of the refugee situation in southern Sudan suggested that those refugees who have been exposed to new methods of farming while in a country of asylum may contribute to a substantial economic transformation and improved agricultural output upon return. He suggested that those refugees who participated in organized settlement schemes or who spontaneously settled in more economically advanced areas and achieved self-reliance will be the most successful in reintegrating following repatriation, whereas those refugees who were totally dependent on aid during their exile will have significantly greater difficulty in readjusting to their homes.

Attitudes towards repatriation are clearly important factors in refugee-related development, particularly in relation to the attitudes of the refugees themselves and of the host government. It is unlikely that refugees who are committed to the idea of returning to their homes will be enthusiastic about participating fully in long-term development programs in the host country. Indeed, they may perceive any participation in these programs as a contradiction to their self-image as refugees and resist such development initiatives. Although the duration of exile may be a factor here, in some cases these attitudes might persist over generations. For its part, the host government may consider refugees as uncommitted to their place of refuge and, therefore, may be unwilling to devote energy, time and resources towards long-term programs related to refugees and development.

However, while attitudes towards repatriation can have an effect on government policies, the reverse is also true. When investigating the situation of Burundi refugees in Tanzania, Ayok-Chol and Mbago (1990) noted a correlation between self-settlement and positive attitudes towards integration within the host society, and found that those refugees who were settled in planned settlements were much more dedicated to the idea of returning to their homes. These researchers also found that in assisted villages where refugees have self-settled, the local inhabitants' attitude towards the refugees was generally positive and they appreciated the skills to be learned from refugees, as well as the services they attracted.

Where repatriation is not an option, there is a clear need to go beyond emergency relief operations to meet refugees' long-term needs. While the hospitality of African host countries has been widely praised, there have also been criticisms of policies that inhibit the full integration of refugees. Few governments are willing to grant citizenship to refugees and there may be limited opportunities for employment, as well as restrictions on movement. Such restrictions inhibit refugees' initiatives and efforts to becoming self-supporting. Yet it is clear that for various economic and political reasons, developed countries severely restrict the number of refugees they accept, particularly the poor and those with uneducated rural backgrounds; none of these countries would be willing to follow the procedures they advise for undeveloped African countries that must cope with much larger refugee populations.

SETTLEMENT CAMPS

Frequently refugees settle in remote areas where services are nonexistent; considerable mobilization of resources is required to establish camps and provide refugees with water, sanitation facilities and medical treatment. In some cases where refugees have settled in a marginal area, another site for the settlement may be chosen, which requires determining the agricultural potential of the proposed site and then clearing the land. Housing, access, communications and education, as well as emergency food supply, have to be provided.

A number of African governments have dealt with the arrival of large numbers of refugees by establishing rural settlement projects that will allow them to become self-supporting. This alternative was developed in the late 1960s as a method of rejuvenating agricultural production and coping with refugee groups; by 1981, sixty-six such schemes existed in fourteen African countries (Bascom 1983, 79).

As noted, however, most refugees try to avoid being settled in such camps (United Nations 1979). In part, this may be due to suspicion regarding the purpose of these camps, but, as Hansen (1982) has indicated, the process of uprooting involves numerous losses and dislocated people will attempt to preserve whatever autonomy they can over their lives. In these circumstances, settlement camps may not be an appealing option. As Hansen found in his study of Angolan refugees in Zambia, even though settling in the camps provided material advantages, refugees seemed to prefer a course of self-settlement because it provided them with a greater sense of autonomy. Some have suggested that the refugees' attitude towards resettlement is the key factor affecting success of settlement schemes (Bascom 1983; Cuénod 1989). Refugees may be reluctant to be institutionalized in organized settlements and prefer to remain near border areas where they may have kin or because they believe they will soon be able to return to their homes (Rogge 1986). This desire may conflict with the priorities of the host government, which may want to avoid security problems in border regions.

One of the main controversies in studies of African refugee issues has concerned this matter of self-settlement or settlement in organized camps. Betts (1981) suggests that the "social advantages of self-settlement far outweigh the material advantages of formal settlements." Self-settled Angolan refugees in Zambia appear to be materially poorer but better integrated with the local population than those refugees living in the settlement schemes; the self-settled refugees do not seek to return to Angola, while those in the settlements are resented by the local population and hope to return to their homes (Mijere 1990). As indicated, better prospects for integration among self-settled refugees and tension between refugees in aid-receiving settlement schemes and the local population were noted in Tanzania (Ayok-Chol and Mbago 1990). Yet Chambers (1979) argues that spontaneous integration is a reassuring myth that absolves host governments and international donors of the responsibility to provide support.

In his view, spontaneous settlement means instant impoverishment, with refugees having restricted access to land and sometimes encountering a hostile reception in the host country where they remain legally and politically vulnerable and a source of cheap, exploitable labour. As the wealthier classes profit from cheap labour and an increased market for goods, the poorest, including refugees, suffer from decreased wages and competition for scarce resources.

Settlement schemes have been seen as a uniquely African response to the refugee problem (Refugee Policy Group 1988). Since the 1960s, these schemes have been promoted as a means of helping refugees to become self-sufficient through agriculture. Zaire developed a number of such settlements for refugees from Botswana, and similar programs were started in the Sudan, Tanzania and Uganda. The settlement approach has since spread throughout Africa. Settlement schemes have been seen as a means of not only reducing the burden on host countries but also as a way of contributing to the development of local, regional and national economies. The need to integrate such settlements with zonal planning by host governments has long been recognized (Rubin 1974; United Nations 1981). The goal of assisting refugees in such settlement schemes should not simply be to maintain them at a level of impoverishment comparable to that of the local population but to use the settlement projects as an impetus towards raising living standards for both refugees and local inhabitants. Furthermore, sharing medical and educational services, for example, eases tensions and assists with integrating refugees into the host society (Kibreab 1985, 96).

Kibreab (1987) analysed the settlement schemes established by the Sudanese government for Eritrean refugees in eastern Sudan. He critiqued the emphasis on mechanized agriculture, inadequate provision of land and failure to consult with the intended beneficiaries of the scheme. Stein (1981) suggested that settler cooperation is crucial to success and that if settlements are established fairly quickly in suitable sites, they may lead to self-sufficiency for refugees and also benefit the host country by providing cash crops, generating surpluses and improving unused hinterlands. This represents an ideal scenario and although some success was achieved with settlements in Tanzania, others were less successful. Not all African states have large areas of land that can be allocated for such settlements. Although many African countries have established settlement camps, little research has been done on them.

Many of the African countries that host large refugee populations do not have adequate infrastructure to support these groups; the typical response has been to establish camps in rural areas. UNHCR has been called upon to develop the infrastructure to deal with refugees, but these efforts were often not integrated with the development programs of the host country (Kozlowski 1982).

In general, UNHCR has not been successful in creating the linkage between refugees and development called for by ICARA II. Rhetoric to the contrary, it is apparent that creating such linkages remains a low priority for international donors, UN agencies and African governments, and "the trend is toward diminishing rather than increased support for refugee-related development projects" (Gorman 1990, 21). At present, UNHCR "seems to be moving away from activities that could be called developmental," in spite of the fact that these programs are widely recognized as necessary (Kilgour 1991, 134).

REFUGEE PARTICIPATION AND DEVELOPMENT

While the need to take the wishes of refugees into consideration is consistently mentioned, it does not occur frequently in actual practice. Discourse analysis allows us to examine the ideological construction of relief and development aid to Africa (Sorenson 1989). Development discourse in general constructs the recipients of aid as "passive targets, obstacles or beneficiaries who are receiving a handout for which they have not worked" (Stamp 1989, 157). Refugees are doubly disadvantaged within such a discourse. There is a rhetoric of participation, but few attempts to involve refugees in decision making (Bulcha 1988). All control is retained by host governments and the aid agencies that provide support and thus play a significant role in determining what sort of assistance is provided. Most agencies dealing with refugees have an antiparticipatory approach, and the most common one is to impose solutions rather than attempt to involve refugees (Harrell-Bond 1986). For example, the administrators of one settlement scheme in Uganda failed to see the wisdom in using existing social relationships for encouraging cooperation and participation and actively blocked the meetings of family heads among the refugees (Bascom 1983). Furthermore, a typical problem has been the fact that settlements have been planned by men for men, marginalizing women both economically and socially (Scudder and Colson 1982, 284); only recently has African women's key productive role been recognized. While there is more literature on gender and development, there is very little information on the role of refugee women specifically (Daley 1991; Moussa 1992; Spring 1982).

A typical example of this tendency to overlook refugee participation occurs in the research of Stein (1981). Stein acknowledged that refugee cooperation is essential for the success of settlements, but then proceeded to dismiss the views of refugees as typically romantic, unrealistic and unstable. He argued that refugees will often resist what is in their best interest (as determined by others) and recommended that they be given "guidance and a firm hand" from host governments whose preferred role should be "autocratic paternalism" (Stein 1981, 71). However, such an approach will be doomed to failure. In contrast to this view are the conclusions of a recent symposium at the University of Oxford: "... refugees' own livelihood strategies play the most important role in securing their welfare. Therefore ... host governments and assistance agencies should maximise refugees' abilities to engage in self-sustaining economic activities, including the freedom of movement, work and trade, in line with that of the host communities" (Refugee Studies Programme 1991, 21). Furthermore, the desire of uprooted people to control their own lives may lead them to actively resist the schemes imposed by the state or experts from outside; this may be so even when the alternatives to those schemes appear extremely bleak (Oliver-Smith 1991; Pankhurst 1991).

Discourse concerning refugees and aid in general frequently reiterates concerns that assisting refugees and others will create a sense of dependency and lack of initiative. African refugees are not dependent or passive but instead must work continually to maintain themselves (Kibreab 1990). There has been very little attention given to the efforts of refugees to help themselves.

Aid itself does not create dependency; that is determined by the manner in which it is given. "Autocratic paternalism" will almost certainly undermine refugee initiatives and create dependency. Restrictions on movement, cooperative activity and decision making will reduce refugees' initiatives to help themselves. Regarding refugees as passive recipients of external assistance rather than as active agents capable of making effective decisions and helping themselves will greatly reduce the utility of any development program.

REFERENCES

Adepoju, Aderanti. 1982–1983. "Undocumented Migration in Africa: Trends and Policies." *International Migration* 20/21:204–17.

Akol, Joshua. 1986. "Refugee Migration and Repatriation: Case Studies of Some Affected Rural Communities in Southern Sudan." Ph.D. dissertation, University of Manitoba. Unpublished.

Anthony, Constance G. 1991. "Africa's Refugee Crisis: State Building in Historical Perspective." *International Migration Review* XXV, no. 3:574–91.

Ayok-Chol, Anthony, and Maurice Mbago. 1990. "Refugee Settlements in Tanzania: A Case Study of the Burundi Refugees." A paper presented at the International Seminar on Refugees in Africa, Arusha,Tanzania, July 30–August 3.

Bascom, Johnathan. 1983. "The Nature of Refugee Resettlement Patterns in Africa." MA thesis, Department of Geography, Kansas State University. Unpublished.

Betts, T. 1981. "Rural Refugees in Africa." *International Migration Review* 15, no. 1:213–18.

Bulcha, Mekuria. 1988. *Flight and Integration: Causes of Mass Exodus from Ethiopia and Problems of Integration in the Sudan.* Uppsala: Scandinavian Institute of African Studies.

Chambers, Robert. 1979. "Rural Refugees in Africa: What the Eye Does Not See." *Disasters* 3, no. 4:381–92.

———. 1983. *Rural Development.* London: Longman.

CIMADE, INODEP and MINK. 1986. *Africa's Refugee Crisis.* London: Zed Books.

Crisp, Jeffrey. 1984a. "The Politics of Repatriation: Ethiopian Refugees in Djibouti, 1977–83." *Review of African Political Economy* 30 (September) 73–82.

———. 1984b. "Voluntary Repatriation Programmes for African Refugees: A Critical Examination." *Refugee Issues* I, no. 2:20–24.

———. 1986. "Ugandan Refugees in Sudan and Zaire: The Problem of Repatriation." *African Affairs* 85, no. 339:163–80.

Cuénod, Jacques. 1989. "Refugees: Development or Relief?" In *Refugees and International Relations*, edited by Gil Loescher and Laila Monahan, 219–53. Oxford: Oxford University Press.

Cuny, Fred, and Barry Stein. 1989. "Prospects for and Promotion of Spontaneous Repatriation." In *Refugees and International Relations*, edited by Gil Loescher and Laila Monahan, 293–312. London: Oxford University Press.

Daley, Patricia. 1991. "Gender, Displacement and Social Reproduction: Settling Burundi Refugees in Western Tanzania." *Journal of Refugee Studies* 4, no. 3:248–66.

Franke, Richard W., and Barbara H. Chasin. 1980. *Seeds of Famine*. Totowa: Rowman & Allanheld.

Gorman, Robert F. 1990. "Linking Refugee Aid and Development in Africa: International and Local Responses." A paper presented at the International Seminar on Refugees in Africa, Arusha, Tanzania, July 30–August 3.

Griffin, Keith. 1991. "Foreign Aid after the Cold War." *Development and Change* 22:645–85.

Hansen, Art. 1982. "Self-Settled Rural Refugees in Africa: The Case of Angolans in Zambian Villages." In *Involuntary Migration and Resettlement: The Problems and Responses of Dislocated People*, edited by Art Hansen and Anthony Oliver-Smith, 13–35. Boulder: Westview Press.

Harrell-Bond, Barbara E. 1986. *Imposing Aid: Emergency Relief to Refugees*. Oxford: Oxford University Press.

Ingram, James 1988. "Sustaining Refugees' Human Dignity: International Responsibility and Practical Reality." *Journal of Refugee Studies* 2, no. 3:329–39.

Karadawi, Ahmed. 1980. "Urban Refugees in the Sudan." Khartoum: Office of the Commissioner for Refugees.

Kibreab, Gaim. 1985. *African Refugees*. Trenton: Red Sea Press.

———. 1987. *Refugees and Development in Africa: The Case of Eritrea*. Trenton: Red Sea Press.

———. 1990. "The State of the Art Review of Refugee Studies in Africa." A paper presented at the International Seminar on Refugees in Africa: Improving Relief Assistance and the Search for Durable Solutions, Arusha, Tanzania, July 30–August 3.

Kilgour, Mary C. 1991. "Refugees and Development: Dissonance in Sudan." In *Sudan State and Society*, edited by John O. Voll, 123–36. Bloomington: Indiana University Press.

Kozlowski, Anthony J. 1982. "Refugees and Development in Africa." A paper presented to the Refugee Seminar, Khartoum, Sudan, September 11–14.

Kuhlman, Tom. 1990. *Burden Or Boon? A Study of Eritrean Refugees in the Sudan*. Amsterdam: Free University Press.

Lewis, L.A., and L. Berry, 1988. *African Environments and Resources*. Boston: Unwin Hyman.

Liebenow, Gus J. 1986. *African Politics*. Bloomington: Indiana University Press.

Matas, David, with Ilana Simon. 1989. *Closing the Doors*. Toronto: Summerhill Press.

Mijere, Nsolo. 1990. "The Long Term Impact and Consequences of Two Refugee Settlement Options: The Case of Angolan Refugees in Zambia." A paper presented at the International Seminar on Refugees in Africa, Arusha, Tanzania, July 30–August 3.

Moussa, Helene. 1992. "Caught Between Two Worlds: Eritrean Women Refugees and Voluntary Repatriation." A paper presented at the Development After Disaster Horn of Africa Conference, University of Manitoba, Winnipeg, May 29–30.

Oliver-Smith, Anthony. 1991. "Disaster and Development." Lecture presented at the Disaster Research Unit, University of Manitoba, Winnipeg, February 21.

Pankhurst, Alula. 1991. "People on the Move: Settlers Leaving Ethiopian Resettlement Villages." *Disasters* 15, no. 1:61–67.

Refugee Policy Group. 1988. "Increasing the Rights of Longer-Term Refugees in Africa." Washington: Refugee Policy Group.

Refugee Studies Programme. 1991. "Responding to the Nutrition Crisis among Refugees: The Need for New Approaches." Report of the International Symposium. Oxford: University of Oxford.

Rogge, John R. 1977. " A Geography of Refugees: Some Illustrations from Africa." *The Professional Geographer* XXIX, no. 2:186–93.

———. 1985. "Africa's Displaced Population: Dependency or Self-Sufficiency?" In *Population and Development Projects in Africa*, edited by J.I. Clarke, M. Khogali, L.A. Kosinski, 68–83. Cambridge: Cambridge University Press.

Rubin, Neville. 1974. "Africa and Refugees." *African Affairs* 73, no. 292:290–311.

Scudder, Thayer, and Elizabeth Colson. 1982. "From Welfare to Development: A Conceptual Framework for the Analysis of Dislocated People." In *Involuntary Migration and Resettlement*, edited by Art Hansen and Anthony Oliver-Smith, 267–87. Boulder: Westview Press.

Sorenson, John. 1989. "An African Nightmare: Discourse on War and Famine in the Horn of Africa." Ph.D. dissertation, York University. Unpublished.

Spring, Anita. 1982. "Women and Men as Refugees: Differential Assimilation of Angolan Refugees in Zambia." In *Involuntary Migration and Resettlement*, edited by Art Hansen and Anthony Oliver-Smith, 37–47. Boulder: Westview Press.

Stamp, Patricia. 1989. *Technology, Gender and Power in Africa*. Ottawa: International Development Research Centre.

Stein, Barry. 1981. "Refugees and Economic Activities in Africa." Research report. Washington: Agency for International Development.

United Nations. 1979. "Report of the Conference on the Situation of Refugees in Africa." New York: United Nations. A/AC. 96/INF.158.

———. 1981. "The Refugee Situation in Africa: Assistance Measures Proposed." Geneva: United Nations. A/Conf.106.

U.S. Committee for Refugees. 1991. *World Refugee Survey*. Washington: U.S. Committee for Refugees.

Whitaker, Reg. 1987. *Double Standard*. Toronto: Lester and Orpen Dennys.

10

Refugees and Rural Development:
A Comparative Analysis of Project Aid
in Sudan and Tanzania

Jan Sterkenburg, John Kirkby and Phil O'Keefe

Refugees in Africa who cross international borders do not normally plan for permanent asylum status. They hope, as all refugees hope, to return to home within relatively short periods of time. Governments in host countries prefer refugees to return and usually grant them no more than temporary rights of residence and usufruct, though not ownership, of local productive resources. In many parts of Africa, refugees are long-term residents of host countries because of long-lasting conflicts in their homelands.

In some African countries the scale of displacement is immense. For example, it is estimated that by 1989 the ongoing war in Mozambique resulted in 200,000 civilian deaths and 300,000 orphaned children. Over three million people in rural areas faced food shortages because of displacement (1.1 million) or disruption of the agricultural production system (2.2 million). Another three million people who fled to the urban centres were almost entirely dependent on imported food supplies. Over one million refugees fled to the neighbouring countries of Malawi and Zimbabwe from the ongoing wars. In short, some eight million people—half the population of Mozambique—were directly displaced (Cherrett et al. 1990).

This scale of displacement is not unique for Mozambique—Somalia, Ethiopia, the Sudan, Chad, Liberia and Angola experience similar problems—nor is the problem simply one of scale. These displacements are ongoing. Many of the refugee areas have been problem areas for at least twenty years. The refugees' dream of returning home seems to be overly optimistic, given the scale and duration of conflict.

Their extended stay in asylum states calls for a change in strategy towards the refugee problem, for a development approach to underpin relief measures. This change in strategy is based on the assumption that relief measures will keep the refugees in a dependent position, but a development strategy will lead to self-sufficiency (Rogge 1985a). Such a policy implies that both host government and relief organizations enable refugees to improve their production and living conditions. As the vast majority of refugees in Africa come from rural areas and are settled in rural areas in the host country, the strategy must focus on sustainable rural development.

Sustainability has a wide range of meanings (World Commission on Environment and Development 1987; Turner 1988; Pearce et al. 1989). In analysing the impact of project aid, sustainability is defined as "the ability to deliver an appropriate level of benefits for an extended period of time after major financial, managerial and technical assistance from an external donor is terminated" (Development Assistance Committee of the OECD 1988). For sustainable refugee settlement, access to consumption is not sufficient—what is required is access to production. For this reason, in this chapter the notion of sustainable rural development is used more broadly with reference to social reproduction as an obligation to provide production opportunities that can be controlled and managed by present and future generations. In this latter sense, sustainability is counterposed against marginalization, which has been described elsewhere as a process in which people are more vulnerable to displacement.

The elements of social reproduction can best be understood by relating them to how household income is spent. A sustainable household income needs to provide for subsistence for reproduction of labour, for replacement value of means of production, and for sociocultural obligations within and beyond the household.

Relief aid covers refugees' immediate subsistence needs. The move to development aid seldom extends beyond the reproduction of labour where, in particular, health and education problems are favoured. Rarely is the replacement value of the means of production addressed, especially the recurring costs of maintaining a productive agricultural landscape. Development aid never provides for meeting sociocultural obligations because relief agencies inappropriately assume that refugees do not continue these obligations.

This discussion of sustainable household income for refugees takes place in a broader national macroeconomic context and often specifically in a donor-funded refugee program framework. This chapter considers the sustainability of refugee projects in the Sudan and Tanzania, taking into account their refugee policies and the approaches followed in three refugee programs cofunded by the Dutch government: the Qala en Nahal and Eastern Refugee Programme in the Sudan and the Burundi refugee settlements in Tanzania. The chapter assesses the perceptions of sustainability of four different actors—the host country, the donor, the delivering agency and the refugee—and how these perceptions match the conditions for project sustainability that would encourage rural development.[1]

SUDAN AND TANZANIA:
COMPARATIVE FRAMEWORKS FOR REFUGEE ASSISTANCE

There are over 1,200,000 international refugees in the Sudan, although some 425,000 Sudanese have also fled the country. Over 2.5 million Sudanese are displaced within the Sudan, and over 1.8 million live as squatters around Khartoum. Most foreign refugees—over 780,000 from Ethiopia—are settled in eastern Sudan, with others in Khartoum, Kosti, Wad Medani and Port Sudan. The Sudan has traditionally provided refugees with a hospitable reception (Rogge 1985b). Refugees receive support structured by the Sudanese government from the UNHCR, the World Food Programme, the European Community, bilateral commodity aid and NGO programs. In recent years, as the refugee displaced population has increased and as its own economy has declined, the Sudanese government has indicated to donors that it cannot accept more refugees. Simultaneously, it has requested more aid from the international community when donors were reducing their resource transfers to the Sudan (Kilgour 1990).

The administrative structure for all donors is dominated by the Sudanese Commissioner for Refugees, who operates at a quasi-ministerial level, while the Commission for Refugees has the authority to handle financial planning matters and relations with donors that are more usually associated with government ministries. The Commission for Refugees is dominated by former or current military officers. Its military hierarchy is not necessarily conducive to sustainable rural development. At a regional level, the Regional Commissioner for Refugees has responsibility for all legal issues, including land allocation.

There are five aspects of Sudanese policies that are particularly relevant to the projects considered here: (1) a settlement should not provide the refugees with more resources or care than is extended to nationals in the area, or more than they formerly had access to in their own country; (2) settlements will be set up so as not to dispossess nationals in the area of land or of opportunity; (3) services provided to the refugees must also be available to the local population; (4) settlements must be attractive enough to retain refugees, while at the same time not attract a further influx; (5) refugees in the Sudan are not entitled to take up employment outside the specified settlement area. It is clear that in the Sudan, if the success of refugee settlements is to be constrained by the Sudanese government's five aims, the potential for developing the settlements is very low.

At the present time, there are over 250,000 refugees in Tanzania (United Nations 1990). Tanzania is a hospitable host country for refugees with an open-door policy backed by a commitment to the principle of *nonrefoulement* (i.e., no refugee should be forced to return to his or her area of origin). Permanent settlements are away from border areas to minimize conflict. Refugee settlements have been developed under regulations covering the establishment of *ujamaa* villages with communal forms of agricultural production (Rogge 1985a). The Tanzanian government considers granting citizenship to refugees who stay longer than seven years. The financing for the settlements is through a tripartite arrangement between the government of Tanzania, UNHCR and the Tanganyikan Christian Refugee Services (TCRS), which is tied to the Lutheran World Federation. The government of Tanzania provides land and community services; UNHCR provides funds and technical advice; and TCRS provides staff coordinators, particularly for health and education services.

There are significant differences between the rights of the host and refugee populations. The refugee population does not have automatic access to secondary education, to work permits or to freedom of association and movement. A settlement is overseen by a Tanzanian administrator who is responsible for law and order, and who is assisted by a TCRS coordinator for development activities.

In general, rights of refugees are stronger in Tanzania than in the Sudan. Land grants in Tanzania to facilitate rural development are, in most cases, more favourable than in the Sudan, where the policy is not directed towards self-sufficient farms. In many ways, this reflects not only greater land availability in Tanzanian refugee settlement areas but also a different rural development policy in general. It may also reflect the Tanzanian government's more realistic assessment of the refugees' rather limited possibilities for returning home. In the Sudan the situation is quite different. Both the Sudanese government and the refugees, who are mostly from Ethiopia, never give up the hope of returning, even strengthening that hope by maintaining the cultural differences that set them apart from the host population.

RURAL DEVELOPMENT AND REFUGEE SETTLEMENTS IN EASTERN SUDAN

There are probably about 1.2 million international refugees in the Sudan, of whom approximately 780,000 are in Kassala province (ETC 1990b). In 1988 the total population of Kassala province was 2.7 million. The population increase, including the refugee influx, was about 5.6 percent per annum. Refugees from Ethiopia started to arrive in 1967. Initially they were held in transit camps, but when short-term repatriation seemed unfeasible, they were relocated to more than thirty permanent settlements, many of them along the Khartoum to Kassala highway. Earlier refugees found agricultural jobs in this area, but those who followed later were unable to find similar employment. In order to enable refugees to become self-sufficient, the later settlements have been smaller, with populations from 5,000 to 10,000. Access to land for farming is easier where settlements are smaller.

The Qala en Nahal (QEN) and Eastern Sudan Refugee Programme (ESRF) settlements are in the zone of mechanized farming near Gedaref. The climate is semiarid with a highly variable rainfall and a long dry season. The soil is fertile, but requires crop rotation and a fallow period every other year to maintain fertility, particularly if the tree cover is removed. Approximately half of the clay plains are cultivated, while the rocky areas are used for livestock grazing. Deforestation for agriculture and charcoal production has reduced the tree cover to less than 5 percent of the area. Before the land was cleared, much of the area was wooded rangeland.

Qala en Nahal

Qala en Nahal (QEN) is the largest and oldest of the Ethiopian refugee settlements. Approximately 30,000 refugees live in six villages. Four of the villages have Sudanese populations. The Sudanese households have been allocated areas of land that are approximately five to six times larger than those allocated to the refugees. This was justified as a compensation for loss of the local population's traditional rights to land in the area of the scheme. The refugees had to clear their land before project machinery prepared it for cultivation, whereas the Sudanese had their land both cleared and prepared for them.

QEN was originally established by the government of Sudan to create self-sufficient agricultural settlements. The first refugee families were all granted land. A fleet of tractors was provided by UNHCR. Responsibility was transferred to local government in 1974, but the scheme rapidly declined until 1978 when UNHCR undertook responsibility with the cooperation of ACORD, a consortium of NGOs.

Land within the QEN project was divided into blocks of about 4 hectares. Each refugee family was initially allocated one block, though later families received as little as 1 hectare, and the most recent did not receive any land at all. This land shortage is a critical problem. Agriculture, livestock rearing (the preferred activity), wage employment and small business activity are the economic bases of refugee subsistence. Approximately 40 percent of households have some cattle and about 30 percent have small stock and donkeys. Poorer households depend on casual wage employment. Major crops are sorghum and sesame; the QEN project is attempting to promote sesame, legumes and a range of other crops, such as sunflower and millet. When the project was started in 1968, it had three immediate objectives: to relocate 23,000 refugees from nearby Kassala; to make the refugees self-supporting as quickly as possible; and to use a potentially productive but mainly unused area of land that was at that time well wooded, 75 percent of which was considered cultivable (Rogge 1975).

Since 1980 the project's aim of making refugees self-sufficient continues, but it is also meant to help the local Sudanese in the same way. Initially this was to be achieved by providing tractors for hire on small holdings. Subsequently, broader support for agriculture and pastoralism was to be given through a research and extension program. Attempts are being made to widen the economic basis of self-sufficiency.

From 1981 onwards, ACORD concentrated on maintaining and renewing the tractor fleet, but in 1986 it started to tackle problems associated with farming the area—investigating the suitability of crop varieties, controlling weeds and pests and land rotation. At the same time, *hafirs* (reservoirs) were constructed for livestock water supply and drinking water supply. During the 1985–1986 droughts, the project had to revert to food distribution, and refugee dependence increased for some time. The current 1989–1993 program aims to achieve phased withdrawal of support, so that the settlements should be self-sustaining by 1993. The 1981 program included tractor hire, improved crop production, extension of credit, grain security, livestock health, water supply, afforestation and women's activities.

Since a redefinition of goals in 1990, emphasis has been on providing tractors on credit rather than for hire, establishing privately-run rather than ACORD-run repair workshops, and generating small businesses and other sources of self-sustaining income, including those through women's groups. In this way, the project attempts an integrated rural development approach covering a wide variety of activities that include broadening the range of cropping, extending the use of tractors to some 30,000 hectares of land preparation, improving livestock quality and water supply for herders, establishing forest nurseries and setting up a special women's program. These activities have resulted in improved incomes. The credit program has had less success because of severe problems with debt repayments, grain security and reforestation. Environmental deterioration is evident in the marked reduction of tree cover that is lost mostly through commercial charcoal production, in soil deterioration and pressure on limited water supplies.

Eastern Sudan Refugee Programme

The Eastern Sudan Refugee Programme began in 1976 at Wad Hileau in six main areas: Umrakoba, Umgurgur, Aburakham, Umgulja, Es Suki and Um Sagata. There was a large increase in the number of refugees in 1985. By 1986 there were sixteen settlements providing health services, social services and primary education for over 100,000 Ethiopian refugees from Tigray, Gonder and Welo, though initially most of the refugees were from Eritrea. They were provided with some land for cultivation.

Sorghum, the traditional subsistence crop in this region, has been cultivated by refugees, who have also undertaken paid seasonal agricultural work. Droughts between 1985 and 1987 led to a 75 percent decline in rainfed sorghum, and because there were insufficient smallholder plots to supply enough sorghum, emergency food supplies were urgently needed for the influx of new refugees. ESRP administered a program of supplementary feeding for vulnerable groups, which included those on low incomes, pregnant women, nursing mothers and young children.

By 1990 the settlements had stabilized, and there was a small surplus of food production. There is some diversification of farming into poultry and vegetable production and diversification of small businesses within older settlements. Unfortunately, land is available for refugees in only four of the six areas. Consequently, refugee families must rely on mostly illegal wage labour or migrate to Khartoum in search of work. All land remains the property of the government of Sudan.

The Sudan Council of Churches (SCC) is responsible for managing the ESRP. The project's general objective is to improve the basic living conditions for refugees through health, education and social services, and to assist in employment creation. These aims were to be implemented through developing preventive health care programs, maintaining the level of medical services, improving delivery of consumer goods, providing food at reception centres, providing supplementary feeding to vulnerable groups, monitoring social programs (counselling, education, self-help), providing support to women's groups and strengthening agricultural extension services.

To undertake these activities, the ESRP program employs a staff of about 700, one-third of whom are refugees. Limited access to land is a severe constraint on success, and the focus of the project and its major expenditure is on health care provision. More attention has been given to social welfare and agriculture in recent years. Some 250 refugee staff members, led by an expatriate doctor and five other expatriates, work on the health program, which consists mainly of curative services through a system of clinics. The health service covers a wider area than the six settlements, and is also available to the Sudanese population.

The social program has three components: education, social counselling (from which a separate women's program has developed) and self-help activities, including employment creation in family businesses, such as butcher shops, tea shops, leather works and cotton weaving.

To some extent, the project has been successful in creating stable settlements, since these are the delivery points of a range of services. Furthermore, the population's health and nutrition standards have improved, and immunization programs have been very successful. Moreover, the Sudanese have access to free health care. Up to 60 percent of out-patient consultations in some clinics are with Sudanese, some of whom travel long distances for the free service. There has been some success in broadening the range of economic activities. The supplementary feeding program has been used by up to 38 percent of children under five during crisis years, as in 1986. Primary health care, staffed mostly by refugee women, is well developed.

The focus of the whole program has been on welfare rather than production. If donor finances were withdrawn, the project would collapse from rapid staff turnover, bureaucratic inefficiency and irregular cash flow. In particular, the limited availability of land critically reduces the possibility of building a sustainable base in agriculture, and the limited support for agriculture (2 percent of total expenditure) implies a lack of will to build the economic base. Women's activities have been taken up by less than 0.5 percent of those women who are eligible. Environmental degradation, particularly soil deterioration and deforestation, has led to a 75 percent decline in crop yields in five years. Population growth through natural increase and immigration adds to environmental degradation of the limited land available. The focus on welfare provision rather than production makes this project unsustainable. Consequently, the project ran into a financial crisis in 1990. In addition, the provision of services encountered sociocultural obstacles. For example, delivery of primary education to children and adults is made difficult by the Sudanese government's insistence that secondary education must be Arabic-based. However, refugees want to maintain their Amharic culture and language, which is reasonable as they intend to return to Ethiopia.

RURAL DEVELOPMENT AND REFUGEE SETTLEMENTS IN TANZANIA

Refugees from Burundi arrived in 1972–1973 after ethnic conflicts between the Tutsi and Hutu. An estimated total of 100,000 Hutu fled from Burundi to Tanzania. After a short period of emergency aid, the refugees were placed in two settlements: the Ulyankulu area (in the Urambo district, Tabora province) and the Katumba area (in the Mpanda district, Rukwa province). In 1978–1979 some 25,000 refugees from Ulyankulu were transferred to a third settlement, Mishamo, together with approximately 3,000 new refugees. The total population of the three settlements was estimated at 132,000 by the end of the 1980s (Gasarasi 1984; United Nations 1990).

In 1972 the area of the settlements was almost uninhabited woodland at an altitude of some 1,000 metres with an average precipitation of 750 mm per annum. The area is rather inhospitable because of mosquitoes and tsetse flies. Population densities are low—seven to ten people per square kilometre, and uncultivated land is easily available. In the Mpanda district, for example, only one quarter of the area is under cultivation. The settlement areas are also isolated; roads have been constructed, but many are impassible during the rainy season.

Immediately after their arrival, refugees received plots of land, tools and seeds. After clearing the bush, they started cultivating food crops (maize, beans, cassava) and became self-sufficient in food within four to five years. During the initial period, additional food was issued through the World Food Programme. After a few years cash crops, such as ground-nuts, tobacco, soya beans, sesame and rice were introduced. In addition, refugees took up other activities, such as poultry farming, brick and charcoal burning, carpentry and trade. Many refugee households now produce a surplus, but marketing crops is difficult due to the isolation of the area and the poor functioning of the cooperatives. Consequently, many households have only a meagre cash income. In Ulyankulu, for example, the average income level was two-thirds of the Tabora Region's average (Christensen 1985).

Refugees live in villages; 250 to 600 households form a village. A varying number of villages form a settlement. Katumba, the largest of the three settlements, consists of twenty-nine villages. Construction of roads, houses and buildings for various community services started immediately after the selection of the area. Much of the construction work was done by the refugees, but they were also employed as wage labourers. At present, the settlements are well provided with primary schools, community development centres, health centres and dispensaries, post offices, bus services, etc. These services are better than average for rural Tanzania.

The project, "Strengthening Refugee Health and Community Services," was the result of an earmarked contribution to the TCRS program, which followed ICARA II (the second International Conference on Assistance to Refugees in Africa). This project, which was financed by the Netherlands, had three components: training health staff (thirty health assistants, fifteen mother-and-child aids, 192 village health workers) from the refugee communities; establishing health libraries at a district school for health assistants and a district hospital, and constructing three rural development centres (RDCs).

The purpose of training refugee health workers was to ease the pressure of the refugee population on district health facilities. The training institutions themselves were assisted by being given health library facilities. The RDCs were intended to enhance the refugee communities' socio-economic development by providing facilities for offices, shops, day-care centres, cooperative enterprises, adult education and meetings of different refugee groups.

The project has been only partly successful. RDCs were constructed mostly by refugees. Libraries were established, but two years after the start of the project, some of the books and equipment had still not arrived. Health staff training was never started at all, due to a last-minute change of mind by the Tanzanian authorities, who were opposed to a separate school for training refugees and could not or would not guarantee employing health-care personnel because it had to reduce its health budget.

The project's contribution to rural development is meagre, when one considers that the Netherlands' assistance was meant to expand social services. For unknown reasons, the Netherlands rejected the idea of contributing to the improvement of production-oriented activities. The sustainability of the Netherlands' contribution (RDCs and libraries) is doubtful. Overall, the favourable conditions for production (particularly the availability of adequate land resources) for refugees and the sound institutional setting contribute strongly to the sustainability of the project.

PROBLEMS IN ESTABLISHING THE REFUGEE SETTLEMENTS

Sudan

A number of problems were common to both the QEN and SCC refugee settlements; in particular, politics and the environment put severe constraints on project success. The Sudanese government's insistence that living conditions for refugees should not be better than those for Sudanese nationals, and that Sudanese nationals should have at least equal access to facilities, curtailed the success of the project by limiting inputs of aid and ensuring that the beneficial effects for refugees would be spread thinly. This is particularly clear in health care provision in SCC settlements. It can be argued that benefits to Sudanese nationals contribute to rural development. Nevertheless, their gain is the refugees' loss.

Environmental problems—such as soil erosion and degradation, deforestation, overgrazing, inadequate water supply and weed infestation—are common to both areas. Decreased yields and increased time spent in gathering fuelwood and water have resulted. Many of the problems were predictable in a semiarid climate with variable rainfall, yet the ultimate explanation for limited success lies in the land-use systems and the limited access to resources.

It must be noted that limited land availability is explained partly by the government's policy on land allocation and partly by competition with absentee owners of large mechanized farms, who have considerable political influence. Access to fuelwood has been made difficult by competition with tree-cutting charcoal producers, and off-site grazing leads to competition with local Sudanese pastoralists. In QEN farmers preferred the security of livestock rearing rather than crop production because many of the refugees came from areas where pastoralism was the norm and crop yields were decreasing. Both schemes were forced to return to famine relief in 1985–1986 when harvests failed, which set back considerably the hope of long-term sustainable development.

The project delivery agencies' contrasting attitudes explain some of the SCC settlement difficulties. At QEN the focus on self-sufficiency and sustainability was built in at the start of the project and has been reinforced at various stages. SCC settlements, in contrast, have been very dependent on external inputs because the focus has been on welfare rather than production, and on the health sector rather than agriculture. In addition, a large proportion of the budget was needed to finance administration and transport.

Tanzania

Problems in establishing the Tanzanian refugee settlements were caused by the natural environment, the government's policies and the implementing agency's approach. The environment in which the refugees were settled was given inadequate attention during the initial phase of setting up the settlements. Agriculture was soil-exhaustive without the use of crop rotation or fertilizer. The introduction of cattle encountered serious difficulties because of tsetse flies (Christensen 1985). These problems have been tackled successfully. The most significant development was the resettlement of some 25,000 refugees when a soil survey in Ulyankulu showed that the size of the refugee population exceeded the carrying capacity of the land. In addition, different farming methods were introduced and soil conservation practices were encouraged.

Tanzanian government policies clashed with the refugees' ideas on farming methods. The refugee settlers rejected communal production by means of block farms and mechanization, and continued to use family farms and hoe cultivation. The introduction of tobacco created a conflict between Tanzanian authorities and Pentecostal church leaders, who dissuaded their followers from growing this crop. As one commentator noted, "the Tanzanian authorities took corrective measures and the situation became [sic] under control" (Gasarasi 1984, 40).

A much more serious obstacle in agricultural production was the cooperative system's poor performance. Although primary societies were operating quite efficiently, the regional cooperative union in Tabora could not afford to purchase seeds for the crops from the primary societies in 1987–1989. Private traders did not regard the settlements as an important area of supply, so the settlements had to sell their crops at lower prices and were subject to irregular collection of their produce.

Finally, there were some problems related to project design and TCRS policy, such as the initial lack of attention to refugee participation in planning and decision making, and the priority given to physical infrastructure and social services, to the detriment of production. At a later stage, village leaders were elected, communication with refugees improved, and priorities reflected the ideas of the refugee community to a greater extent.

In spite of these problems, the establishment of the refugee settlement was fairly successful. Within a relatively short period, refugees were self-sufficient in food, earned incomes through the production of cash crops, and had access to relatively good quality community services.

FACTORS DETERMINING THE SUSTAINABILITY OF THE PROJECTS

Sustainability of development projects has been defined as the ability to deliver an appropriate level of benefits after the termination of major financial, technical and managerial assistance from an external donor. The Development Assistance Committee of the OECD's report (1988) identified factors that influence the sustainability of project results. These factors may be grouped into three categories: project design features; financial, organizational, sociocultural and environmental characteristics of the project area; and the wider macroeconomic and policy environment of the country in which the project is implemented. In the case of a multidonor project—and most refugee projects are of this type—it is not appropriate to limit the sustainability analysis to one individual donor's contribution. Such analysis must consider the project as a whole.

Project design features with a positive influence on sustainability were the formulation of clear goals, the execution of a feasibility study with due attention to the resource base, detailed work plans, a high degree of flexibility and opportunities to experiment and learn from experience. These features were observed in the QEN and the Tanzanian refugee settlements. Such features are necessary preconditions for sustainability, as they determine project results during the donor support phase. They also lay the foundation for success after the termination of support.

Financial sustainability is influenced to a larger extent by the availability of adequate productive resources. With limited nonagricultural employment opportunities for refugees in the Sudan and Tanzania, this effectively means that there must be sufficient land and livestock resources to generate household incomes to sustain social reproduction. All three projects showed striking deficiencies in this respect, with the SCC refugee project in the weakest position, as productive resources were severely limited here and the project basically operated relief services that were not financially sustainable. The QEN scheme had improved its resource base and achieved self-sufficiency in food, but opportunities for cash income were limited and fodder for the increasing herds of livestock had to be collected partly outside the project area. The Tanzanian settlements enjoyed the most favourable situation with large tracts of uncultivated land around the settlements. This allowed for self-sufficiency, the production of surplus food and sufficient land for the refugees to cultivate cash crops.

In all three project areas, primary education, health services and drinking water supplies were made available. Facilities were constructed through donor aid and provided free of charge, with the exception of water supply in the QEN scheme. Maintenance of the services requires either some form of user charges to recover costs or permanent support from the government budget. Under the present conditions in the Sudan and Tanzania, such permanent government support is not to be expected and priority must be given to cost recovery. The QEN project showed a weakness in many cost recovery systems. The payment arrangement applied in QEN did not adequately sustain the drinking water facilities, as the money "disappeared" in provincial government coffers.

Project management, the incorporation of the project into the framework of administration and the degree of people's participation in both planning and implementation affect sustainability. There are significant contrasts in this respect between the Sudan and Tanzania. Whereas the government of Sudan set up a structure under the Commissioner's Office for Refugees, the government of Tanzania incorporated the refugee settlements into the normal administration system and created a balance of power between the settlement commander and the TCRS coordinator within the framework of the tripartite agreement.

Both the Tanzanian settlements and QEN were fortunate in having experienced executing organizations and significant participation through elected bodies, although the latter only materialized gradually. During the initial period of settlement, little attention was paid to refugee participation, apart from having them provide free labour. The SCC had a hierarchical and centralized administration with little devolution of authority to the field staff.

Environmental factors were important in both countries, as refugees were settled in relatively inhospitable natural environments. In both the Tanzanian settlements of Ulyankulu and the Sudanese settlement of QEN, insufficient attention was given initially to the land's long-term carrying capacity. In both projects, however, agricultural practices were modified to fit the environmental situation in order to enhance sustainability. These modifications were not entirely successful. For example, the QEN refugees showed little interest in tree planting and preferred to expand their herds as a form of mobile capital that could be taken back to their area of origin, even though fodder had to be collected partly outside the project area. The environmental factor was of little relevance in the SCC project, as the refugees had limited access to land.

Sociocultural factors played a role in both the Tanzanian settlements and QEN, but in different ways. In the Tanzanian settlements the Hutu refugees were familiar with agricultural practices in general, but they also quickly adopted new crops and appropriate crop husbandry. In QEN the refugees were mostly nomadic and seminomadic pastoralists who had to change their lifestyles drastically and become arable farmers practising crop rotation. Although a substantial number of refugees had problems in adjusting, they succeeded in making the switch.

A particular problem in the SCC program was the government of Sudan's insistence on using Arabic as the medium of instruction for secondary education versus the refugees' desire to maintain their Amharic culture, so the refugees arranged an education program to support their own culture and language. At QEN the credit scheme has been threatened because lending for profit is not acceptable under Sharia law. Furthermore, rates of repayment have been poor. Sheiks were unwilling to undertake debt collection since they claimed that they were not involved or insufficiently involved in the initial lending procedures.

Differing sociocultural frameworks of governments, refugees and agencies often lead to conflicts. These may appear tiresome, sometimes even ridiculous. It would, however, be inequitable if the refugees' cultural system were to be singled out as the obstacle to progress and the only part of the system requiring change. Regardless of whether the refugees settle permanently or are ultimately repatriated, their sociocultural system should not bear the brunt of changes.

Government policies towards refugees were more favourable in Tanzania than in the Sudan. In Tanzania refugees were provided with adequate land and standard services by government organizations. The government of Tanzania seriously considers granting citizenship to long-term residents. In the Sudan provision of land to both refugees and Sudanese was hampered by government priorities for large-scale mechanized farming. Land, equipment, seeds and fertilizers for this type of farming were available at subsidized rates, with preferential access to these resources for the urban elite.

Macroeconomic conditions in both countries have had a negative impact on rural development in general and sustainability of project results in particular. This is, however, much more serious in the Sudan than in Tanzania. Tanzania, under structural adjustment policies, has experienced a shift in rural-urban trade with higher food prices in urban areas and a substantial increase of private traders' share in the marketing of food crops. Because of competitive market conditions, private traders carefully consider transport costs, which have led to lower prices paid to growers in the remoter parts of Tanzania, including the refugee settlements. Export crops are still, to a large extent, marketed through the cooperative system, but cooperatives have serious financial and management problems that negatively influence the sustainability of the refugee settlements.

In the Sudan macroeconomic conditions have been disastrous for rural development due to the civil war between north and south, enormous foreign debts, high inflation rates and serious balance of payment problems. In addition, the country has been declared a noncooperating country by the International Monetary Fund, which blocks its access to IMF loan facilities. Finally, Sudanese development policies favour the urban areas, irrigated agriculture, large-scale mechanized farms and higher income groups. Under these conditions, it seems impossible to achieve sustainability in refugee projects.

The preceding analysis reveals the overriding importance of macroeconomic conditions and policies and availability of productive resources to generate income for the sustainability of project results. Environmental limitations and the degradation of environmental resources are evident in the areas of refugee settlements and influence the potential for income generation, thus limiting the settlements' sustainability.

CONCLUSIONS

Long-term refugee settlements require developmental initiatives, not merely relief activities. Relief programs, particularly those employing large numbers of refugees, are difficult to refocus from relief to developmental activities, not least because of the reduction in direct project employment. Ironically, given the commitment of donor NGOs to long-term relationships with local partners, these relief programs are frequently sustainable as programs even if they do not contribute to a broader goal of sustainable rural development. Most long-term relief programs move at some stage from food distribution to broader welfare services, particularly health and education, but find it difficult to develop further. This is partly because different skills and methods are needed, partly because a switch to development implies that the host government will make a political commitment to quasi-permanent settlement and that the refugees will realize that a return to the homeland may be impossible, at least in the immediate future.

Projects with a developmental perspective, particularly those emphasizing sustainable development, have a commitment to providing means of production, especially land. Yet in both Tanzania and the Sudan, the provision of land was not in itself sufficient to create opportunities for sustainable development. Lack of access to markets and income opportunities beyond the settlements, especially because of employment restrictions, have limited refugees' access to the development process. As a consequence, refugee settlements in the Sudan have faced limited availability of land and subsistence production.

These conclusions lead back to four perceptions of sustainability in refugee projects. For the donor a sustainable project is defined by its support, including long-term financing for an identifiable local group. This definition is restricted to project goals that can be focused on relief and that often loosely address sustainability in a macroeconomic and national policy context.

For the host country sustainability is defined as development without cost to the national capital, revenue budgets and local politics. This latter cost is hard to avoid if refugees appear to have more development inputs than the local host population. It would, in any case, be politically undesirable that refugees should appear to prosper more than hosts—even if the prosperity were not due to higher inputs of resources. From a political perspective, the host country does not wish refugee settlements to fail absolutely, nor does it wish them to succeed to the extent that it shows up government failure to support its own nationals. It is politically convenient if they just subsist. For a number of reasons, host countries limit refugees' access to productive resources and government services, and thus restrict sustainable development.

To the program delivery agency sustainability is probably, but not necessarily, the ultimate aim. Conventional wisdom is that NGOs do not have the political constraints of donor and host governments, and can thus be more "objective." Objectivity is always bounded, in this case, by the aims and ethos of the agency. For fund-raising purposes, it is valuable for agencies to be seen relieving suffering, saving lives, fighting disease, spreading education, "spreading the word," in other words, effectively providing relief. Few agencies have the skills needed for development of long-term sustainability. Some may, in truth, have little commitment to sustainability as opposed to relief.

For the refugees themselves, sustainability implies the maintenance of social reproduction. However, quite often the possibilities for this are limited, forcing them to find illegal sources of income. This, coupled with the hope of returning home, encourages short- rather than long-term strategies, such as developing a sustainable rural landscape and putting down roots for their children's children.

NOTES

1. Much of the empirical data in this chapter is taken from internal reports for the Netherlands' Ministry of Foreign Affairs, in particular CDP (Consultants for Development Programmes) and ETC (Netherlands). The data were collected in the framework of an evaluation study of the Netherlands' sector program for rural development, coordinated by the Operations Review Unit of the Directorate General for International Cooperation of the Netherlands' Ministry of Foreign Affairs. The authors wish to thank Karel Ungheim for his assistance in the analysis of the Tanzania material and data, and Ian Cherrett for his comments on the paper.

REFERENCES

Cherrett, I., J. Kirkby, O. Marleyn, B. Munslow and P. O'Keefe. 1990. "Norwegian Aid and the Environment in Mozambique: The Issues, DERAP Working Paper D. 1990:16." Bergen: Christian Michelson Institute.

Christensen, H. 1985. "Refugees and Pioneers: History and Field Study of a Burundian Settlement in Tanzania." Report No. 85.4. Geneva: United National Research Institute for Social Development.

Consultants for Development Programmes. 1990. "ICARA II: Refugee Support." Utrecht: Consultants for Development Programmes. Internal report of a project evaluation of Netherlands assistance to refugee settlements in Rukwa and Tabora regions, Tanzania.

Development Assistance Committee of the OECD. 1988. *Sustainability of Development Programmes: A Compendium of Donor Experience.* Paris: Development Assistance Committee of the OECD.

ETC (Netherlands) 1990a. "Ethiopian Refugees, ICCO/SCC." Internal report of a project evaluation of Netherlands assistance to refugees in Sudan. Leusden: ETC Foundation.

———. 1990b. "The Qala en Nahal Refugee Scheme." Internal report of a project evaluation of Netherlands assistance to refugees in Sudan. Leusden: ETC Foundation.

Gasarasi, C.P. 1984. "The Tripartite Approach to the Resettlement and Integration of Rural Refugees in Tanzania." Report No. 71. Uppsala: Scandinavian Institute of African Studies.

Kilgour, M. 1990. "Refugees and Development: Dissonance in Sudan." *Middle East Journal* 44.

Pearce, D., A. Markandya and E. Barber. 1989. *Blueprint for a Green Economy*. London: Earthscan.

Rogge, J.R. 1975. "The Qala en Nahal Refugee Settlement Scheme." *Sudan Notes and Records* 54:130–46.

————. 1985a. "Africa's Displaced Population: Dependency or Self-Sufficiency?" In *Population and Development Projects in Africa*, edited by J.I. Clarke, M. Khogali and L.A. Kosinski, 68–83. Cambridge: Cambridge University Press.

————. 1985b. *Too Many, Too Long: Sudan's Twenty-Year Refugee Dilemma*. Totowa: Rowman & Allanheld.

Turner, R.K., ed. 1988. *Sustainable Environmental Management: Principles and Practice*. London: Belhaven.

United Nations. 1990. "UNHCR Activities Financed by Voluntary Funds: Report for 1989–90 and Proposed Programmes and Budget for 1991, Part I, Africa." Report A/AC 96/751 (Part I). Geneva: United Nations.

World Commission on Environment and Development. 1987. *Our Common Future*. Oxford: Oxford University Press.

11

Government-Sponsored Agricultural Schemes for Involuntary Migrants in Africa: Some Key Obstacles to Their Economic Viability

Véronique Lassailly-Jacob

A wide range of land resettlement schemes have been implemented in Africa since the colonial period. The purposes of early large-scale settlements were either political (to establish European settlements) or humanitarian (to evacuate areas infected with sleeping sickness). Neither implied agricultural development.[1] People continued to practise traditional farming systems before and after the move (Chambers 1969).

This chapter deals with land resettlement schemes that attempt agricultural development. Such schemes have been sponsored by governments and international agencies as part of a rural development strategy in Africa. They imply a planned and controlled transfer of population towards underused or unused arable lands that should be exploited through agricultural intensification. Creating new economically and socially viable rural communities that foster regional and even national development are the main purposes.

Two types can be identified, depending on the nature of the migration. The first and most widespread comprises motivated risk taking and selected households willing to settle in planned agricultural projects for economic reasons. These settlers are usually called voluntary migrants or economic migrants because they have a degree of choice about migrating.

The subject of this chapter is the second, more contained community. It comprises entire rural communities that are forced to move temporarily or permanently from their homelands and that are channelled by governments towards agricultural schemes. These are involuntary migrants; their forced migration is used by the authorities as an opportunity for developing new lands. Among involuntary migrants are refugees who are channelled towards agricultural schemes in order to regain self-sufficiency in host countries.

The overall purposes of such schemes are to assist the settlers in becoming economically self-sufficient and even to raise their previous standard of living. They should also contribute to national development by producing surplus food crops and cash crops. Despite commendable governmental efforts and substantial assistance, the results have been disappointing. It often takes many years before newcomers achieve self-sufficiency or even their previous standard of living. By comparing some agricultural schemes implemented for involuntary migrants, this chapter points out some key obstacles that prevent such schemes from achieving economic viability.

WHO ARE THE INVOLUNTARY MIGRANTS?

Forced relocation towards agricultural schemes can be caused by three major agents: national development policies, wars and political turmoil, and ecological and natural disasters.

National Development Policies

Resettlement can be an element of planned change undertaken by governments for national or regional development. Planned agricultural schemes involving involuntary settlers appeared during the colonial period. Between 1946 and 1950, for example, almost 50,000 families, virtually the whole Azande population in southern Sudan, was forcibly resettled on organized holdings where cotton cultivation was compulsory (Reining 1982).

Since the 1960s, a new generation of resettlement projects, including agricultural development programs, has started in independent states. Most remarkable has been the compulsory relocation of large communities resulting from dam construction and the formation of man-made lakes. The Akosombo dam, built in 1964 across the Volta River in Ghana, disrupted the life of 80,000 people. The Aswan High Dam, built in Egypt in 1969, flooded the homeland of over 100,000 Nubian people. Half were resettled around Kom-Ombo (New Nubia) in Upper Egypt, and the other half around Khashm el-Girba (New Halfa) in the Sudan. The Kossou dam, built in 1970 on the Bandama River in Côte d'Ivoire, forced 75,000 people to move. The Kariba dam, built in 1968 on the Zambezi River in Zambia, and the Kainji dam built in 1968 on the Niger River in Nigeria, each affected about 50,000 people. Recently, the Manantali dam built on a Senegal river's tributary in

Mali caused the relocation of 10,000 people. All these evacuees were re-settled on government-sponsored agricultural schemes and development assistance is provided to help them regain their self-sufficiency and even to raise their standard of living as compensation. Several other dam projects that will disrupt the lives of many people are under construction or have been planned.

Another example of planned resettlement resulting from development policy is massive population redistribution. Three major reasons are advanced: maximized utilization of a nation's resources, strategic considerations or counterinsurgency policy and apartheid policies. Most planned mass population removals are accompanied by agricultural programs.

In Ethiopia, especially after the revolution and the nationalization of rural lands, planned agricultural settlement schemes were carried out for the scattered rural population (Wood 1985). In Tanzania, the so-called "villagization program" meant a massive redistribution that shifted over five million peasants from scattered homesteads into nucleated settlements of 250 to 600 households each. The government's objective was to bring farmers together in villages to benefit from improved services, agricultural intensification and the advantages of cooperative agriculture (McCall 1985). In Mozambique, after the 1975 independence, the government declared that rural development would be based on "communal villages." Scattered and isolated family compounds were forcibly regrouped along the roads (De Araujo 1985).

Another example of forced relocation is the "sedentarization" of pastoral nomads or shifting cultivators. This policy is usually motivated by governments' own administrative and economic purposes. Nomads are introduced to settled agriculture through irrigation schemes that are sometimes located on their traditional dry-season grazing areas, such as in the Khashm el-Girba scheme in the Sudan (Hoyle 1977) or in the Ogaden desert in Ethiopia (Wood 1985).

Redistributing the population because of strategic considerations is yet another example. During the armed struggle for national liberation in Mozambique during the 1970s, the Portuguese colonizers forcibly resettled the rural population into protected villages (De Araujo 1985). As a counter-insurgency policy, the French army undertook a massive policy of *regroupment* during the 1954–1961 Algerian war of independence. This policy was implemented in order to protect the rural population and prevent them from actively assisting the guerrillas; a few years later it was turned into an attempt at rural development (Sutton 1977, 285).

In South Africa, forced and mass population displacements have been linked to implementing apartheid policies. More than seven million blacks were affected by resettlement into areas known as the "homelands." One type of displacement involved resettlement schemes for the "agricultural betterment" of the homelands. This meant reorganizing dispersed rural communities into a series of planned agricultural villages (Rogerson and Letsoalo 1985).

Wars and Political Turmoil

Anticolonial insurrections and civil wars are the main reasons behind population displacement in Africa. In the late 1980s, one African migrant out of five was a refugee; about six million uprooted people—at least half of the world's refugee population—were located in Africa.

For many years, refugee assistance amounted mainly to emergency relief provided in reception camps. Contemporary refugee movements, however, have been on a much larger scale and of a much longer duration. Maintaining large refugee communities creates enormous economic and social burdens for the asylum countries. They ask for international assistance to help them resettle refugees with programs for agricultural development. The United Nations High Commissioner for Refugees (UNHCR), many nongovernmental organizations and some host governments have attempted to achieve local integration and economic self-sufficiency of refugee communities through organized rural settlements.

Rural development schemes for refugees first appeared as a form of UNHCR assistance in the early 1960s. The first one, Bibwe in Kivu, Zaire, opened in October 1961 for Rwandan Tutsi refugees. From 1961 to 1987, more than 200 refugee settlements were opened in Africa, assisting some one million refugees in the Sudan, Zaire, Tanzania, Uganda, Burundi, Botswana and Zambia (Stein and Clark 1990).

Ecological and Natural Disasters

Relief assistance is generally the only form of assistance provided to victims of disasters. However, mass movements of population caused by natural calamities were channelled towards resettlement schemes. A number of resettlement projects were carried out as a result of ecological disasters, especially drought. In Ethiopia, famine victims affected by recurring drought in Welo and Tigray provinces in 1977–1978 were resettled in development villages (Wood 1985). The drought in northern Kenya in the early 1970s forced Somali nomads to resettle on irrigated farms along the Tana River (Merryman 1982). Frequent flooding has also created mass population movements.

Assistance in Agricultural Schemes

Agricultural settlement schemes have received high priority for government and international aid. They are often initiated by newly created national agencies helped by international agencies, such as the World Bank, the Food and Agricultural Organization, the World Food Programme (WFP), the UNHCR and nongovernmental organizations. The UNHCR is especially involved in assisting rural refugee settlements. Host governments participate by providing arable land and staff. Once these agricultural schemes are deemed self-sufficient, they are handed over to local authorities; this means they are cut off from international assistance and integrated into the local administrative framework.

Most schemes receive high infrastructural investments in order to create modern rural communities. Basic infrastructures are provided, such as access roads, drinking water, cleared sites; less often provided are ready-built houses or building materials, education, health services and other community services. Food rations are usually supplied by the WFP for two or more years. Most schemes are also conceived to develop new lands under agricultural intensification. Major land development around the newly created villages is often achieved through reclamation, clearing, levelling or irrigation. Settlers are allotted farms, tools, seeds and fertilizers, and are provided with technical assistance and expertise. Such new communities are supposed to become economically and socially integrated through high infrastructural investments and improved agricultural programs.

A new settlement's economic viability is attained when the settlers reach a level of self-sufficiency and are productive members of the host society. However, self-sufficiency is a relative concept that is difficult to evaluate. Speaking of refugees living in organized settlements, Rogge finds the term self-sufficiency is used "to denote the subsequent attainment of complete independence from any form of external help, when refugees are not only self-reliant in their food production but are able to generate all their own infrastructural needs and requirements, so that settlements are fully self-contained units" (Rogge 1987, 87).

He points out the unreality of this definition since no rural community can be totally independent from any form of government assistance or subsidy. Criteria of self-sufficiency are usually defined according to the general standard of living achieved by the host communities: "Self- sufficiency can be seen as including reaching the economic level and general standard of living of the local community and being integrated into the economic life of the area on a sustainable basis" (Stein and Clark 1990, 8).

Being better off economically than the host population usually results in strained relationships. But can we speak of self-sufficiency when the economic level and general standard of living of the local community is below subsistence level, as is often the case (Kibreab 1987)? A refugee community is declared self-sufficient when, as a whole, it has reached a level of staple food self-sufficiency. However, discrepancies can exist among subgroups (Clark 1987, 17).

When an agricultural settlement is declared self-sufficient, vulnerable groups—the old, the disabled—are also declared self-sufficient even though they require permanent support and welfare. For the purpose of this chapter, economic viability of a new settlement means that settlers are self-reliant in food production and have surplus cash crops or income-generating activities that allow them to meet their other basic needs.

Let us now observe the situation of some agricultural resettlement schemes. With regard to organized refugee settlements, Stein and Clark (1990) mentioned that of 117 refugee settlements set up between 1961 and 1982, only fifty-nine were still operating in 1990. Eleven were abandoned and forty-seven were closed due to repatriation. Of those still operating, only thirty-two have sporadically been considered self-sufficient, although twenty-four of these have required renewed international aid. Thus, twenty-seven settlements had not yet attained self-sufficiency by 1982.

In the case of evacuees from man-made lakes, the results are no better, despite a greater level of assistance. Seven years after relocation on the Volta project in Ghana, for example, the relocatees were still on World Food Programme relief due to lack of arable lands. Some new towns became ghost towns as settlers left for the cities. In Côte d'Ivoire, the mechanized farming system introduced in the Kossou project failed after ten years, and many settlers left the area while others today are landless farmers. In New Nubia, Egypt, and New Halfa, Sudan, settlers have started leaving the re-settlement area to return and settle spontaneously on the lakeshore (Lassailly-Jacob 1983). In the Zande project as well, resettlement was soon regarded as a burden by those who were to benefit from it (Reining 1982).

Why do these development settlements, which receive such significant assistance, encounter so many difficulties in becoming viable communities? Many factors impede viability. All three partners involved in the resettle-ment process—the planners, the resettlers and the local population—share responsibilities in achieving economic viability.

OBSTACLES LINKED TO THE PLANNERS

Planners or developers are represented by governments, the international community and nongovernmental organizations. They are responsible for allocating the resources that settlers need to become an economically viable community: arable land, clean water, appropriate farming programs, income-generating activities and community services. They are also in charge of supervising the settlements, but first let us examine the geographical locations selected by planners.

Geographical Situation of the New Sites

While proper geographical location is critical, governments are usually solely responsible for selecting the new sites. In the case of evacuees from man-made lakes, two resettlement policies have been implemented with different consequences for self-sufficiency. The first considered where evacuees wanted to move—usually, as close as possible to their former habitat. While constituting a less painful move for evacuees, this may involve problems in connection with less fertile soils or lands already owned and farmed by host farmers. This was the case in the Kossou project (Côte d'Ivoire), the Volta project (Ghana) and the Kainji project (Nigeria).

The second policy imposed a new resettlement area on evacuees, sometimes far from their former habitat, as in the case of Nubian Sudanese who were moved more than 2,000 km. The farther the people are moved, the greater their resistance, but in the new areas selected by the authorities, settlers received large tracts of arable land (Lassailly-Jacob 1992).

Refugee agricultural settlements are often located in marginal and isolated areas where accessibility is a major problem. Most settlements are isolated. The official reason for putting them far from the borders is to protect them from potential guerrilla attacks. However, remoteness hinders marketing and trade and, thus, viability. Host governments choose remote and isolated areas to prevent refugees from integrating into local communities and competing with nationals for scarce resources and employment opportunities (Kibreab 1989).

Land and Hydrological Surveys

Availability and quality of arable land are basic prerequisites for attaining self-sufficiency in food production. This is, however, often neglected by planners when they rush to select new sites. Many settlements are selected after inadequate baseline surveys or land feasibility studies. For example, a faulty land survey in Ulyankulu (a refugee settlement in Tanzania), resulted in a mass transfer of 25,000 of 60,000 refugees to a new settlement. It was found that the soils were unsuitable and that there was an inadequate water supply (Gasarasi 1987, 107).

Another example is the Tanzanian villagization program. While people were displaced short distances in order to be regrouped along roads, new sites were selected without much consideration for soil quality. Following subsequent land deterioration around new settlements, peasants had to walk considerable distances to get to their fields. In some cases, new settlements were again displaced to new sites. McCall (1985) notes that some communities were shifted three times to "better sites."

In Mozambique, most communal villages assembled 4,000 to 5,000 people, far from fertile farmland, forcing peasants to walk for hours to reach their fields (De Araujo 1985). Resettlement in the South African homelands is another illustration of faulty land surveys. People were moved to locations where opportunities for farming were considerably reduced or non-existent. As a result, participation in South Africa's migratory labour system has become the major means of household survival (Rogerson and Letsoalo 1985).

Viability also depends on an accurate hydrological survey. In many cases, people are relocated to areas with inadequate supplies of drinking water: "It is one of the ironies of large-scale man-made lakes in Africa that several miles inland from the lake margin, relocated communities are frequently plagued by inadequate water for themselves and their livestock" (Scudder 1975, 462).

This is also true in many refugee rural settlements that suffer from inadequate water supply. To provide water, resettlement authorities sometimes use sophisticated technologies, such as piped water systems or pumps that soon present maintenance problems. A lack of this basic resource threatens settlements' viability.

Size of the Settlements

Agricultural resettlement schemes often house large populations. Planners use relocation as an opportunity to aggregate relocatees into large settlements and to facilitate administration and community services. In the Volta project, for example, 170 scattered hamlets were regrouped in fifty-two new settlements. Planners, however, do not accurately study the human carrying capacity of the resettlement area. Many are overpopulated, especially those that house refugees: "Once a settlement has opened there is a great temptation to continue to send newly arrived refugees (or spontaneously settled refugees who have been rounded up by the host government) to the site. Ndzevane in Swaziland and Meheba in Zambia recently doubled in size to accommodate new arrivals" (Stein and Clark 1990, 24).

Overpopulation requires a densely settled population to survive on reduced resources. It results in shortage of arable land and acute environmental pressure, both threatening viability of settlements. In the Kariba project, relocation of the Tonga in the Lusitu area increased the population densities by a factor of four. The result was desertification, which turned the

Lusitu area into a dust bowl (Scudder 1980). Deforestation and overused land and water resources usually result in conflict with the host communities.

Agricultural Programs

A new settlement's viability is based on agriculture. Many governments see relocation as a means for rapid economic change through intensification of agriculture. Settlers should be brought to a state of self-sufficiency by producing food and cash crops. Mechanized block farming, irrigation projects and improved farming systems are often introduced. However, the programs have often been unsuccessful. Several factors have contributed to these disappointing results.

Farms allocated to the settlers are often not their property. Settlers may be considered tenants on government land, especially when the land has been cleared and prepared by agencies. This is the case in the Sudan's New Halfa scheme, where tenancies were distributed to the newcomers to grow compulsory crops of cotton, wheat and ground-nuts. Lack of control over their allocated farms discourages settlers from fully committing themselves to agricultural production.

Farms are not always allocated to all the entitled households because of lack of land (as in the Kossou project) or the arable land is not prepared to be farmed at the time of resettlement (as is the Aswan High Dam project). In the Kossou project, arable land was given to a small number of settlers, provided that they respected the rules of a new mechanized farming system. Other settlers had to beg for land from host landowners. In New Nubia at the time of resettlement, less than 10 percent of the relocatees' new land was reclaimed for irrigation purposes.

Plot sizes have often been too small to provide sufficient crops and to maintain soil fertility by allowing the soil to remain fallow. Villagization in Tanzania reduced acreage per household without any intensification and with a significant reduction of fallowing, resulting in declining soil fertility and increased erosion (McCall 1985). Furthermore, tracts of land allocated are often fixed without considering the size of the family. Future demands for land, based on natural population growth or soil depletion, are not taken into account. Relocatees' grown children must share their parents' land or leave.

Availability of labour is another requisite for success. Often planners offer programs requiring a high degree of labour not consistent with the availability of family members. In many settlements, the stronger members of the population are often away in search of livelihood. They leave behind the elderly, women and children. Many resettled nomads leave resettlement areas to care for their cattle because they are not allowed to raise livestock in or around the settlement; they only return at crucial times when sowing and harvesting are required, meaning that crop yields fall below expected levels (Hoyle 1977).

As far as farm inputs are concerned, tractors, improved seeds, fertilizers, insecticides, etc., are often used for cultivation. They are part of the capital invested in the resettlement area by external aid. However, they are often wasted. Even in Etsha (set up in Botswana for Hambukushu Angolan refugees), which is considered a successful resettlement scheme because most refugees opted for the Botswana citizenship offered to them, the improved agricultural program failed:

> Destumping was emphasized, although it led to wind erosion, and was unnecessary as the Hambukushu cultivated mainly with the hoe. The kinds of seed were not geared to their preferences (sorghum was provided initially, although the Hambukushu staple diet is millet). More than 600 donkeys were bought for the settlers, although they were accustomed to ploughing with donkeys, and the beasts proved vulnerable to the few tsetse remaining in the area. Several hundred ploughs were purchased, but not more than 30% were ever used (Potten 1976, 116).

Agricultural schemes often operate as agricultural pilot schemes and are not consistent with the settlers' needs and wants. Another problem is linked to the long-term economic viability of settlements whose future depends on mechanized farming. Agencies may purchase and replace tractors, spare parts, fuel, oil and lubricants, but when they withdraw aid, there are no funds to maintain the equipment.

Income-Generating Activities and Innovative Programs

Rural people usually diversify their economic strategies to maximize their livelihood. They do not rely only on farming, which is a seasonal activity. Other income-generating activities should allow settlers to acquire basic items. Often there is no alternative income source provided. Planners neglect the wide range of income-generating activities, such as cattle rearing, brick burning, charcoal burning, carpentry, wood carving, etc. Planners too often consider settlers only as farmers. They give them arable land for improved farming but not for other activities, such as gathering, hunting or stock farming. Planners take into account only what they see as productive activities, forgetting other needs, so subsequent impoverishment follows.

For example, during the villagization program in Tanzania, slight consideration was given to potential for village crafts, small industries or alternative energy sources (McCall 1985). Furthermore, many innovative programs, especially those involving women (gardens, nutrition) are undertaken during the first few years of resettlement. After resettlement schemes are handed over, such programs are rarely pursued because they cannot be financed by local districts.

Community Services

Community services, such as clinics, schools, electricity, water supply, etc., improve the newcomers' quality of life. McCall (1985) stated that the most successful aspect of villagization in Tanzania has been the provision of services to formerly isolated populations. In New Nubia, Egypt, each new settlement is provided with electricity, a supply of drinking water, a school, a health unit, a mosque and youth club. Community services also play an important role in settlements' viability, especially with regard to education. Despite the lack of arable land in the Kossou area, many settlements are still inhabited because of the presence of schools; the elderly and children stay in the settlement while adults work in southern coffee and cocoa plantations (Lassailly 1980).

However, problems of maintaining infrastructure arise when agencies withdraw aid. This is especially true for water systems that use pumps and piped water. Such systems rarely continue to function after schemes are handed over.

This is the case in the Qala en Nahal scheme in the Sudan, where the costly and elaborate pump system has frequent maintenance problems (Rogge 1981; Asfaha 1988). Planners introduce machinery and equipment, which, in order to be maintained and operated, require resources and skills not found in the local areas. These rural development settlements often create modern dependent enclaves in the regions concerned.

Administration of the Settlements

Chambers (1969) was one of the first scholars to examine the role of organization and management in settlement schemes. Even when a resettlement scheme is planned well in advance, as in the case of a development project, settler involvement in the site selection, layout of the new village and crop selection is always very limited. Settlers are often excluded from decision making and running the settlement: "Big projects constitute development from above; they are superimposed by national or regional agencies upon a local population which has virtually no say during the stages of feasibility studies, planning, and implementation" (Scudder 1973, 45). Lack of participation in managing the settlement may become a major constraint on development.

OBSTACLES LINKED TO THE SETTLERS

Settlers are usually considered responsible for the agricultural programs' failure. For example, the day after their arrival at New Halfa, Nubian evacuees were invited by the authorities to take over their farms and start sowing wheat, but they refused to cooperate (Dafalla 1975). Planners did not understand or ignored the psychological conditions of forced migrants.

Regardless of the causes of displacement, forced relocation results in considerable stress and trauma: "From the perspective of displaced people, forced resettlement is always a disaster" (Partridge 1989, 375). This is especially true when the forced migrants are low-income rural inhabitants with strong ties to their homelands, or when governments coerce the move. Strong resistance to villagization in Tanzania prompted the government to use the militia in violent operations: "The ultimate sanction was always force and the militia were quite widely used in violent operations, burning houses, food stores and crops, and there were some deaths. The operation arguably has left a legacy of peasant alienation, mistrust and antagonism towards state rural development programmes, and of superiority and paternalism from the bureaucrats" (McCall 1985, 125–26).

Stress and trauma are common among refugees who have fled to another country, who are cut off from family members, stranded without their belongings and exposed to violence and persecution. By contrast, victims of development stay in their own country, are displaced among their kin, have their belongings and usually know where they will be resettled and how they will be compensated.

Thayer Scudder (1973, 1975, 1980; Scudder and Colson 1982) analysed the enormous multidimensional stress, which includes physiological, psychological and sociocultural factors, that accompanies involuntary relocation linked to man-made lakes. Resettled communities attempt to reduce stress by maintaining their social, economic and cultural characteristics: "In clinging to the familiar, relocatees attempt to move the shortest distance not only in space, to remain in contact with a familiar habitat, but also in terms of the psychological and sociocultural context of their lives" (Scudder and Colson 1982, 273).

As a result, they develop a very conservative attitude and refuse to participate in innovative agricultural programs. However, behavioural patterns of forced migrants may differ slightly according to one factor—their notion of permanency. Most refugees intend to go home as soon as possible. They are often reluctant to settle in planned settlement areas because these suggest permanence. Refugees do not want to put down roots in the host country because they feel they are temporary settlers; this behaviour does not promote the effective implementation of settlement programs. Evacuees from man-made lakes or from natural disasters, by contrast, know they can never return to their destroyed homelands; hence, their behaviour may be more cooperative.

When authorities introduce improved farming systems to newly arrived relocatees, they erroneously identify them as a carefully recruited group of initiative-prone, risk-taking and motivated settlers, in other words as voluntary migrants. They forget or misunderstand that involuntary settlers behave in a completely different way. According to Scudder, involuntary settlers need a transition phase, during which they attempt to cope with their new environment. No development should be undertaken during this phase.

Another behavioural pattern among relocatees is linked to a dependency syndrome. Basic facilities—which often include cleared land, housing and food—are provided at the time of resettlement. Provision of free inputs may foster dependence and paternalism, which inhibit the long-term viability of resettled communities. Settlers continue to expect that everything will be done for them and may develop a welfare syndrome.

OBSTACLES LINKED TO THE LOCAL POPULATION

Local people play an important role in the success or failure of a new settlement. They may have to give land to the newcomers and share resources, such as wood, water, fruits, plants or wild game. When host populations are not compensated, they develop feelings of hostility towards the newcomers, and their reactions may threaten the settlements' viability.

For example, in the Kossou project, landowners refused to lease their land to newcomers because they were neither compensated for their loss nor integrated into the development program. Acute tension between the two communities followed (Lassailly-Jacob 1983). In the Qala en Nahal scheme, disparities in living standards between refugees and local communities developed. This aggravated the already strained relationships that resulted when the local people lost their lands to the settlement scheme (Rogge 1981). The larger a new settlement, the higher the chances of conflict with the host population.

Local people may be affected by an infrastructural project, such as a dam, but are not entitled to resettlement. Fishermen-farmers living downstream from the impounded river may suffer from destruction of their flood-recession farming systems. For example, in Ghana thousands of downstream fishermen migrated spontaneously to the Volta lake area, competing with new settlers for farming the drawdown area.

Planners rarely undertake comprehensive development plans. Because they take into account only those who resettle, they envision only a small part of the population who will be affected by their project. Resettlers appear to be awarded too much assistance, while the local population is neglected. Provision of community services to a resettlement area can create disparity with the surrounding area if local people have no access to them. As a result, resettlers can attain a standard of living superior to that of the surrounding population. This increases the chances of conflict as settlers are perceived as privileged and therefore resented by the local population, thus hindering integration. By assisting only resettlers, planners create modern enclaves that cannot be extended to the host population. Their piecemeal plans create unbalanced regional development.

CONCLUSION

Key obstacles linked to any of the three partners in agricultural resettlement threaten the economic viability of such schemes. Planners, however, play the most important role. As long as they pay little attention to basic requisites, such as geographical location, availability and quality of arable land and clean water, agricultural settlements will never achieve economic viability. Resettlement schemes will only be an opportunity for governments to plead for international assistance to develop marginal or underused areas.

If planners pay too little attention to the carrying capacity of the selected area, overcrowding and resource depletion will follow, threatening the new settlement's viability and integration. As long as planners implement one model of intensive farming programs for all new settlers, they will fail as far as involuntary settlers are concerned. Involuntary settlers react in a completely different way than voluntary settlers do and planners should adapt their programs to their conservative attitudes.

Finally, if a resettlement area is conceived as a modern enclave, disputes will arise with the host population. Settlers should not be perceived as privileged by forgotten hosts, who may develop unexpected reactions, thus impeding proper implementation of the development project.

NOTES

1. This chapter is partly based on data collected by the author during fieldwork in Côte d'Ivoire (the Kossou project), Ghana (the Volta project) and Egypt (the Aswan High Dam project). I am grateful to Professor Michael Lanphier, Agnès Callamard and Valerie Ahwee for their valuable comments on the draft of this chapter.

REFERENCES

Asfaha, S. 1988. "De l'Erythrée au Soudan: Contribution géographique à l'étude d'une politique d'assistance aux réfugiés." Doctoral dissertation, Ecole des Hautes Etudes en Sciences Sociales, Paris.

Cernea, M.M. 1988. "Involuntary Resettlement in Development Projects: Policy Guidelines in World Bank-Financed Projects." World Bank Technical Paper No. 80.

————. 1990. "Internal Refugee Flows and Development-Induced Population Displacement." Journal of Refugee Studies 3, no. 4:320–39.

Chambers, R. 1969. Settlement Schemes in Tropical Africa: A Study of Organizations and Development. London: Routledge and Kegan Paul.

Clark, L. 1987. Key Issues in Post-Emergency Refugee Assistance in Eastern and Southern Africa, Vol. III. Washington: Refugee Policy Group.

Dafalla, H. 1975. The Nubian Exodus. Khartoum: Khartoum University Press.

De Araujo, M.G. 1985. "Communal Villages and the Distribution of the Rural Population in the People's Republic of Mozambique." In Population and Development Projects in Africa, edited by J.I. Clarke, M. Khogali and L.A. Kosinski, 153–62. Cambridge: Cambridge University Press.

Gasarasi, C.P. 1987. "The Tripartite Approach to the Resettlement and Integration of Rural Refugees in Tanzania." In Refugees: A Third World Dilemma, edited by J.R. Rogge, 99–114. Totowa: Rowman & Littlefield.

Horowitz, M.M. "Victims Upstream and Down." Journal of Refugee Studies 4, no. 2:164–81.

Hoyle, S. 1977. "The Khashm El Girba Agricultural Scheme: An Example of an Attempt to Settle Nomads." In Land Use and Development, edited by P. O'Keefe and B. Wisner, 116–31. London: International African Institute.

Kibreab, G. 1987. "Rural Refugee Land Settlements in Eastern Sudan: On the Road to Self-Sufficiency?" In Refugees and Development in Africa, edited by P. Nobel, 63–71. Uppsala: Scandinavian Institute of African Studies.

————. 1989. "Local Settlements in Africa: A Misconceived Option?" Journal of Refugee Studies 2, no. 4:468–89.

Lassailly, V. 1980. "Espace utile et transfert de population en amont du barrage de Kossou." Paris: Centre National de la Recherche Scientifique. (Mémoires et Documents de Géographie).

Lassailly-Jacob, V. 1983. "Grands barrages africains et prise en compte des populations locales." Espace Géographique 1:46–58.

————. 1992. "Les politiques de transferts de populations liés aux aménagements hydrauliques: Etude comparée de cinq barrages-réservoirs africains." In Les terrains du développement, Approche pluridisciplinaire des économies du Sud, edited by C. Robineau, 221–34. Paris: ORSTOM.

McCall, M. 1985. "Environmental and Agricultural Impacts of Tanzania's Villagization Programme." In *Population and Development Projects in Africa*, edited by J.I. Clarke, M. Khogali and L.A. Kosinski, 123–40. Cambridge: Cambridge University Press.

Merryman, J.L. 1982. "Pastoral Nomad Settlement in Response to Drought: The Case of the Kenya Somali." In *Involuntary Migration and Resettlement: The Problems and Responses of Dislocated People*, edited by Art Hansen and Anthony Oliver-Smith, 105–19. Boulder: Westview Press.

Palmer, G. 1974. "The Ecology of Resettlement Schemes." *Human Organization* 33, no. 3:239–50.

Partridge, W. 1989. "Involuntary Resettlement in Development Projects." *Journal of Refugee Studies* 2, no. 3:373–84.

Potten, D. 1976. "Etsha: A Successful Resettlement Scheme." *Botswana Notes and Records* 8:105–17.

Reining, C.R. 1982. "Resettlement in the Zande Development Scheme." In *Involuntary Migration and Resettlement: The Problems and Responses of Dislocated People*, edited by Art Hansen and Anthony Oliver-Smith, 201–24. Boulder: Westview Press.

Rogerson, C.M., and E.M. Letsoalo. 1985. "Resettlement and Underdevelopment in the Black 'Homelands' of South Africa." In *Population and Development Projects in Africa*, edited by J.I. Clarke, M. Khogali and L.A. Kosinski, 176–93. Cambridge: Cambridge University Press.

Rogge, J.R. 1981. "Africa's Resettlement Strategies." *International Migration Review* 15, no. 1:195–212.

———. 1985. "Africa's Displaced Population: Dependency or Self-Sufficiency?" In *Population and Development Projects in Africa*, edited by J.I. Clarke, M. Khogali and L.A. Kosinski, 68–83. Cambridge: Cambridge University Press.

———. 1987. "When Is Self-Sufficiency Achieved? The Case of Rural Settlements in Sudan." In *Refugees: A Third World Dilemma*, edited by J.R. Rogge, 86–98. Totowa: Rowman & Littlefield.

Scudder, T. 1973. "The Human Ecology of Big Projects: River Basin Development and Resettlement." *Annual Review of Anthropology* 2:45–55.

———. 1975. "Resettlement." In *Man-Made Lakes and Human Health*, edited by N.F. Stanley and M.P. Alpers, 453–71. London: Academic Press.

———. 1980. "River-Basin Development and Local Initiative in African Savanna Environments." In *Human Ecology in Savanna Environments*, edited by D.R. Harris, 383–405. London: Academic Press.

Scudder, T., and E. Colson. 1982. "From Welfare to Development: A Conceptual Framework for the Analysis of Dislocated People." In *Involuntary Migration and Resettlement*, edited by Art Hansen and Anthony Oliver-Smith, 267–87. Boulder: Westview Press.

Stein, B.N., and L. Clark. 1990. "Refugee Integration and Older Refugee Settlements in Africa." A paper presented at the 1990 meeting of the American Anthropological Association, New Orleans, Louisiana, November 28, 1990.

Sutton, K. 1977. "Population Resettlement: Traumatic Upheavals and the Algerian Experience." *The Journal of Modern African Studies* 15, no. 2:279–300.

Wood, A.P. 1985. "Population Redistribution and Agricultural Settlement Schemes in Ethiopia, 1958–80." In *Population and Development Projects in Africa*, edited by J.I. Clarke, M. Khogali and L.A. Kosinski, 84–109. Cambridge: Cambridge University Press.

12

Refugee Aid and Development in Africa: Research and Policy Needs from the Local Perspective

Robert F. Gorman

This chapter examines and evaluates a decade of effort by the international community to link refugee aid and development in Africa. Drawing upon the discussions, conclusions and recommendations of the International Seminar on Refugees in Africa, held in Arusha, Tanzania, from July 30 to August 3, 1990, the chapter outlines policy recommendations and research issues needed to improve international and local efforts to link refugee and development assistance more effectively. An attempt is made here to emphasize the local African context in which this linkage must take place without ignoring the more widely studied and better understood (albeit inadequate and problematical) international mechanisms for linking refugee aid and development. Before proceeding with an evaluation of policy and proffering recommendations, it is useful to recount briefly how the refugee aid and development dialogue of the 1980s unfolded and to review the principles that emerged from it.

THE DIALOGUE

The idea of linking refugee aid to the wider development agenda, though hardly a new notion, attracted increased attention during the 1980s (Gorman 1987a; Betts 1984; Goodwillie 1983). Much of this recent debate focused on Africa, where substantial growth in refugee populations during the early 1980s, combined with deteriorating economic conditions in refugee-hosting countries, raised concern that the traditional hospitality shown by Africans to their exiled kin and neighbours was in danger of widespread decline.

These conditions prompted the United Nations General Assembly, the United Nations High Commissioner for Refugees (UNHCR), host and donor governments to convene two international conferences on assistance to refugees in Africa. Held in 1981, the first International Conference on Assistance to Refugees in Africa (ICARA I) addressed principally the emergency assistance needs of African refugees (Birido 1982). Although African governments also sought assistance to cope with the effects of large numbers of refugees on their social and economic infrastructures, donors largely ignored their requests, which often inadequately justified and poorly documented. Three years later, Africa's economic condition was in even worse shape, refugee populations were even larger and the threat to first asylum was growing increasingly tenuous.

The second International Conference on Assistance to Refugees in Africa (ICARA II) was convened in 1984 under these inauspicious circumstances. However, with assistance from UN technical teams, African host countries elaborated project submissions that were more successful than the ICARA I submissions at attracting greater donor interest and support (Gorman 1987a). These projects addressed host countries' infrastructural weaknesses, so that they could better cope with large numbers of refugees. For instance, when large numbers of destitute, hungry and ill refugees move into remote and arid regions, they place additional demands on local water and fuelwood supplies, often depleting both and precipitating desertification. They place demands on the local health infrastructure. Host country hospitals and clinics, doctors and paramedical personnel must accommodate larger numbers of patients and cope with the refugees' effect on the health of the local population. Refugee children place a heavy demand on local schools. Security personnel must often be increased to ensure public safety in refugee-affected regions. Local roads are often inadequate for handling the traffic of heavy trucks that carry relief supplies, and often deteriorate as relief shipments overtax their carrying capacity. ICARA II projects sought to identify and ameliorate such infrastructural strains. In short, ICARA II moved beyond ICARA I by placing less emphasis on emergency assistance and more on the implications of refugee settlement and repatriation for host country infrastructure and development. In this sense, ICARA II was a milestone in linking refugee aid and development.

While governments were elaborating projects and programs of action through the ICARA process, debates among researchers, academics and assistance agency personnel began to elaborate key principles on how refugee aid and development might be successfully linked (Chambers 1979, 1982; Gallagher and Stein 1984). Numerous conferences, meetings and colloquiums of these experts and interested parties took place in the early 1980s to rationalize a strategy for linking refugee aid and development (Goodwillie 1983; European Communities 1983; Refugee Policy Group 1984; United Nations High Commissioner for Refugees 1981, 1983; World

Bank 1983). Emerging from this dialogue and from actual practice were a number of central principles:

- Refugees' basic needs must be met in ways that do not prejudice the condition of host country nationals. Refugees should be assisted on a level that does not place them in an advantageous position relative to local people. However, if adherence to this principle results in unacceptably low standards of living or abject poverty for refugees and their hosts, then every effort should be made to raise the living standards of both.

- Assistance should encourage and enable refugees to attain self-reliance, so that they can eventually provide for their own basic needs. Agricultural self-sufficiency and income-generating projects should be undertaken to this end. As refugee productivity increases, more significant income generation benefits for locals should result and should be encouraged.

- Development assistance should anticipate the impact that refugee populations have on the economic and social infrastructures of host countries. Where negative effects occur, the donor community should work to ease the stress on host country infrastructure. In short, development assistance should take into account the development-related effects of refugee flows.

- Identification, formulation and implementation of refugee programs and refugee-related infrastructural assistance should involve input and participation from refugees and local hosts, and careful co-ordination among existing refugee and development arms of governments, nongovernmental organizations and intergovernmental organizations.

These principles provided a basic orientation for a strategy of linking refugee aid and development. However, proper orientation is one thing and effective implementation quite another. Indeed, the promising dialogue of the early 1980s on first principles has not been followed by truly effective implementation.

DIFFICULTIES AND OBSTACLES

Numerous difficulties and obstacles have hampered effective linkage of refugee aid and development. First, such a linkage implies either the creation of new bureaucratic mechanisms or the effective coordination of existing ones. The international community explicitly chose the latter option to avoid unnecessary duplication of functions that would have required new UN and national bureaucracies. However, given the very different styles, modes of operation and assumptions under which refugee and development agencies function, effective coordination has been difficult. UNHCR and the United Nations Development Programme (UNDP) signed letters of agreement on coordinating their respective mandates and joint technical missions were sent to some refugee-hosting countries to assess refugee-related development needs. But routine coordination, at both headquarters and in the field, often eludes UN refugee and development agencies. Some donor governments, notably the United States, have failed to achieve adequate coordination between their refugee and development agencies. Regrettably, the same can be said of some African governments, too. At all levels, bureaucratic imperatives, turf disputes, budget considerations, planning cycles and styles of operation have made it difficult for refugee agencies and their development counterparts to coordinate effectively (Gorman 1987a, 1987b).

A second related problem complicates the first: efforts to coordinate refugee aid and development assistance are decentralized in nature. Although UNDP was given primary responsibility to coordinate the ICARA II follow-up in consultation with UNHCR, the reality is that the effort to link refugee aid and development assistance remains largely a country-by-country exercise, with most of the rather limited assistance for refugee-related development projects funnelled through bilateral channels. Coordination under these circumstances is more vital and difficult. To a very large extent, effective coordination rests with the personalities and energies of development and refugee specialists residing in the affected countries—that is, UNDP and UNHCR country representatives; UN specialized agency personnel; the officials of host country development, national refugee ministries and local governments; and the representatives of donor country development and refugee agencies. There are mechanisms to combine all of them into an effective unit for identifying and addressing refugee-related development needs and linking the two forms of assistance through local round-table discussions, elaboration of country development strategy statements and even World Bank consultations. But whether they work effectively depends very much on a country's particular circumstances. In the absence of aggressive stewardship from UNDP headquarters in New York, each refugee-affected country is left to fashion its own strategies for linking refugee aid and development.

A third obstacle is the lack of resources committed by donors. Comparatively little money has been dedicated to projects that address refugee-related development needs. More than fifty ICARA II or ICARA II-related projects received some funding in the course of the past decade, but this was insufficient compared to the need. Donor governments are under budgetary pressure and have not been enthusiastic about pumping substantial resources into refugee-related development efforts, especially when the emergency assistance needs of Africa in the past decade demanded large sums of money merely to save lives. When governments must choose between spending money on new and untested refugee-related development programs or emergency aid, they consistently opt for the latter. For some African governments, the lack of resources provides little incentive to link development efforts to what they often view as ephemeral refugee movements. Lacking additional resources, money spent on these *ignes fatui* is money lost to their regular and more pressing development programs. By the same token, if additional resources were available, they might have greater incentive to integrate, link and harmonize their refugee and development assistance programs.

But even if more money were available, a fourth obstacle—the absorptive capacity problem—would hamper successful implementation of refugee-related development projects. This problem refers to the inability of many refugee-hosting countries in Africa to absorb resources effectively. If a country lacks the managerial and technical capability to identify, implement and monitor a large number of innovative projects, resources are easily wasted. Moreover, many host governments lack the capacity to meet future running costs, especially in connection with the ICARA II infrastructural assistance for such things as roads, schools and hospitals. Hospitals and schools without supplies or adequate staffing and roads without adequate ongoing maintenance may not be worth building in the first place. The development of managerial capacity, in other words, may be as central to linking refugee aid and development, as is the application of resources to "brick-and-mortar" projects.

These obstacles underscore the daunting challenges facing African governments and the international community in their efforts to link refugee aid and development. Many obstacles cannot, by their very nature, be eliminated or wished away. Resource stringencies will not disappear overnight, nor will a centralized system of linking refugee aid and development suddenly appear. Given these realities, it is necessary to identify strategies for doing better within the existing institutional and resource environment. To do this—as the Seminar on Refugees in Africa concluded —requires better information and better policy.

Both the academic and policy-making communities have a role to play in devising coping strategies. At the Seminar on Refugees in Africa, the working group on refugee aid and development explored ways in which academic and policy communities could undertake further research on and implementation of effective strategies for linking refugee aid and development. What follows is my interpretation of those deliberations and my own views on the subject.

A RESEARCH AGENDA FOR THE ACADEMIC COMMUNITY

The first item on the research (as well as the policy) agenda is the issue of data. One of the central tenets of the refugee aid and development dialogue is that large numbers of refugees impose burdens on host countries' economies and populations. But what actually are these burdens? Indeed, should the term "burden" even be employed, since in some cases refugees may represent a net asset to a host country? The effects of refugees on host countries' economies, budgets and infrastructure are not precisely known and very little research has been done on the matter. Existing research suggests that the presence of large refugee populations can have both positive and negative effects.

One study indicates that different elements of the host population are variably affected by the presence of refugees, some negatively, others positively, still others neutrally (Chambers 1986). A recent World Bank study of the effect of Mozambican refugees in Malawi concluded that the Malawi government expended over U.S. $20 million in terms of seconded personnel and logistical support to cope with Mozambican refugees under its care. The expenditure was a drain on its already strained national budget (World Bank et al. 1990). On the other hand, in Tanzania and Rwanda, refugees have brought new lands under cultivation, paid taxes and/or increased regional productivity and stimulated economic development (Gorman 1987a). The effects of refugee populations appear to vary widely between countries and even between regions of the same country. This conclusion seems supported by unsystematic evidence, but complete verification requires a meticulous survey of the patterns of the impact of refugees on the host country or of returnees on the country of origin. Academics and governments should encourage basic research so that these patterns can be identified. Presumably, more reliable and concrete information will result in better projects and policies. Donors might even be persuaded to provide greater assistance, if the existence and nature of a burden is clearly identified.

A second area for study and research concerns existing refugee-related development projects. As mentioned, more than fifty such projects have received some funding and are in various stages of implementation. These projects should be evaluated to determine how well they helped to relieve refugee-related strains on the host country's economy, infrastructure and population. Since the majority of the ICARA II projects focus on strengthening economic infrastructure, a central question should be the pattern of infrastructure utilization by refugees and the host population before and after project implementation. Do the infrastructural projects stimulate integrated refugee and host utilization as intended? Apart from strengthening infrastructure, refugee-related development projects are often intended to stimulate income generation and regional economic growth. How well do they do this? To what extent are local materials and local/refugee labour used in construction projects? How does this affect the local economy? In some cases, projects are intended to promote acquisition of new skills among refugees or the host population. To what extent do ICARA II or other refugee-related development projects actually accomplish this? Do participants in such projects subsequently utilize the acquired skills to the advantage of the local economy? Evaluation of existing ongoing and completed ICARA II projects provides an opportunity to understand better the effects of such projects and to modify those that are judged deficient.

One axiom of the refugee aid and development dialogue is that refugees and the affected host population should participate in the formulation and implementation of projects and policies that are intended to benefit them. A corollary of this axiom is that projects and policies lacking such participation are more likely to fail, while those including it are more likely to succeed. Although this proposition might seem self-evident, empirical support for it is still wanting. Even if our expectations are fulfilled, the dynamics of participation need to be explored in greater detail. For instance, what are the best modalities of participation? How should conflicts of interests between and among refugees, the local population and the often forgotten or ignored local administration be resolved? And how should these local interests be reconciled with the interests of the host country's national government, the donor countries, UN agencies and NGOs? Existing projects that have such participation may begin to provide us with tentative answers to such questions.

Finally, the academic community should not shy away from studying the operation of the existing institutions and policies that deliver refugee-related development assistance. A host country that has marshalled effective linkages between refugee aid and development may serve as a model. Institutional analysis of successes and failures should be conducted to determine what helps and hinders an effective response. This, ultimately, is the most sensitive area for academics or government. Indeed, an extensive analysis of the policies and institutional make-up of refugee-receiving countries was undertaken prior to ICARA II as part of the technical team report on each African country submitting project proposals. However, this portion of the original report was so sensitive that only a very sanitized and sketchy version of the analysis was included in the conference documentation. Still, the policies of governments and of agencies within governments, perhaps more than any other factor, determine whether or not refugee aid and development assistance can be effectively linked. On this note, let us turn to the policy agenda itself.

A POLICY AGENDA FOR HOST COUNTRIES AND
THE INTERNATIONAL COMMUNITY

We assume that linking refugee aid and development will continue to be essentially a decentralized activity. It is most unlikely that governments will consent to the creation of a new international bureaucracy for promoting and sustaining this enterprise. If this is so, then coordination of existing agencies and institutions must be the principal preoccupation of policy makers at all levels. Better policy coordination, in turn, depends on the quality of data used to inform programs and projects. Hence, governments and international agencies need to encourage systematic data collection and analysis of many of the issues mentioned earlier.

SUBNATIONAL PARTICIPATION AND COORDINATION

If accurate information is critical to better coordination, so is communication between the relevant development and refugee arms of the UN system, NGOs, donor governments and the regional, district and local governments in host countries. Let us begin by examining the subnational (regional, district and local) levels, since in the absence of effective cooperation there, the best-intentioned efforts of national governments and the international community are likely to be frustrated or even sabotaged. Indeed, the least explored and perhaps most crucial link in effective coordination of refugee-related development assistance lies in the hands of local politicians, mayors, chiefs, district officers and regional managers. The structure and functioning of regional and local governments within a host country can either facilitate or hinder implementation of effective refugee-related development assistance strategies. When national governments and the international community ignore the concerns and interests of local government officials, they run the risk of inviting their resistance and/or apathy. On the other hand, consulting with local officials when formulating projects and programs, and requesting their input and suggestions, coopts them into the policy-making process and gives them a stake in the outcome. Although this kind of consultation process may be time-consuming and at times even exasperating, policy implementation should run more smoothly if refugee-related development strategies have the cooperation rather than the resistance of local authorities at the outset.

But including these authorities in the planning process should be seen as more than an effort to avoid offending local egos. Indeed, given the widespread lack of managerial absorptive capacity in many African countries, participation of local officials in development and refugee aid strategies and projects should be considered a major part of the development process itself. Strong and effective local governments increase the absorptive capacity of countries. In other words, when local officials (as opposed to expatriates) can be called upon to implement or manage projects, or to conduct project evaluations, national self-reliance is promoted. The effectiveness and the role of local governments is very much within the province of a country's domestic affairs. Many national governments are suspicious of local governments and often want to minimize their power and control their functions. However, whether or not an autonomous tradition of local government exists, local officials cannot be wholly denied participation in policy making if policies are to be effective. As a matter of principle, then, local and district administrators should be regularly involved in formulating and implementing refugee-related development assistance.

We have already observed that the local population and refugees should participate in the process of linking refugee aid and development. Any effort by national governments and international agencies to do this directly, while ignoring local administrative structures, would be a mistake. Representatives of refugees and of local host groups should be engaged in the process of linking refugee aid and development, and so should local government officials. The interaction of such disparate groups will not always result in consensus, and at times the interests of one group will prevail over another. However, all affected groups should have an opportunity to voice their interests and concerns before policies are finally adopted, if only to find out beforehand where potential problems and obstacles to implementation lie.

NATIONAL LEVEL COORDINATION

If the participation of local government in the hinterlands is important to effective policy implementation, national level planning is even more critical to success in linking refugee aid and development, since it is at the national level that a host country's development plan is articulated in conjunction with relevant UN bodies and donor agencies. There are a number of difficulties involved in effective coordination at the host country level. They include:

- resistance by many African governments to the notion that refugees should be integrated into the national economy (preference being given to the view that refugees should and will eventually repatriate)
- a lack of enthusiasm among host country development agencies for including refugee-related development projects in the regular development planning process

- genuine differences in orientation, planning cycles and assistance priorities between national development and refugee agencies (a problem that afflicts donor governments and UN agencies as well)
- tendencies by national governments to ignore local participation in the policy-making process
- the fluidity and fast-changing nature of refugee movements that hamper long-term planning
- varying degrees of enthusiasm among UNDP resident representatives, who, though principally responsible for UN in-country coordination, often view involving refugees in the development planning process difficult and/or inappropriate
- varying degrees of cooperation between UNDP and UNHCR country representatives, and widespread failure to involve UNHCR representatives meaningfully in the country development strategy process
- a lack of domestic and foreign resources to finance refugee-related development activities.

The effort to link refugee aid and development assistance in Africa, then, faces numerous though surmountable obstacles. Governments, such as Tanzania and Burundi, which have development ministries that are responsible for dealing with refugees, avoid many of the difficulties that exist where separate refugee agencies have been established. There were examples of the latter in Somalia and Ethiopia, where coordination of national refugee rehabilitation commissions with development ministries proved problematical. Governments that permit refugees to integrate into the local economy, to secure professional and business licences, to purchase or own land, or even to apply for citizenship, are more likely to encourage linkage of refugee aid and the development planning process. Tanzania represents a good example of these liberal attitudes towards refugee integration, although it actively discourages secondary migration of refugees from rural to urban areas by denying assistance to urban refugees.

Where governments have separate agencies for refugee policy and development planning, coordination (though more difficult) still can be achieved. Steering committees have been established in some countries to ensure coordination of these different bodies, and in some cases round-table discussions and World Bank consultations have directly addressed the development impact of refugees. However, often national development ministries view the refugee situation as temporary, one that does not require long-term planning, and as secondary to more ambitious development planning. The changeable nature of many refugee situations, in fact, corroborates this perspective. Where development ministries' built-in biases against including refugee-related considerations in the development planning process are reinforced by a UNDP resident representative with similar views, little progress in linking refugee aid with development can be expected. Indeed, a UNDP resident representative need not actively oppose coordination to subvert the linkage process. Passivity alone is enough to stymie progress. Inertia and uncoordinated action can be overcome only by aggressive leadership by those charged with coordination. Lacking enthusiastic local UNDP leadership, UNHCR representatives should be encouraged to promote greater attention to refugee-related development opportunities among development-oriented sister agencies. In short, UNHCR must continue to play a catalytic role in apprising and energizing UN agency country representatives, as recent General Assembly conference documents (A/AC.96/737 and A/AC.96/742) have reiterated.

Clearly, much of the success of linkage efforts depends on the determination of a government and UN agency representatives. If there is a genuine desire to coordinate and harmonize refugee aid and development, successful methods can be found. But even where the will exists, the forging of an effective team of host, donor, NGO and UN representatives depends on the interplay of personalities.

The bottom line is that if a host government does not want to promote refugee integration, and if it does not want refugee assistance to be linked with development planning, these goals will never be achieved, external pressure to the contrary notwithstanding. On the other hand, progress is possible through a variety of means if national policy really promotes these goals. Governments could establish a jointly administered UNDP/UNHCR national trust fund (as distinct from the UNDP trust fund in New York) for refugee-related development projects. By insisting on joint administration, governments would enable the UNHCR to play its catalytic role in identifying what programs are needed and encouraging the UNDP to exercise its development-oriented technical skills in conjunction with UNHCR's sensitivity to refugees. The government then might more successfully solicit additional donor government contributions into this fund, especially if they actively involve the donors in the development of projects. By documenting project need and identifying a specific burden, the government might convince donors to supply additional revenues, so that the regular development program will not experience a corresponding decrease in funding. The government might further insist that the impact of refugees on its economy be an ongoing item on the agenda of round-table discussions on development and World Bank consultations, thus giving refugee issues more prominence and perhaps attracting greater donor interest. In short, host governments could take the lead in promoting coordination by actively seeking donor participation and encouraging, even requiring, that relevant UN agencies undertake their respective roles more aggressively. If host governments choose not to do this, the process of linking refugee aid and development in Africa will remain a largely rhetorical exercise.

Host country activism, then, is essential. The case of Malawi illustrates the point. Malawi now hosts over 980,000 Mozambican refugees—about one-tenth of its own population. The vast majority of these refugees have been accommodated in Malawian villages. The government has resisted the temptation to create a separate refugee agency, and instead provides assistance through its regular national ministries and district civil service system. This avoids duplicating existing governmental infrastructure and encourages better utilization of limited resources. While the UNHCR, the World Food Programme, donor governments and NGOs contribute substantial sums to meet the refugees' ongoing care and maintenance needs, the government of Malawi has incurred substantial additional costs to its civil service, social and economic infrastructure. There is also a substantially higher demand for public goods, such as water and fuelwood. Moreover, all this pressure occurred after ICARA II, so that Malawi did not have the opportunity of discussing its needs in an international forum, thus complicating efforts to convince donors to provide additional assistance, despite obvious evidence of need.

In an effort to gain support, Malawi called upon the World Bank, UNHCR and the UNDP to work with it to study the impact of the refugee influx on its public expenditures program. A technical team composed of representatives from these agencies conducted an exhaustive study that was published as a report to the Consultative Group for Malawi in April 1990 (World Bank et al. 1990). Based on conservative estimates, this model study demonstrated that the Malawi government absorbed substantial costs in direct public expenditures for refugee assistance and even larger amounts to rehabilitate infrastructure or restore services to a level enjoyed by Malawians prior to the influx. To compensate partially for these measurable budgetary costs, the report called upon the international community in 1990–1991 to provide additional assistance to Malawi to upgrade and rehabilitate roads (U.S. $7.9 million), to rehabilitate and restore health services (U.S. $5 million), to rehabilitate and restore education, water, community service and social welfare services (U.S. $2.2 million), to cope with deforestation and land degradation (U.S. $7.3 million), and to strengthen veterinary services in order to cope with deteriorating livestock health (U.S. $2.6 million). The report represents precisely the kind of work that can and should be done to identify refugee-related development burdens. Although Malawi's modest requests (about U.S. $25 million in infrastructural assistance and budgetary support) may eventually attract some donor interest, the initial response was neither enthusiastic nor encouraging. Despite a clear need for support and generous and responsible policies towards refugees and linking refugee aid to development, Malawi's situation may be neglected by donors. When the effort to link refugee aid and development is done properly, donors should be prepared to reward it.

It appears that host country activism, though necessary, is not sufficient to ensure a successful linkage of refugee aid and development. Success also hinges on how well local governments, refugees and host population interests are incorporated into the policy process, on how effectively the UN system supports host countries' bilateral programs and, at some point, on whether donors will provide additional resources.

INTERNATIONAL COORDINATION

Coordination of international assistance for refugee aid and development lies principally with UNDP and UNHCR. The former is responsible for monitoring refugee-related development assistance and the latter for promoting refugee integration schemes and durable solutions. Clearly, each form of assistance must meet both refugee and development needs. For this reason, each agency must be keenly aware of the other's activities and coordinate their respective efforts. Still, there is insufficient contact at the headquarters' level. Instructions to UNDP and UNHCR country representatives are still issued separately from New York and Geneva, and there is little ongoing or operational contact between the two organizations.

Moreover, UNDP operates budgets on a five-year indicative planning cycle, while the UNHCR budget is an annual affair. Any effort to improve UNDP/UNHCR coordination must account for this crucial difference. Indeed, the Executive Committee of the UNHCR and the UN General Assembly have recently recognized the importance of this issue and have asked the high commissioner to identify program components, such as local settlement assistance for refugees, that might be financed for up to three years. They have also asked the UNDP to include refugees in its population estimates, which in turn are essential for indicative planning (United Nations General Assembly 1989c, 13–14, 25). Clearly, ongoing contact between the operational counterparts of UNDP New York and UNHCR Geneva should be encouraged. The sooner a closer relationship is established, the more likely it will be that a comprehensive and effective coordination will take place. The UNHCR Executive Committee's call for a joint UNHCR/UNDP task force on refugees to work out such a relationship is heartening. So are its recommendations that joint letters of instruction be sent to the field to ensure that coordination at that crucial level is further underscored. In a decentralized system for linking refugee aid and development, this kind of coordination is absolutely essential.

Beyond UNDP/UNHCR relations, refugee aid and development must be made an ongoing and more visible part of the global development agenda. There are numerous UN and regional bodies that already deal with some aspect of refugees or development: World Food Programme, the International Organization for Migration, the World Bank, various regional banks, UNICEF, the International Fund for Agricultural Development, the World Health Organization, HABITAT, the United Nations Environment Programme and the Development Assistance Committee of the Organization for Economic Cooperation and Development. These and other bodies should be more involved in the refugee aid and development dialogue. The Office of the United Nations Secretary-General should promote this wider scope of cooperation—a point urged by the UNHCR's Executive Committee when it called for the high commissioner to take up the issue with the secretary-general in the context of the UN's Administrative Committee on Coordination (United Nations General Assembly 1989c, 22; 1989a).

These policy coordination efforts are worthwhile and necessary. However, whether they are effective depends on the actions of governmental representatives to the governing bodies of the various UN agencies and on the amount of attention given by high-ranking officials of those agencies to effective coordination. The Executive Committee of the UNHCR is composed of governmental representatives who are very aware of the refugee component in the development process. Its desire to see refugee aid and development effectively coordinated may not be as enthusiastically shared by representatives in the governing bodies of UN development agencies or by the secretariats of these agencies. Part of the problem is that development officials of many donor governments are still not convinced that refugee-related development projects deserve priority consideration in face of the more extensive needs of developing countries. This resistance will not be readily overcome. Thus, refugee advocates must press for inclusion of refugee issues on the development agenda, so that it is not overlooked by development agencies whose interests and instincts lie elsewhere.

The UN might develop a well-honed system for linking refugee aid and development, for coordinating its agencies, and for ensuring that this coordination extends from headquarters into the field. Host governments might be persuaded to coordinate their development and refugee agencies so as to complement such a UN effort. However, if donor governments, after calling for more systematic coordination, decide not to finance concrete projects for refugee-related development needs, then much of the fuss over coordination will have been unnecessary. Careful coordination, of course, is desirable in its own right, but donor governments should commit themselves up front to providing additional assistance to meet refugee-related development needs. Problems cannot be solved by just throwing money at them, nor are they solved by denying resources to those who are trying to find solutions. Indeed, even very modest levels of donor support to refugee-related development projects would go a long way towards meeting needs and encouraging responsible spending. Whether the United States, the European countries and other donors will come forward with sufficient resources to keep alive efforts to link refugee aid and development remains to be seen.

CONCLUSIONS

Sometimes it is hard for advocates of refugee assistance to admit that the problem of refugees and refugee aid in Africa is dwarfed in comparison to the continent's poverty, famine and environmental degradation. Still, the refugee problem is by no means insignificant, nor the plight of the refugees any less critical. Moreover, to the extent that refugees worsen economic conditions for the local population and frustrate local development, they must be viewed as a component of this wider development crisis facing Africa. It is laudable that the refugee advocacy community has drawn attention to these connections. But the development community, in close cooperation with refugee assistance bodies, must take a less hesitant and more enthusiastic role in linking the two kinds of assistance. This effort, in turn, should document the effects of refugees' presence on host country populations and economies. It should be a combined effort by local groups, host country populations, local administrators and refugees to identify policies and programs that are meant to address measurable burdens. Donors should be prepared to provide additional resources for clearly identified burdens.

What is the price of failure? Clearly, the failure to link effectively refugee aid and development in Africa will not lead to catastrophe. On the other hand, successful linkage would meet needs, strengthen local infrastructures, impart usable skills and avoid unnecessary and wasteful duplication of effort. The enterprise, though modest, nevertheless makes good sense. The development of the African hinterlands, where most refugees reside, will be enhanced by such linkage efforts if they are pursued in a systematic and intelligent manner. Refugee-affected regions are among the most sensitive to drought and environmental degradation. They are often the sites of emergency famine operations and have the least developed infrastructure—a fact, in turn, that often hinders effective emergency response. Refugee problems and development in Africa are linked in very concrete ways. Our assistance policies should take this reality into consideration.

The international community became more aware of linkages between refugee aid and development in Africa during the past decade. It has responded by holding international conferences, by identifying relevant project interventions, by funding some of them, and by attempting to coordinate decentralized response mechanisms. This system is not perfect. It lacks systematic cooperation, strong leadership and sufficient funds. But there is some cooperation, some leadership and some money—just enough of each to give hope that efforts to link refugee aid and development are alive, if not wholly well. Instead of a coordinated Africa-wide strategy of linkage, we see a country-by-country process, in which some countries have fared better than others. Lessons learned from the more successful cases need to be applied elsewhere and, as the International Seminar on Refugees in Africa concluded, both the academic and international communities should be actively engaged in this task of assessment and promotion. Indeed, success even at the host country level requires policy coordination at the international level. It is essential that UNDP, UNHCR and other relevant international agencies strengthen their respective capacities to promote linkage of refugee aid and development, and that they do so in mutual and close cooperation.

REFERENCES

Betts, T.F. 1984. "Evolution and Promotion of the Integrated Rural Development Approach to Refugee Policy in Africa." *Africa Today* 35, no. 1:7–24.

Birido, Omer. 1982. "International Conference on Assistance to Refugees in Africa (ICARA) and Its Aftermath." A paper presented at the Khartoum Seminar on Refugees, Khartoum, September 11–14.

Chambers, Robert. 1979. "Rural Refugees in Africa: What the Eye Does Not See." *Disasters* 3, no. 4:381–92.

————. 1982. "Rural Refugees in Africa: Past Experience, Future Pointers." *Disasters* 6:21–30.

————. 1986. "Hidden Losers: The Impact of Rural Refugees and Refugee Programs on Poorer Hosts." *International Migration Review* 20, no. 2:245–63.

European Communities. 1983. "Draft Report on Assistance to Refugees in Developing Countries." Brussels: Committee on Development and Cooperation for the European Parliament.

Gallagher, Dennis, and Barry Stein. 1984. "ICARA II: Burden Sharing and Durable Solutions." Washington: Refugee Policy Group.

Goodwillie, Susan. 1983. "Refugees in the Developing World: A Challenge to the International Community." Prepared for the UNHCR-sponsored Meeting of Experts on Refugee Aid and Development, Mont Pèlerin, Switzerland.

Gorman, Robert. 1987a. *Coping With Africa's Refugee Burden: A Time for Solutions.* New York: Martinus-Nijhoff and UNITAR.

———. 1987b. "Taking Stock of the Second International Conference on Assistance to Refugees in Africa (ICARA II)." *Journal of African Studies* 14, no. 1:4–11.

Refugee Policy Group. 1984. *ICARA II: Future Directions for Assistance to Refugees in Africa*. Washington: Refugee Policy Group.

United Nations General Assembly. 1989a. *Resolution 44/137*. New York: UNGA.

———. 1989b. A/AC.96/737. "Report of the Fortieth Session of the Executive Committee of the Programme of the UNHCR." New York: UNGA.

———. 1989c. A/AC.96/742. "Report of the Executive Committee Temporary Working Group to the Extraordinary Session of the Executive Committee of the UNHCR." New York: UNGA.

———. 1990. A/AC.96/747. "Report on the Extraordinary Session of the Executive Committee of the Programme of the UNHCR." New York: UNGA.

United Nations High Commissioner for Refugees. 1981. "The Refugee Problem in a Development Context." Prepared for the Organization for Economic Co-operation and Development. Geneva: UNHCR.

———. 1983. "Report of the Meeting of Experts on Refugee Aid and Development." Mont Pèlerin: UNHCR.

World Bank. 1983. "Staff Appraisal Report: Pakistan: Income Generating Project for Refugee Areas." Washington: World Bank.

World Bank, Malawi, United Nations General Assembly and United Nations High Commissioner for Refugees. 1990. "Report to the Consultative Group for Malawi on the Impact of Refugees on the Government Public Expenditure Program." Unpublished.

About the Editors and Contributors

Howard Adelman is a professor of philosophy and director of the Centre for Refugee Studies at York University.

Chris J. Bakwesegha is the head of the Division of Conflict Prevention and Resolution at the Organization of African Unity. He has written extensively on refugee matters.

Robert F. Gorman is professor of political science at Southwest Texas State University. He has served in the African Office of the Bureau for Refugee Programs in the U.S. Department of State and as a visiting scholar at Africare. He is the author of numerous articles on African politics and refugee affairs, and has written or edited several books on these subjects.

Tsegaye Hailu is a hydro-geologist in Littleton, Colorado. As a field geologist between 1968 and 1976, he became very familiar with life in rural Tigray and other parts of northern Ethiopia. He is a consultant on rural water supply and sanitation.

Edward Khiddu-Makubuya is an associate professor of law at Makerere University in Kampala, Uganda. He has written extensively on repatriation, human rights and refugees in Uganda.

Gaim Kibreab is an associate professor in economic history at Uppsala University in Sweden. He has written books and articles on refugee issues, and is currently researching population resource management and environment in eastern Sudan.

John Kirkby is a senior lecturer in environment at the University of Northumbria. He has been a consultant on environmental issues in several African and Asian countries.

Peter H. Koehn is a professor of political science and the director of international programs at the University of Montana. He has written books, articles and reviews on refugee issues and Ethiopian politics.

Tom Kuhlman has worked in rural development programs for over ten years, mostly in Africa. During 1986–1987, he carried out research on the integration of spontaneous refugees in the Sudan. Until 1991 he was a lecturer in economic anthropology at the Free University.

Véronique Lassailly-Jacob is a French geographer and research fellow at the Centre for African Studies in Paris, which is part of the French National Centre for Scientific Research. She is presently a visiting research fellow at the Centre for Refugee Studies at York University in Toronto. Her research field includes forced migration and rural development in Africa. She specialized in the study of land resettlement schemes implemented for involuntary migrants and conducted fieldwork in Côte d'Ivoire, Ghana and Egypt.

Phil O'Keefe is a professor and reader in environmental management at the University of Northumbria. He has worked extensively in development and environmental consultancy throughout the developing world.

John Sorenson is a research associate of the Centre for Refugee Studies at York University and the Disaster Research Unit at the University of Manitoba, and has written extensively on refugee matters.

Jan Sterkenburg is with the Department of Geography of Developing Countries at Utrecht University and the Operations Review Unit of the Directorate General of International Cooperation, Ministry of Foreign Affairs. His main interest is in rural development in Africa. He has worked in several countries in eastern and southern Africa, including the Sudan, Kenya, Tanzania and Botswana.

Peter W. Van Arsdale is a refugee, immigrant and American Indian specialist at the Colorado Division of Mental Health; adjunct associate professor of international studies at the University of Denver, and chairperson of the Center for Cultural Dynamics.

Roger Winter has been the director of the U.S. Committee for Refugees since 1981. In that capacity, he has visited most of Africa's refugee-producing and receiving countries.

Tsegay Wolde-Georgis is a doctoral candidate at the Graduate School of International Studies at the University of Denver. His dissertation is about the constraints on the coping mechanisms of Tigrayan famine in the 1980s.

Index